WHAT SHALL WE SAY THEN?

*Questions and Answers
Concerning Primitive Baptist
Beliefs and Practices*

Elder Jeff Winfrey

Sovereign Grace Publications
Shallotte, North Carolina

WHAT SHALL WE SAY THEN? Questions and Answers Concerning Primitive Baptist Beliefs and Practices
Published by Sovereign Grace Publications
Post Office Box 1150
Shallotte, NC 28459
www.sovgrace.net
sovgracepublications@gmail.com

ISBN 978-1-929635-28-3

Scripture quotations are from the *King James Version.*

Printed in the United States of America.

CONTENTS

1
What Do Primitive Baptists Believe?

Two simple statements sum up Primitive Baptist beliefs: 1) **Primitive Baptists believe in sin**; 2) **Primitive Baptists believe in grace**. Some might counter, "All Bible believing Christians believe in sin and grace." Yet Primitive Baptists believe in sin and grace, the way the Bible describes sin and grace. The Bible does not teach a not-so-bad, 'white-washed' version of sin, which just needs a little help, so the sinner can be saved. Nor does it teach a not-so-good, 'off-white' version of grace, which needs just a little help, so the sinner can be saved.

God's description of sin is such that *there is so much bad in the best of men, that salvation by grace is the only possibility*. Further, God's description of grace is such that *there is not so much bad in the worst of men, that salvation by grace is an impossibility*. According to God's word, salvation by grace, and grace alone, is essential for the best of men, and sufficient for the worst of men. Salvation, which is solely by grace, and wholly by grace, is the only salvation that intermeshes with Bible truth.

Primitive Baptists believe in sin: the way the Bible describes sin. First of all, we believe in the doctrine of original sin, even that all who were in Adam became sinners by Adam's original sin. *Wherefore, as by one man sin entered into the world, and death by sin; and so death passed upon all men, for that all have sinned* (Rom 5:12). When Adam sinned, God judged all whom Adam would father to be sinners. Adam's sin not only condemned Adam to death, but also condemned to death every person who would come from Adam.

Secondly, we believe all men are sinners by nature. A man does not become a sinner when he commits his first sin. A man commits sin because he is a sinner by nature. Adam passed his fallen nature to his offspring. *And Adam...begat a son in his own likeness, after his image...* (Gen 5:3). Sinners can father nothing but sinners. *Who can bring a clean thing out of an unclean? Not one* (Job 14:4). We are judged to be sinners from conception. *Behold, I was shapen in iniquity; and in sin did my mother conceive me* (Ps 51:5). We are sinners at birth. *They go astray as soon as they be born, speaking lies* (Ps 58:3). We are sinners by our very nature: *by nature the children of wrath, even as others* (Eph 2:3).

Thirdly, we believe that the Bible condemns all men to be sinners by practice. *There is none righteous, no, not one...there is none that doeth good, no, not one* (Rom 3:10-12). All commit sins through their actions. All commit sins with their words. *The tongue can no man tame; it is an unruly evil* (Jas 3:8). The Bible condemns whisperers, backbiters, slanderers and talebearers. Foolish talk and jesting are condemned (Eph 5:4). Jesus even forbade idle words. *Every idle word that men shall speak, they shall give account thereof in the day of judgment* (Mt 12:36).

Yet it is not just what we do or say. Our wicked hearts are sufficient to condemn us to hell. *The heart is deceitful above all things, and desperately wicked: who can know it?* (Jer 17:9). We commit sin when our hearts lust. *Whosoever looketh on a woman to lust after her hath committed adultery with her already in his heart* (Mt 5:28). Our thoughts condemn us. *Whosoever is angry with his brother without a cause shall be in danger of the judgment* (Mat 5:22). Surely covetousness is a sin that occurs in the mind.

Moreover, sin is not just what we do, say or think. Sin is also what we do not do, that should be done. *To him that knoweth to do good, and doeth it not, to him it is sin* (Jas 4:17). When Jesus condemned the goats to hell, it was not for wrongs they had done, but for the 'right' that they had failed to do. *Inasmuch as ye did it not to one of the least of these, ye did it not to me. And these shall go away into everlasting punishment* (Mt 25:45-46).

Who can meet Jesus' standard of good? *Love your enemies, do good to them which hate you* (Lk 6:27). Who can say that they have no sin? *If we say that we have not sinned, we make him a liar* (1Jno 1:10). It does not help to say we are just 'little sinners'. *For whosoever shall keep the whole law, and yet offend in one point, he is guilty of all* (Jas 2:10). If Paul never ceased from being a sinner, what hope do we have of ceasing? *For the good that I would I do not: but the evil which I would not, that I do... O wretched man that I am! who shall deliver me from the body of this death?* (Rom 7:19, 7:24). Paul summed up all men's guilt. *What things soever the law saith, it saith to them who are under the law: that every mouth may be stopped, and all the world may become guilty before God. Therefore by the deeds of the law there shall no flesh be justified in his sight* (Rom 3:19-20).

So God judges all of us to be sinners by Adam's sin, by our natures, and by our personal sins, which come through our actions, words and thoughts. We all are sinners by what we do, but also sinners by what we fail to do. If we say we are not sinners, we just sinned again by telling such a lie. To claim to be a 'little sinner' makes hell no cooler. To say we have ceased from sin makes us better than Paul. Moreover, we are impotent by our own will and ability to recover ourselves from the fallen state, which we are in by nature. An unborn again man has no will to come to God, neither does he have a *'want to'*. Jesus said, *ye will not come to me, that ye might have life* (Jno 5:40). The unborn again natural man is a hater of God (Rom 1:30). The carnal mind considers God as an enemy (Rom 8:7). The natural man has no fear of God (Rom 3:18). The wicked do not even think about God (Ps 10:4). *The natural man receiveth not the things of the Spirit of God: for they are foolishness unto him* (1 Cor 2:14). What would motivate a man who thinks like this to come to God? He will not!

Furthermore, the unborn again man cannot come to God. He has no *'can do'*. Jesus said: *No man can come to me, except the Father which hath sent me draw him* (Jno 6:44). A natural man cannot know spiritual things (1Cor 2:14). He cannot understand, so that he would seek after God (Rom 3:11). The unborn again cannot see the things of the kingdom of God (Jno 3:3). Neither can he enter into that which he cannot see (Jno 3:5). The unborn again cannot hear spiritual words (Jno 8:43). The unborn again cannot believe (Jno 10:26). Nor can he be converted and become a believer (Jno 12:40). This unconvertible unbeliever cannot please God (Heb 11:6). Natural man cannot cease from sin (2Pe 2:14). The carnal mind cannot be subject to God's law (Rom 8:7). This *'cannot'* man is what he is by nature, and he cannot change. The *'cannot'* cannot become a spiritual *'can'* (Jer 13:23). How can an unborn again man with all these Bible-stated *'cannots'* ever be able to come to God? He cannot!

The scriptures liken regeneration to a birth. *The wind bloweth where it listeth...so is every one that is born of the Spirit* (Jno 3:3). Can a man help bring to pass his own birth? What did you do before you were you? The scriptures liken regeneration to a resurrection from the dead. *And you hath he quickened, who were dead in trespasses and sins* (Eph 2:1). Can a dead man help raise himself? How dead is dead? The scriptures liken regeneration to a new creation. *If any man be in Christ, he is a new creature* (2 Cor 5:17). Can the uncreated man help create himself? Did Adam help God create Adam? Regeneration is God's sovereign act, without any help from the yet-to-be born, still dead, yet-to-be created sinner. Primitive Baptists believe in sin to such an extent that if salvation is going to occur, it must totally be of God's will, God's power and God's choosing. **There is so much bad in the best of men, that salvation by grace is the only possibility.**

Primitive Baptists believe in the sovereign God who *doeth according to his will in the army of heaven, and among the inhabitants of the earth: and none can stay his hand* (Dan 4:35). This sovereign God's eternal will and purpose has always been to save His people by sovereign grace. This God is not the world's kind of god, who needs man's help so He can be God. Neither is this grace the world's kind of grace, which needs man's help to make it grace.

Let me lay out the sovereign God's plan of salvation by sovereign grace, which leaves no loopholes, even no chance of failure. Before creation, this sovereign God had His salvation so worked out that He could declare *the end from the beginning... saying, My counsel shall stand, and I will do all my pleasure ...yea, I have spoken it, I will also bring it to pass; I have purposed it, I will also do it* (Is 46:9-11). God's purpose in salvation began by God electing His children, even before He created. *He hath chosen us in him before the foundation of the world...* (Eph 1:4). God predetermined to give eternal salvation to each of His chosen. *Having predestinated us unto the adoption of children...* (Eph 1:5). The God, who rules heaven and earth, was not wrong in choosing people to be His children. *Hath not the potter power over the clay, of the same lump to make one vessel unto honour, and another unto dishonour?* (Rom 9:21). God did not elect His children based on any good that He saw in them. *For the children being not yet born, neither having done any good or evil, that the purpose of God according to election might stand, not of works, but of him that calleth* (Rom 9:11). God simply elected His people unconditionally *according to the good pleasure of his will* (Eph 1:5).

Salvation is not by man's will, or man's actions. Salvation is of God's will, God's action and God's mercy. *So then it is not of him that willeth, nor of him that runneth, but of God that sheweth mercy* (Rom 9:16). No one could possibly end up in heaven, if not for God's election of specific individuals to such an end. Let us reason together. Since salvation is not of man that *willeth* to come (*Ye will not come to me, that ye might have life* – cf. Jno 5:40), God has to be the one who has the will to come. Since salvation is not of him that *runneth*, in that man cannot come to God (*No man can come to me* – cf. Jno 6:44), God has to be the one who has the ability to come. Since man will not choose God, God has to be the one to do the choosing. *Ye have not chosen me, but I have chosen you* (Jno 15:16). In order for any to be saved, God had to choose particular individuals that He would come to and save. So we see that election is as essential to salvation as crucifixion and 'born again'. Thus election should not be ignored and ridiculed. God's election of a vast host from every nation and family under heaven is *to the praise of the glory of his grace* (Eph 1:6).

Primitive Baptists believe that God gave His elect people to Christ in the Covenant of Grace before time began, in order that Christ would save each and every one of them, when time is no more. Jesus often spoke of this eternal agreement from eternity past. He also spoke of the certain fulfillment of the terms of the covenant in eternity future. In John 6:37, we see the transaction in eternity past: *All that the Father giveth me...* We then see the certain success in eternity future: *...shall come to me; and him that cometh to me I will in no wise cast out.* In John 6:39, notice the covenant agreement: *...that of* *all which he hath given me...* And the sure success: *...I should lose nothing, but should raise it up again at the last day.* In John 10:29, we find the covenant in eternity past: *My Father, which gave them me...* And the certainty in eternity future: *...no man is able to pluck them out of my Father's hand.* In John 17:2, notice the assurance of the end: *...that he should give eternal life...* And then see that the assurance is for those who were given before the beginning: *to as many as thou hast given him.* In John 17:24, Jesus prayed that each one the Father had given Him in eternity past would be with Him in eternity future: *Father, I will that they also, whom thou hast given me, be with me where I am; that they may behold my glory...* Jesus' victory statement in eternity future will be that He has successfully saved each and every one that the Father had entrusted Him with from eternity past. *Behold I and **the children which God hath given me**.* (Heb 2:13).

It even seems that the transaction that occurred in the Covenant of Grace goes beyond the idea of the Father giving His chosen children '**to**' Christ, but that the Father even placed His children '*in*' Christ. Yet before we pursue this thought, let us digress and look a little deeper into something we have already mentioned. Let us further consider the doctrine of original sin, even the Bible's idea of being '*in*' another man, and receiving what that man earned by his actions. God judged all who were '*in*' Adam to be worthy of death, based on the fact that they were '*in*' Adam. What Adam did, counted as if they did it: *Wherefore, as by one man sin entered into the world, and death by sin; and so death passed upon all men...* (Rom 5:12). This idea of being '*in*' another man goes further than Adam. God also judged all who were '*in*' Christ to be worthy of eternal life, based on the fact that they were '*in*' Christ, and what Christ did, counted as if they did it.

Consider these words: *For as **in Adam** all die, even so **in Christ** shall all be made alive* (1 Cor 15:22) [emphasis added]. As Adam represented all men who were '*in*' him, even so Christ represented all men who were '*in*' Him. All who were '*in*' Adam received the consequences of what Adam earned by his actions: *For as **in Adam** all die...* Even so all who were '*in*' Christ received the consequences of what Christ earned by His actions: *Even so **in Christ** shall all be made alive.*

As Adam's sinfulness was accounted to all who were *'in'* him: *For as by one man's disobedience many were made sinners* (Rom 5:19), even so Christ's righteousness was accounted to all who were *'in'* Him: *By the obedience of one shall many be made righteous* (Rom 5:19). As by the offense of Adam, the judgment of condemnation came upon all who were *'in'* Adam: *Therefore as by the offence of one judgment came upon all men to condemnation* (Rom 5:18), even so by the righteousness of Christ the verdict of justification came upon all who were *'in'* Him: *Even so by the righteousness of one the free gift came upon all men unto justification of life* (Rom 5:18). As by one man's one sin, all who were *'in'* him were condemned to death: *For since by man came death* (1 Cor 15:21), even so by one man's perfect righteousness, all who were *'in'* Him were given eternal life: *By man came also the resurrection of the dead* (1 Cor 15:21).

So let us now return to the thought that the Covenant of Grace went beyond the Father giving His chosen children **'to'** Christ, but that the Father even placed His children *'in'* Christ. *He hath chosen us **in him** before the foundation of the world* (Eph 1:4). It is not of ourselves that we come to be *'in'* Christ. This thing is of God. *But **of him** are ye **in Christ Jesus*** (1 Cor 1:30). Because of our position of being *'in'* Christ, God counts what Christ did, as if we did it. Thus God declared that Christ's righteousness counts, as if it were ours. *For he hath made him to be sin for us, who knew no sin; that we might be made the righteousness of God **in him*** (2 Cor 5:21). Because of our being *'in'* Christ, we lose all condemnation. *There is therefore now no condemnation to them which are **in Christ Jesus**...* (Rom 8:1). From our position of being *'in'* Christ, we are made to be acceptable to God. *He hath made us accepted **in the beloved*** (Eph 1:6). Our being *'in'* Christ, grants us redemption and forgiveness. ***In whom** we have redemption through his blood, the forgiveness of sins* (Eph 1:7). We will be gathered home, because we are *'in'* Christ. *That in the dispensation of the fulness of times he might gather together in one all things **in Christ*** (Eph 1:10). Due to our being *'in'* Christ, we have an eternal inheritance. ***In whom** also we have obtained an inheritance, being* *predestinated according to the purpose of him who worketh all things after the counsel of his own will* (Eph 1:11). It certainly seems that everything about our eternal salvation is based on our having been placed *'in'* Christ Jesus.

Primitive Baptists believe in a successful Savior. Jesus finished His work of salvation to the point that nothing needs to be added in order to let Jesus save a sinner. Christ finished redemption for all for whom He died. *By his own blood he entered in once into the holy place, having obtained eternal redemption for us* (Heb 9:12). Jesus totally cleansed each one for whom He died. *As far as the east is from the west, so far hath he removed our transgressions from us* (Ps 103:12). Jesus reconciled to God all for whom He died. *When we were enemies, we were reconciled to God by the death of his Son* (Rom 5:10). Jesus suffered God's wrath in the place of all for whom He died. *But he was wounded for our transgressions, he was bruised for our iniquities: the chastisement of our peace was upon him; and with his stripes we are healed* (Is 53:5). God has counted Jesus' righteousness to belong to all for whom He died. *For he hath made him to be sin for us, who knew no sin; that we might be made the righteousness of God in him* (2 Cor 5:21). Christ perfected all for whom He died. *For by one offering he hath perfected for ever them that are sanctified* (Heb 10:14). Christ satisfied God concerning all for whom He died. *He shall see of the travail of his soul, and shall be satisfied* (Isa 53:11). God justified (declared to be righteous and innocent) all for whom Christ died. *Being justified freely by his grace through the redemption that is in Christ Jesus* (Rom 3:24). Christ shall eternally save all for whom He died. *Being now justified by his blood, we shall be saved from wrath through him* (Rom 5:9). The angel declared His success ahead of time. *He shall save his people from their sins* (Mt 1:21). Paul declared His success in the past tense. *Who hath saved us...* (2 Tim 1:9). Primitive Baptists believe in the 'successful Savior' who got the job done.

Primitive Baptists believe in Holy Spirit unassisted regeneration. *Not by works of righteousness which we have done, but according to his mercy he saved us, by the washing of regeneration, and renewing of the Holy Ghost* (Titus 3:5). 'Born again' comes only by the sovereign will and power of God. *The wind bloweth where it listeth...so is every one that is born of the Spirit* (Jno 3:8). At some point between natural conception and natural death, the Holy Spirit seeks out, finds, and moves upon each of God's chosen children in order to give them the eternal life, which God predetermined that each of them would have. Primitive Baptists maintain the Biblical truth that this regeneration is a sovereign act of God, and only of God. 'Born again' is not through the means of men. It is not by the help of men. It requires nothing of men. 'Born again' is totally, and only, to the praise of the God, who accomplishes it all by Himself.

Primitive Baptists believe that God's elect shall be preserved in grace, and shall never fall finally away. Jesus proclaimed final preservation in grace. *They shall never perish, neither shall any man pluck them out of my hand* (Jno 10:28). Election demands final preservation in grace. *Moreover whom he did predestinate, them he also called: and whom he called, them he also justified: and whom he justified, them he also glorified* (Rom 8:30). The Covenant of Grace requires final preservation in grace. *Of all which he hath given me I should lose nothing, but should raise it up again at the last day* (Jno 6:39). God's purpose demands final preservation in grace. *Who hath saved us, and called us with an holy calling, not according to our works, but according to his own purpose and grace...* (2 Tim 1:9). God's immutability demands that there will be final preservation in grace. *For I am the LORD, I change not; therefore ye sons of Jacob are not consumed* (Mal 3:6).

God's justice regarding Jesus' finished work demands final preservation in grace. If God is satisfied that each and every one that Jesus died for is paid for, cleansed, reconciled, made to be righteous, declared to be righteous, justified and saved, what can keep a one Jesus died for out of heaven? So if Jesus died for all people, then all must get to heaven. Yet the Bible is clear that all will not be in heaven. Jesus did not die for all people. Jesus died for God's elect people. Jesus saved each of them. Each and every one of them will be in heaven.

Regeneration demands final preservation in grace. God finishes what He started. *He which hath begun a good work in you will perform it until the day of Jesus Christ* (Phi 1:6). Those that Jesus calls shall live. *The hour is coming, and now is, when the dead shall hear the voice of the Son of God: and they that hear shall live* (Jno 5:25). The effectual call is to eternal life. *My sheep hear my voice...And I give unto them eternal life* (Jno 10:27-28). God is faithful to His call. *Who shall also confirm you unto the end, that ye may be blameless in the day of our Lord Jesus Christ. God is faithful, by whom ye were called...* (1 Cor 1:8-9). God will finally preserve in grace all He now calls by grace. *And I pray God your whole spirit and soul and body be preserved blameless unto the coming of our Lord Jesus Christ. Faithful is he that calleth you, who also will do it* (1 Ths 5:23-24).

God's unbreakable chain of salvation demands final preservation in grace. *Moreover whom he did predestinate, them he also called: and whom he called, them he also justified: and whom he justified, them he also glorified* (Rom 8:30). Every *'whom'* God started with, ends up a *'them'* that God will finish with. Nothing can pluck one from this unbreakable chain of salvation. From start to finish salvation is successful, because it is all of the Lord.

Primitive Baptists believe in sin, even sin that plunges all men into such a state that *there is so much bad in the best of men, that salvation by grace is the only possibility.* Primitive Baptists believe in grace, even grace that can raise any man from the lowest state, so that *there is not so much bad in the worst of men, that salvation by grace is an impossibility*. We believe that salvation by grace, and grace alone, is essential for the best of men, and sufficient for the worst of men. We believe that salvation, which is solely by grace and wholly by grace, is the only salvation that intermeshes with Bible truth.

2
Is There a God? If So, Who is He?

Is there really a God? The Bible declares that there is a God, and it goes on to declare that men know that there is a God. Men may not know **who God is**, yet men do know **that God is**. The Bible calls a man a fool, if he says that there is no God: *The fool hath said in his heart, there is no God* (Ps 14:1). The fool may say that there is no God, but God's creation proves that there must be. A reasonable man observes his surroundings and concludes that there has to be a Creator God. *The heavens declare the glory of God; and the firmament sheweth his handywork. Day unto day uttereth speech, and night unto night sheweth knowledge. There is no speech nor language, where their voice is not heard* (Ps 19:1-3). God created man with a sense of rationality that is common to men. Moreover, the wonder of creation declares to man's sense of reasoning that there must be a God. The spectacle of the skies (whether the sun by day or the stars by night) speaks the same common message to the common sense of men of all languages. The heavens declare the glory of God, in that the works of His hands can be seen in the sky.

For the invisible things of him from the creation of the world are clearly seen, being understood by the things that are made, even his eternal power and Godhead; so that they are without excuse (Rom 1:20). Observation of the complexities of the universe (both macro and micro) forces the rational mind to the reasonable conclusion that there must be a Creator. Any position, which does not recognize the wisdom and power of an eternally existent God, is a senseless and defenseless position.

Yet even with the God-given ability to know that there must be a God, many people refuse to acknowledge and believe that there is. *Because that, when they knew God, they glorified him not as God, neither were thankful; but became vain in their imaginations, and their foolish heart was darkened. Professing themselves to be wise, they became fools* (Rom 1:21-22). How can intelligent educated men, who even study the intricacies of God's creation, conclude that it all just happened by chance and time? They profess themselves to be wise, yet they have the thoughts of fools. To use the scientific method to study God's creation, and then to declare that science proves that there is no God, is to declare yourself not to be a true scientist, but to be a fool. Observation of creation teaches common sense reasoning that there must be an intelligent and powerful designer of it all.

As men know that there is a God, even without the Bible's testimony, they can also know that there must be only one God without the Bible. Now the Bible does repeatedly declare that there is only one God. *Hear, O Israel: The LORD our God is one LORD* (Deut 6:4). *For I am God, and there is none else; I am God, and there is none like me* (Is 46:9). *I am the LORD, and there is none else, there is no God beside me* (Is 45:5). *Before me there was no God formed, neither shall there be after me* (Isa 43:10).

Yet even without the Bible, men can come to the logical conclusion that there is only one God. If observation of creation teaches common sense reasoning that there must be a God, then contemplation of creation teaches common sense reasoning that there is only one God. As observation of creation says, "God caused everything," even so contemplation of creation asks, "Who caused the Cause?" If God is the cause of all things, then who is the cause of the cause of all things? Did something cause God? Is it possible that there is a creator of the Creator?

Come let us reason together. If God had a beginning, then something must have caused Him to be. If something caused God to be, then that something (which would have been both prior to God and superior over God) would be God. So if God was caused to be, then He is not God. God's cause would be God.[1]

So by necessity, at some point there must have been a 'First Cause' that caused everything, and that 'First Cause' must be eternal, without beginning. The One (and only one) Being of God

---

[1] If we say that God caused Himself to be, that would make God before Himself, which is an absurdity.

must have always existed. One God, the 'First Cause', is without cause, and is the cause of all. One God, the Eternal Being, is the cause of all other beings. All live, and move, and have their being in Him, yet He receives His Being from none. He is dependent on none — independent of all. This can be said of only one Being — and none other. Thus, there is one, and only one, God.

Well who is this one God? Eastern mystics claim 'God is everything'. Western scoffers claim 'God is not'. A 'Doctor of Philosophy' rants his sacrileges. A 'Medicine Man' chants his superstitions. Heathen idolaters make gods with their hands. Visionary dreamers form gods in their minds. Some trust a four-leafed clover. Some sign a cross. Some worship deceased ancestors. Some reverence sacred cows. Moses declared the God of the mountain. Mohammed declared the god of the mosque. Nebuchadnezzar declared a God on a throne. Jesus declared a God on a cross. The hippies said, "God is dead." The angel said, "He is risen."

So who is God? And what is He? Will the real God please stand up? Is it even possible to know who God is? My gut feelings tell me that I know who the real God is. My gut feelings further tell me that I can trust my gut feelings. I know who God is, and I know that what I know is right. Surely the God of my parents, the God of my church, the God of my preacher is the true God. I am certain that my God is the real God. He must be. You see, I believe it with all my heart. So it must be so!

Yet reasoning and observation tell me that strong gut feelings can sometimes be wrong feelings. Think about the false prophets of Elijah's day. They surely had strong gut feelings about their gods, in that they cut themselves and sacrificed their own blood to those gods who were not God. It cannot be denied that their feelings were strong feelings, but it is certain that their feelings were wrong feelings. By the end of the day, the real God proved them to be wrong. With conviction they strongly believed in the reality of their gods, but their strong beliefs did not make them right, nor did their wrong beliefs turn their unreal gods into the real God.

Consider the suicide bombers of our day. They willingly martyr their lives to kill Christians. I do not believe in the god they believe in. I do not see how they can believe in the god they claim. Yet I cannot deny that they sincerely believe in their god. Though I know that their gut feelings are wrong feelings, I cannot deny that their gut feelings are strong feelings. I believe that they believe in their god with all their hearts.

So my conclusion is that strong gut feelings can be wrong gut feelings, and even the strongest wrong feelings cannot make the wrong to be right. Moreover, sincere belief can believe in untruth, and even the greatest belief in an unreal god cannot make the unreal god real. Yet in spite of these observations about how gut feelings can be undependable, my gut feelings still tell me that all these things apply to others, who have wrong gut feelings, but not to me. My gut feelings still tell me, that my gut feelings are right gut feelings.

Yet I know what the suicide bomber would say about my gut feelings. While my gut feelings continue to tell me that my feelings are right feelings, I expect that his feelings are telling him that he is right. At this point I might say, "I have the answer; I have the book of answers. My Bible not only declared the false prophets in Elijah's day to be wrong, but it also declares the beliefs of the suicide bombers to be wrong."

Yet at that point the suicide bomber might reply, "Oh, but I have a book, too!" Then the eastern mystics pipe in, "Look at all our books." The PhD boasts, "I have more books than you all." The scoffers say, "Bah! Who needs books? The world is full of books, and books are full of baloney!"

So can we ever get beyond gut feelings? Is it possible to get past men's opinions? Man can look at creation and know that there must be a God. Yet as we look back through history, and around at cultures, it seems that there are gods many and lords many. Is God just to be pondered, or can He be known? Men have always pondered the idea of God, and in all their pondering, men have churned out lots of ideas about God. Men have reasoned and speculated. Men have fought and debated. Yet left to themselves, men have figured out very little about God. Men can know by common sense reasoning **that God is**, but men have no way of knowing **who God is**. Left to man's own limited ideas and imaginations, God would forever remain past our finding out. Truly the only way for men to discover the identity of the real God would be if the real God revealed Himself to men.

Yet if we are waiting for a revelation from God concerning His identity, we need to wait no longer. God has revealed Himself to men, and men can know who the real God is through God's revelation. We were on the right track when we grabbed for the Bible to prove who God is, because the Bible is God's revelation concerning Himself, and many other things. It is only through the Bible that men can know God. The scriptures of the Old and New Testament are the word of God. The Bible is a special book beyond all books — beyond their books. The scriptures were not actually penned by God. The Bible was written by men, but the men wrote what God inspired them to write. The Bible is truly God's book, wherein God reveals Himself to man. Men can know that there has to be such a thing as God without the Bible, but men cannot know who God is without the Bible. The scriptures tell us who the one true God is.

This takes us back a step. We cannot just take for granted that the scriptures of the Old and New Testament are the inspired revelation of God. Before we use the Bible to discover who God is, we need to be satisfied that the Bible is a book that merits its use for such a purpose. Lots of people have lots of books, but what makes our Bible better than any other book? Why do we say the Bible is the word of God? How can we know the Bible is inspired by God, and not just another book written by men? How can we know which god of all the books is the real God? If we can prove the Bible to be the revelation of God, and not just another book by a man, then we have grounds to take the Bible as the book for our only rule of faith and practice. Let us see if we can prove that the Old and New Testament Bible is truly the book that is inspired by the one and only, true and living God.

The Bible accurately prophesied countless future events. What are the odds of predicting hundreds of events with 100% accuracy? In God's book, all predictions come to pass in full accuracy, because the God who can see the future wrote the book. There were dozens of prophecies in the Old Testament that came to pass in the coming of Jesus. Who, but God, could have declared the details from the coming of the babe to His rising from the grave? The Bible recorded where Christ would be born, even centuries ahead of time. God alone could have named Bethlehem as the place. Who, but God, could have known of the killing of the babes and the fleeing into Egypt? Who would have dreamed of Jesus coming out of Nazareth? How could Psalm 22 have declared all those particular things that Jesus would say on the cross? How could it be known how He would die, where He would die, and hundreds of years before, when He would die? Who could have predicted resurrection? From the manger to the resurrection, the details were foretold. Moreover, every minute detail came to pass, even dozens of prophecies all happened just as it was written.

Let us contemplate other amazing prophecies, not related to Jesus. Let us consider two different Old Testament kings, beginning with a King of Judah named Josiah. *And he cried against the altar in the word of the LORD, and said, O altar, altar, thus saith the LORD; Behold, a child shall be born unto the house of David, Josiah by name; and upon thee shall he offer the priests of the high places that burn incense upon thee, and men's bones shall be burnt upon thee* (1 Kings 13:2). So what is the big deal? The verse calls Josiah by name and declares what he will do. Yet the amazing thing is that these words were written about 300 years before the birth of this man named Josiah. It is impossible for men to even be sure about what will happen tomorrow, but here we are given details about a particular man, and things this particular man would do, even 300 years into the future.

Now let us observe the verse that describes the fulfillment of the prophecy, even 300 years later. *And as Josiah turned himself, he spied the sepulchres that were there in the mount, and sent, and took the bones out of the sepulchres, and burned them upon the altar, and polluted it, according to the word of the LORD which the man of God proclaimed, who proclaimed these words* (2 Kings 23:16). Who, but God, could have called Josiah by name 300 years before he was born? Who, but God, can see 300 years into the future? Who, but the real God, could have written such a book that records not only the past and the present, but with equal accuracy, the Bible records the future?

Next, consider the words of prophecy written about a King who would be named Cyrus.[2] *That saith of Cyrus, He is my shepherd, and shall perform all my pleasure: even saying to Jerusalem, Thou shalt be built; and to the temple, Thy foundation shall be laid* (Is 44:28). Now observe the fulfillment of the prophecy. *Now in the first year of Cyrus king of Persia, that the word of the LORD by the mouth of Jeremiah might be fulfilled, the LORD stirred up the spirit of Cyrus king of Persia, that he made a proclamation throughout all his kingdom, and put it also in writing, saying, Thus saith Cyrus king of Persia, The LORD God of heaven hath given me all the kingdoms of the earth; and he hath charged me to build him an house at Jerusalem, which is in Judah* (Ez 1:1-2).

There are three outlandish things about this prophecy. First of all, God called a king by name, writing it down 175 years ahead of time. Secondly, God predicted the rebuilding of a city, well before the time that it was destroyed. Finally, God predicted an event that no reasonable person could have expected to happen. This was not like predicting that the sun would rise tomorrow.

The thing that God wrote down, which He would accomplish through Cyrus, was a thing unheard of in history. Who could have imagined that any king would voluntarily release a nation of slaves from captivity? Yet, God made the long shot prediction that even the very king named Cyrus would act so out of character. Nearer the time of the fulfillment of the prophecy, God raised Cyrus to be one of the most powerful kings that the world has ever known. Then God stirred the spirit of Cyrus, whose heart God held in His hand, to release a nation of slaves. The King of kings was in control of it all. The God of the Bible ruled over this king on the earth, just

---

[2] It should be noted that these words were written about 175 years before the time of Cyrus.

like He had said He would nearly two centuries before. What a God! What a book!

Let us evaluate the Bible, as it relates to science. The Bible is not a science book. Yet where it speaks of science, it speaks correctly. Ponder the words: *It is he that sitteth upon the circle of the earth, and the inhabitants thereof are as grasshoppers; that stretcheth out the heavens as a curtain, and spreadeth them out as a tent to dwell in* (Is 40:22). Why did Isaiah say *the circle of the earth*, when men of his day very probably still considered the earth to be flat? Why did Isaiah particularly say that God *stretcheth out the heavens*, even using a verb tense that indicated an ongoing process? If Isaiah had been speaking of God stretching out the heavens in creation, he should have said that God *stretched out the heavens*. Yet instead of saying that God *stretched out the heavens*, Isaiah said that God *stretcheth out the heavens*, indicating that God not only did stretch out the heavens in creation, but that he is also still stretching out the heavens. Isaiah might have gazed at the stars, but he was not a modern day physicist. Isaiah could not have known of an ever expanding universe. Yet the God, who told Isaiah how to say what he said, knew all about it. Wow! God did write the book! It is a book beyond the capabilities of man.

The archeologist's spade continues to prove the Bible to be an accurate book. From the Dead Sea scrolls, to the writings of the ancient Hittites, to the way the walls of Jericho fell, to the pyramids and tombs of Egypt, to the plains of Sodom and Gomorrah, to the tetrarchs of Rome, every dig just adds more evidence to the Bible's historical accuracy.

So the Bible itself proves that it could only have been written by revelation from the real God. The Bible establishes itself to be God-inspired by its multitudes of prophecies that time has proved to be true, by its multitudes of statements that science has proved to be true, and by its historical accuracy that archeology has proved to be true.

The Bible not only proves itself to be God-inspired, it even declares itself to be thus. *All scripture is given by inspiration of God* (2 Tim 3:16). The Bible claims its very words to be God's words. *For the prophecy came not in old time by the will of man: but holy men of God spake as they were moved by the Holy Ghost* (2 Pet 1:21).

Beyond the Bible proving itself to be true, and declaring itself to be true, as a final point as to the authenticity of the Bible, Jesus said of God's word: *Thy word is truth* (Jno 17:17). A scoffer might say, "So what, who is this Jesus?" This Jesus said of Himself: *I am the truth*. All He said was truth. All He did was truth. He is the one who repeatedly stated that He would rise from the grave after three days. If you had been there and heard Jesus say such a thing, you might have laughed Him to scorn, that is, until He really did it. Then you would have been assured that you could count on what this man said to be the truth.

So since the Bible itself proves itself to be truth, and since the Bible itself declares itself to be truth, and since Jesus (who is truth) proclaimed the Bible to be truth, then we can surely trust the Bible concerning who the real God is. Our answer, as to who the real God is, can be found in the book of truth, even the book that must have been written by revelations originating from the real God.

So after a long side road of proofs as to where to find our answer, we finally come to the conclusion that we can trust God's book to tell us the truth about who the real God is. It should be easy now. Let us find our answer. Ah, here is what God says about Himself. *For there are three that bear record in heaven, the Father, the Word, and the Holy Ghost: and these three are one* (1 Jno 5:7).

What does that say? *These three are one.* Is this who the real God is? How can that be? What does that mean? Left to himself, and in his deepest thinking, man could never have envisioned the God described in these words. A three in one God could only be known by revelation. Revealed truth is stranger than imagination! In man's craziest dreams, he would never have described God as three persons being one. Moreover, the idea of a three in one God is not just beyond the possibilities of imagination. It is also beyond the possibilities of comprehension. In man's deepest intellect, he will never understand God, as three persons being one. So we thought we had it all figured out. Well we do have it figured out as to where to find the answers, but when we begin to look, we learn that the answer is bigger than our thinking.

Now add to that confusion the idea that the man named Jesus is as much God, as God is God. How can the Creator of man be made of a woman? How can the giver of life be born of a womb? How can Sovereignty sigh? How can Eternity die? How can this man be God? How can this thing be?

The Biblical concept of a three in one God (and entwined in that concept, the idea of a God/man Jesus Christ) has caused much confusion throughout the history of the world, and even throughout the history of the church. Men have hated the idea, misunderstood it, and rejected it from the beginning. It was the accusation for which Jesus was crucified. It is an idea that has split churches since the time of Christ. It has ever been, and still is, a concept that is impossible for a natural mind to fully grasp.

So who is God? There is no more difficult task in nature than to attempt to comprehend God. The scriptures are clear that He is past our ability to find out. His ways are past our ways, and He is past our understanding. He has revealed much about Himself in His word, but as finite creatures, we cannot even understand what He has revealed. Yet we do not have to be able to understand all about God in order to believe in Him. God has given His children the gift of faith, so that we are enabled to believe that He is, and that He is who He is said to be. We are told that He is one. We are told that He is three. We may not be able to understand this, much less explain it. Yet by God's gift of faith, we can believe it, and we can praise God for who He is.

As a final practical thought, if the Bible is '*thus saith the Lord*', and proves itself to be the real book of the real God, then we should make the Bible our only rule of faith and practice. God gave us His Bible. God has preserved it for us. We should not try to change it, or even question it. We simply need to believe the Bible and put its teachings into practice.

3
What is the Doctrine of the Trinity?

In his deepest thinking, man could never have envisioned the God described in these words: *For there are three that bear record in heaven, the Father, the Word, and the Holy Ghost: and these three are one* (1 Jno 5:7). The fact that God is three persons in one can only be known by revelation. Moreover, the idea of a three in one God is not just beyond the possibilities of man's imagination. It is also beyond the possibilities of man's comprehension. In man's deepest intellect, he will never understand God, as three persons being one.

Jesus proclaimed His oneness with the Father. *I and my Father are one* (Jno 10:30). Men hated Jesus for such words. As a matter of fact, Jesus' confession to equality with the Father was the so-called crime for which He was crucified. Moreover, things got no better after Jesus' crucifixion. The apostles continued to face stiff resistance, not only for proclaiming the resurrection of Christ, but also for holding to the idea of the plurality of the one God, even that this Jesus was the God Whom He had claimed to be.

The resistance to the idea of a Trinity has continued throughout the history of the church. Rather than accept the idea as truth, many have rejected it as impossible. For example, in the second century Sabellius taught that there was not a trinity of persons in the Godhead, but simply a trinity of offices held by one God. Many still cling to this error, believing that it solves the mystery of the Godhead. Yet, the idea of one person with three offices cannot agree with the words: *For there are three that bear record in heaven, the Father, the Word, and the Holy Ghost: and these three are one.* To 'bear record' is to be a witness, even to be called on to give testimony. In any situation where a person is asked to bear record to something, or to give his testimony concerning the matter, it would be absurd to consider one person to be three witnesses, just because he might hold three offices. If the same man is called to testify once (because he could claim to be the mayor), and again (because he could claim to be a pastor), and yet again (because he could claim to be a salesman), there would still be only one who bears record. The only way that three can *'bear record'* is if there are three distinct and individual persons, and not one person with three offices.

In the fourth century, Arius introduced the false notion that Jesus was the first created being. In the Arian sense, the idea of a Trinity is explained away as one supreme God, and two subordinate and inferior gods created by the supreme God. This kind of thinking is really no different to the false gods of cultures throughout history. The Greeks and the Romans claimed a supreme god and multiple underling gods. So mythology already had this idea long before Arius' day. Whether the claim is two lesser gods, or hundreds, neither fits the revelation that the three are one.

To refute the Arian teaching of a created Christ who would in turn create everything else, consider the following: *In the beginning was the Word, and the Word was with God, and the Word was God. The same was in the beginning with God. All things were made by him; and without him was not any thing made that was made* (Jno 1:1-3). Arian thinking acknowledges that Christ created all things, but with the one exception that Christ did not create Himself.

This error is destroyed in the statement: *without him was not any thing made that was made.* It is impossible to make these words fit the idea of a created Christ. If Christ was created by another, then there can be no truth to the thought that *without him was not any thing made that was made,* in that He Himself would have been made without Him. Thus, this one text alone refutes the whole Arian notion of a created Christ.

So either the Bible is wrong, or Arius was wrong. We may choose to believe what God has revealed about God, or we may choose to believe what we imagine about God, or we may choose to believe only what we can reason out with our finite minds. There is no doubt that a finite mind cannot fully comprehend a being of God that is three persons. Yet, by the gift of faith, the mind can believe the things that it cannot understand.

Though we admit that we cannot understand such a thing as the Trinity, let us attempt to reason about what must be involved in the truth: the three are one. As we begin to think about the idea that the three are one, let us present an initial thought that **the idea of Trinity without unity is absurdity**. Consider these words: *The grace of the Lord Jesus Christ, and the love of God, and the communion of the Holy Ghost, be with you all. Amen* (2 Cor 13:14). Here each of the three persons of the Trinity is presented as possessing three distinct and different things.

As I ponder *the grace of the Lord Jesus Christ, and the love of God, and the communion of the Holy Ghost,* questions come to my mind concerning how intertwined the three persons of the Trinity might be. Does each work independently, even uncooperatively? Like oil and water, individually beneficial, just do not mix well. Does each do His own thing, unconscious of the others? Like the right hand that does not know what the left hand is doing. Does each take care of His own business, knowing where the lines are? Like suburban neighbors, who occasionally wave, but each stays on his side of the fence. Do the three make up a well-balanced triad, each with His talents and failings, but cooperating to get the job done? Like Jack Sprat and his wife. He could eat no fat, and she no lean, yet by combining, they licked the platter clean.

These thoughts are not only absurd, but even border on blasphemy. To view the persons of the Trinity as being uncooperative with each other is ridiculous. The idea that one is unaware of the others' plans and efforts is outlandish. The proposition that each minds His own business and keeps the relationship casual is preposterous. For the persons of the Godhead to be restricted by what they cannot do (as the Sprat couple) is unthinkable.

It would seem that no conscientious believer would ever be guilty of thinking such things as these about God, yet close analysis of the man-made plans of salvation reveals similar absurdities to what we have just described. The plans of salvation created and devised by men do border on blasphemy, in that they present the three persons of the Trinity in an uncooperative relationship. The Father, Son and

Spirit are described as if each is unaware of the others' plans and efforts. Men's so-called proposals for salvation present the Trinity in disunity, each seemingly with His own agenda. The Bible says *the three are one.*

Surely this must be so in the salvation of sinners. Surely the plan is one plan. The work is one work. The end is one end. The Lord our God is one Lord! The one Lord cannot be a divided God. *The three are one!* Though each person of the Trinity sometimes does different things, there are no lines drawn in the sand. The three are a perfectly cooperative unit, always working together in everything. They have common motives, and are in common in their efforts to bring success to their motives. Never divided, and always united. Trinity, yet Unity. *The three are one!*

As we think upon the words: *The grace of the Lord Jesus Christ, and the love of God, and the communion of the Holy Ghost,* what about *the grace of our Lord Jesus Christ?* Is Jesus the only one of the Trinity who has grace? Of course not! The Father is a God of grace: *...continue in the grace of God...* (Act 13:43). The Son is a God of grace: *...the grace of the Lord Jesus Christ...* (Act 15:11). The Holy Spirit is a God of grace: *...the Spirit of grace* (Heb 10:29). Surely Father, Son and Spirit are in unity, as far as grace goes.

What about *the love of God?* Is the Father the only one of the Trinity who shows love to His people? Of course not! The Father is the God of love: *For God so loved the world, that he gave his only begotten Son* (Jno 3:16). The Son is a God of love: *Greater love hath no man than this, that a man lay down his life for his friends* (Jno 15:13). The Holy Spirit is a God of love: *Now I beseech you...for the love of the Spirit...* (Rom 15:30). Surely love is not confined to the love of God, but is as much of the Son and Spirit, as it is of the Father.

What about *the communion of the Holy Ghost?* Is the Holy Ghost the only one of the Trinity who has communion with His people? Of course not! The Father is the God of communion: *...and truly our fellowship is with the Father...* (1 Jno 1:3). The Son is the God of communion: *I will not leave you comfortless: I will come to you* (Jno 14:18). The Holy Spirit is the God of communion: *...if any comfort of love, if any fellowship of the Spirit...* (Phi 2:1). Surely communion and fellowship with God are communion and fellowship with the entire Trinity.

What about the unity of the Trinity in creation? The Bible says that each of the three was united in the common purpose of creation. Of the Father, the Bible declares: *In the beginning God created the heaven and the earth* (Gen 1:1). Of the Son, the Bible declares: *All things were made by him; and without him was not any thing made that was made* (Jno 1:3). Of the Holy Spirit, the Bible declares: *The Spirit of God hath made me...* (Job 33:4). Surely creation was a united work of the Trinity.

What about Jesus' resurrection? Just who is responsible for the greatest event in history? Each of the three was united in raising Jesus from the grave. Of the Father, the Bible says: *This Jesus hath God raised up, whereof we all are witnesses* (Act 2:32). Jesus Himself said: *I have power to lay it down, and I have power to take it again* (Jno 10:18). Of the Holy Spirit, the Bible says: *...being put to death in the flesh, but quickened by the Spirit* (1 Pet 3:18). Surely the resurrection of Jesus is a united work of the Trinity.

No matter the activity that God undertakes, the three Persons of the Godhead always move together in perfect unity and cooperation. Grace, love, and communion are extended from all three. Though any of the three by Himself would have been capable, creation was a joint venture. Jesus' resurrection is to the praise of each, and to the praise of all three.

Surely there must be unity in the Trinity, with never a hint of disunity. Surely the One God, who is three persons, can never be opposed to Himself. Surely the Father, the Son and the Holy Spirit agree in one, and as one. Surely the work of the Father, the work of the Son, and the work of the Holy Spirit are one work. Surely what one does, the others would not hinder. Surely the plan and purpose of one is the plan and purpose of all. Surely the relationship is 'All for one, and one for all'.

So let us revisit salvation. Are the three united in saving sinners? Do they work together in the different aspects of salvation? The Bible speaks of a phase of salvation, where God planned the details before time began. The Bible speaks of a phase of salvation, where

God paid for His peoples' sins on a cross. The Bible speaks of a phase of salvation, where God gives spiritual life individually to each of His children, at some point during their natural lives. The Bible speaks of a phase of salvation, where God finally saves each of His children to glory.

Let us consider one verse which proclaims all these phases of salvation. *Moreover whom he did predestinate, them he also called: and whom he called, them he also justified: and whom he justified, them he also glorified* (Rom 8:30). There is unity in the Trinity in salvation. Each one the Father predestinated—the Spirit called. All that the Spirit called—the Son justified. All the Son justified—end up glorified. This unbreakable chain of salvation is a united effort of the Trinity. This chain describes the three in one God working together in salvation. God working together with God to save God's people is an unstoppable plan of salvation. All the *'whoms'* end up *'thems'*. None is lost along the way. Salvation is of the Lord. Salvation is certain. *The three are one.*

There must be unity of the Trinity in God's plan of salvation. Surely the three persons of the Trinity worked together in the planning phase? It seems absurd to think that the three argued, and that perhaps one stormed out, saying that He would do it His way. It seems doubtful that two of the three knew the plan, while one was left in the dark. It seems unreasonable to think that there would have been any disagreement in the planning phase. After all, the all-wise God was doing the planning. So the plan would be a perfect plan, and they all three would know that the plan was perfect. All three were in on the planning. All three were agreeable to the plan. All three left the planning phase knowing His part in the plan. All three left the planning phase with a purpose to save. The purposes of God always come to pass. God's plan of salvation is a certain plan. In the end, it is certain that all God ever purposed to save will be saved. *The three are one.*

Do you suppose Jesus still remembered the planning phase, when He went to the cross? Did He remember the part where the Father elected His people? Did Jesus still remember that the Father had given the chosen children to Him in the planning phase? Jesus said that He came to do His Father's will. The Father's will and purpose had been established in the planning phase of salvation. Jesus came to save each and every one of God's children that the Father had given to Him. Jesus did save each and every one whom He planned to save. In the final phase none will be lost. *The three are one.*

Do you suppose the Holy Spirit still remembers the planning phase, when He moves as he pleases to born again His children? Does the Holy Spirit remember the part where the Father elected His people? Does the Holy Spirit know each and every one of the children that God gave to Jesus in the planning phase? Does the Holy Spirit know the exact group that Jesus died for? Does the Holy Spirit know just how, and when, and where, to find each one of them? Will the Holy Spirit lose any that He agreed to find? In the end all God's chosen children, for whom Jesus died, will have been born again. *The three are one.*

In God's plan of salvation, the Father elected the ones to be saved. The Father gave the elect to His Son. The Son died for the elect who had been given to Him. The Holy Spirit gives spiritual life to each and every one that Jesus died for. Each of the three was in on the plan. Each knew His part in the plan. Each does His part in the plan. There is unity in the Trinity in the salvation of sinners. Salvation is of the Lord: Father, Son and Holy Spirit. *The three are one.*

Man-made plans of salvation inevitably introduce disunity into the Trinity. Salvation by God's sovereign grace, and grace alone, is the only plan that maintains perfect oneness in the Godhead. A united Trinity can only be preserved in the Bible taught truths: unconditional election, particular redemption, irresistible grace and final preservation. If a reasonable person consents to the essential conclusion that God must agree with God, then he is also forced to conclude that salvation must be by sovereign grace.

Why do I say this? Every other plan, except salvation totally by grace, invariably disrupts the unity of the Trinity. Men's devised plans of salvation describe the three persons of the Godhead with different wills and motives, different degrees of commitment, different levels of ability, and different success rates. Some so-called plans of salvation have one in the Trinity doing for the sinner without measure, while another of the three fails to do. Where one of the three would have great faithfulness to the cause of salvation, another falls short. While one of the Persons would have unquestionable love, another's love seems fickle. Where one acts of His own will, another can only react to man's will. While one moves as He pleases, another is hindered in moving. The God that men describe is pitted against Himself—a Trinity in disunity.

For example, consider men's idea of supposed general atonement. They surmise that Christ died for all men, and that He offers salvation to all who believe and accept. Will all for whom Christ died ultimately be saved in this proposed plan? No! According to the supposed plan, only those who accept His offer will be saved. The error of general atonement proclaims that Christ died for all. Yet it will not allow all that Christ died for to be saved. These statements not only present Christ as a weak and conflicted God, unable to attain what He desires, but also present a lack of unity in the Trinity.

First of all, the idea that Christ died for all, contrasted to the Biblical truth that the Father elected some, creates disunity between these two persons of the Trinity. Secondly, the idea that Christ died for all, contrasted to the notion that the Holy Spirit only saves some, creates disunity between these two persons in the Trinity. This self-opposed general atonement plan of salvation has the Son trying to save, but failing. It has the Father never intending to save in the first place. It has the Spirit not even now trying to save. Thus 'general atonement' says that the Father, Son and Spirit are very different. The Bible says *the three are one.*

In an effort to maintain unity in the Trinity, some try to explain election away by saying that the Father elected those that He foresaw would accept Christ. They go on to explain regeneration by saying that the Holy Spirit gives the new birth to those that He now sees do accept Christ. Though these two premises are untrue, they at least maintain a consistency between the work of the Father and the work of the Spirit, in that the Father is said to have elected a particular group, and the Spirit is said to born again the exact same group. Yet, this supposed plan of salvation still declares that the Son died for everybody. So this proposal has the Father foreseeing whom He would save, and the Spirit now seeing whom He will save, but the Son blindly trying to save everybody. This man-made plan of salvation demands significant disunity in the Trinity. The Bible says *the three are one.*

What about the oneness of God's love? Many claim that God, the Father, loves all people, so much as to give His Son for all. They claim that God, the Son, loved all people, so much as to die for all. Yet God, the Holy Spirit, does not love the people, even so much as to find and save any of them. In this plan, if the sinner wants salvation, he has to ask for it. The Father did not wait to be asked. He just by grace sent His Son. The Son did not wait to be asked. He just by grace went to the cross. Yet the Holy Spirit waits to be asked. He is content just to wait it out, even to the point where it is too late.

This certainly seems to indicate a difference in the love of the persons in the Godhead. To send your Son to die is unquestionable love. To willingly die on the cross is unquestionable love. To refuse to make the first move is questionable love. The Bible says *the three are one.* This so-called plan of salvation says they are different. Again, there is disunity in the Trinity.

The problem is not that the Holy Spirit is the weak link in salvation. The problem is a man-made plan of salvation that makes man the means to his own salvation. To make man the means to his own salvation, not only makes for a weak link in the plan, but it also makes for disunity in the Trinity. If the Spirit has to wait for man, then His hands are tied. He ceases to be the God that acts in accordance to His sovereign will. He becomes the puppet that can only react to the will of man. That is not the sovereign God of the Bible!

If man is an essential link in the chain of salvation, then the certainty of salvation becomes uncertainty. Yet the Bible does not describe God's salvation of His people in uncertain terms. The Bible speaks emphatically when it says: *thou shalt call his name JESUS: for he* **shall save** *his people from their sins* (Mt 1:21). The verse does not say that Jesus will try to save all people, but finally settle for some people. It does not say that Jesus will do His part, and then wait to see who will do their part. The proclamation is that Jesus **shall save** His people. That is a certain statement about a certain salvation. Salvation is certain, because man has no part in his own salvation.

Salvation is certain, because salvation is totally of the Lord. Salvation is certain because salvation is by God, and God alone. Salvation is certain because salvation is by grace, and grace alone. Salvation by grace alone is the only plan of salvation that preserves the unity of the Trinity. God the Father chose a people. God the Son redeemed that same precise people. God the Holy Spirit does born again each one of those same exact people, in that He individually, and personally, calls each of them from spiritual deadness to spiritual life. In the end, not one of those same people shall be lost.

Salvation by grace is the only plan that maintains consistency and harmony from start to finish. From before the beginning, God had a consistent plan to save His people. Each person in the Trinity knew His part in the plan. Each person in the Trinity does His part in the plan. In the end, the Father, the Son, and the Holy Spirit will be satisfied that each has done His part in the plan. Would you expect less from an all wise, all-powerful, sovereign God? In the end, all of God's children who were in the plan from the beginning shall be saved. Salvation is certain, because there is a united consistency within the Godhead. Salvation is certain, because there is unity in the Trinity. *The three are one.*

4
Is Jesus Really God?

According to His own purposes, the real God has oftentimes raised men of this world to positions of great power. Some of these 'pawns' of the true God have claimed that they themselves are gods. The claim itself proves such men to be nothing more than arrogant fools. A rational man observes the scope and complexity of creation, and very sensibly concludes that he is not the cause of such wonders. The fool has said in his heart that there is no God. The greater fool has said in his heart that he is God. The very idea that a man would claim to be the Creator God represents the height of arrogant insanity. As a side note, the mighty man who claims to be God is inevitably, and finally, proved to be the fool. His claims of godhood are soon buried with him in a tomb of death, where the worms consume his mortal flesh.

Yet in spite of the foolishness of the very thought of a man being God, the Old Testament foretold of the coming into the world of a man who would indeed be God. The New Testament gives details of the whole thing, and then describes the significance of it all. The idea that God became man is the theme of the Bible and the theme of salvation. It is the centerpiece of eternity. The Bible does not say that God came into the world in such a way that He just appeared to look like a man. The Bible does not say that God came pretending to be a man. The Bible declares that God really came into this world as a real man.

He even came into the world in the very usual way that men come, in that He was born into this world, just like the sinners that He came to save. Yet His birth was most unusual, in that He was born of a virgin mother. He had no earthly father. God was His Father. The one who came was the Son of God.

Now who would have believed a young girl with such a story as that? Who can believe such a thing, even now? It might have been more believable if God had flown down on a bolt of lightning, or suddenly appeared out of a flaming whirlwind. Yet God chose to do the impossible, rather quietly and without much ado. The God, who fills eternity, entered the womb of a virgin. The God, who had created all, was born into the world as a babe. The whole thing does seem a bit far-fetched. The very idea of a God/man is quite unbelievable from start to finish, and the mental image of God as a helpless baby is indeed hard to swallow. From a rational standpoint, the story seems to border on bizarre.

So let us further explore the apparent contradictions in the paradoxes of the very thought of a God/man. To make matters even more conflicting, let us use the Bible itself to show the seeming impossibility of it all. First of all, think of the God that fills the universe. *Do not I fill heaven and earth? saith the LORD* (Jer 23:24). The question was once posed as to how such an enormous God could possibly dwell on the earth. *But will God indeed dwell on the earth? behold, the heaven and heaven of heavens cannot contain thee...* (1 Kings 8:27). So if God fills the expanse of the universe, and if God is so large that the earth cannot hold Him, then try to explain how God can be confined to a womb for nine months! *Before they came together, she was found with child of the Holy Ghost* (Mt 1:18).

Ponder the Creator of all being made of a woman! This very Son of God is the Creator of all. *For by him were all things created, that are in heaven, and that are in earth...* (Col 1:16). How can the Creator of all, Himself be made? *But when the fulness of the time was come, God sent forth his Son, **made of a woman**...* (Gal 4:4). *Concerning his Son Jesus Christ our Lord, which was **made of the seed of David** according to the flesh* (Rom 1:3). *And the Word **was made flesh*** (Jno 1:14).

Think of the immutable God undergoing mitosis within the placenta! Jesus is none other than the unchangeable God. *For I am the LORD, I change not* (Mal 3:6). The Bible says of Jesus: *Jesus Christ the same yesterday, and to day, and for ever* (Heb 13:8). How can the unchangeable God start as one cell, and end up a child? How can God experience all the changes that go along with nine months in a womb? *Thine eyes did see my substance, yet being unperfect; and in thy book all my members were written, which in continuance were fashioned, when as yet there was none of them* (Ps 139:16).

Consider the idea that 'Omnipresence' walked! (Let that one soak in a second.) God is everywhere, at once, all the time. *Whither shall I flee from thy presence? If I ascend up into heaven, thou are there: if I make my bed in hell, behold, thou art there* (Ps 139:7-8). If Jesus is God (and He is), and if Jesus is everywhere all the time (and He is), then it seems a bit unusual that Jesus would have to walk to get to where He already was. *After these things Jesus walked in Galilee...* (Jno 7:1). *Nevertheless I must walk to day, and to morrow, and the day following: for it cannot be that a prophet perish out of Jerusalem* (Lk 13:33).

Ponder the conflict in the idea that 'Omniscience' learned! God is omniscient. He knows everything about everything. *Great is our Lord, and of great power: his understanding is infinite* (Ps 147:5). *O the depth of the riches both of the wisdom and knowledge of God!* (Rom 11:33). If Jesus is God (and He is), and if Jesus already knew everything about everything (and He did), how can it be possible for Jesus to increase in wisdom? *And Jesus increased in wisdom and stature, and in favour with God and man* (Lk 2:52).[1]

How can 'limitless Strength' grow weary? God is the all-mighty God, and Jesus is that mighty God. *For unto us a child is born, unto us a son is given...and his name shall be called Wonderful, Counselor, The mighty God...* (Isa 9:6). The all-mighty God never gets weary. *Hast thou not known? hast thou not heard, that the everlasting God, the LORD, the Creator of the ends of the earth, fainteth not, neither is weary?* (Isa 40:28). Yet the man Jesus grew weary. *Jesus therefore, being wearied with his journey, sat thus on the well* (Jno 4:6). Indeed, it seems strange to find God asleep. The Bible says of God: *He that keepeth thee will not slumber* (Ps 121:3). Yet, the Bible says of Jesus, who was the all-mighty God: *And he was in the hinder part of the ship, asleep on a pillow* (Mt 4:38). How can this be?

His hands held the world, but He had nowhere to lay His head. God's hands hold everything. *The eternal God is thy refuge, and*

---

[1] This verse is unexplainable in more ways than one.

underneath are the everlasting arms (Deut 33:27). Jesus maintains the whole creation. *By him all things consist* (Col 1:17). Jesus holds all His people in His hands. *And I give unto them eternal life; and they shall never perish, neither shall any man pluck them out of my hand* (Jno 10:28). Yet, while holding His world in His hands, and while holding His people in His hands, Jesus had no place to lay His head to sleep. *And Jesus said unto him, Foxes have holes, and birds of the air have nests; but the Son of man hath not where to lay his head* (Lk 9:58).

Do you not find it outlandish that God could be hungry and thirsty? God is the feeder of the birds. *Behold the fowls of the air: for they sow not, neither do they reap, nor gather into barns; yet your heavenly Father feedeth them* (Mt 6:26). Yet God Himself was hungry. *And when he had fasted forty days and forty nights, he was afterward an hungered* (Mt 4:2). Jesus is the one who gives living water. *Jesus... answered and said unto her, If thou knewest the gift of God, and who it is that saith to thee, Give me to drink; thou wouldest have asked of him, and he would have given thee living water* (Jno 4:10). Yet this same Jesus saith, *I thirst* (Jno 19:28). The same God who rained manna in the wilderness, and the same Christ who was the rock that poured water for the multitudes, experienced hunger and thirst. Amazing indeed!

How can the God, who does whatever He is pleased to do, be troubled? Surely, God is God, and He does His pleasure. *But our God is in the heavens: he hath done whatsoever he hath pleased* (Ps 115:3). It is hard to envision the God who always does His pleasure being in a situation that would trouble Him. Yet the man, Jesus, was often troubled. *He groaned in the spirit, and was troubled* (Jno 11:33). *Now is my soul troubled* (Jno 12:27). *When Jesus had thus said, he was troubled in spirit* (Jno 13:21). If Jesus was God (and He was), and if God does what He pleases (and He does), then why did Jesus not just fix whatever was troubling Him, and cease from His troubles?

Do you find it a bit confusing that 'Sovereignty' sighed? Jesus is the sovereign King of heaven and earth. He is the King of kings and Lord of lords. *For he spake, and it was done; he commanded, and it stood fast* (Ps 33:9). Yet this sovereign ruler over everything came to a point where He sighed. *And looking up to heaven, he sighed* (Mr 7:34).

People sigh in despair, when they do not know where to turn, even when they do not have the answers. How can this be of God? How can the real God ever come to the point of a sigh?

Is it not a bit confusing how 'Omnipotence' could ever come to tears? Jesus is omnipotent. He has all power. *And Jesus came and spake unto them, saying, All power is given unto me in heaven and in earth* (Mt 28:18). Yet, *Jesus wept* (Jno 11:35). At another time, Jesus prayed to His Father and wept bitterly. *Who in the days of his flesh, when he had offered up prayers and supplications with strong crying and tears unto him that was able to save him from death* (Heb 5:7). How can the God, who has all power to fix anything, ever experience *strong crying and tears*?

It seems impossible that the Almighty would ever say, "If it be possible." God is all-mighty. *I am the Almighty God* (Gen 17:1). Jesus Himself spoke the words. *With God all things are possible* (Mt 19:26). Yet the God, Jesus Christ, groaned the words: 'if it be possible'. *If it be possible, let this cup pass from me* (Mt 26:39).

How can the all-wise God ask, "Why?" God understands everything. God has all wisdom in all things. *In whom are hid all the treasures of wisdom and knowledge...* (Col 2:3). Surely God knows all the 'whys' to all the situations. Yet Jesus, who is God, asked "Why?" *My God, my God, why hast thou forsaken me?* (Mt 27:46).

Who can constrain God? *None can stay his hand* (Dan 4:35). Do you find it a bit contradictory that a man-made nail held the hand that none could stay? *In his hands the print of the nails...* (Jno 20:25). How can such a thing be?

Perhaps the most contradictory of all the paradoxes concerning the God/man Jesus Christ is how 'Eternity' can die. Jesus is the God who encompasses eternity. *In the beginning was the Word, and the Word was with God, and the Word was God* (Jno 1:1). Yet how can He which is eternal die? *When Jesus therefore had received the vinegar, he said, It is finished: and he bowed his head, and gave up the ghost* (Jno 19:30). The Bible further says: *For when we were yet without strength, in due time Christ died for the ungodly* (Rom 5:6). The wonder of salvation is that Jesus would die for sinners! Perhaps the bigger wonder is that Jesus **could** die for sinners! In the whole scheme of things, perhaps Jesus' death is as big a miracle as His resurrection! How can 'Eternity' die?

After considering all these impossible to explain paradoxes in the whole idea of God being man, you might think that I do not believe in such an irrational absurdity. Yet, as I go back to the Bible and look at the details about this man Jesus, I find a fact that I cannot ignore, even a truth that absolutely convinces me to believe what common sense says cannot be. What if this man, Jesus, did what the arrogant fool could not do? What if this man Jesus saw no corruption? Oh, but I am getting ahead of myself. Let us first tell the story of this man, Jesus.

At about the age of thirty, this Jesus began to prove Himself to be very special. His many miracles drew attention from far and wide. At His command, the devils would flee, and the blind could see. He touched the untouchable lepers, and they were cleansed. He spoke to the deaf, and they could hear. At His word, the dumb could speak, the lame could leap, and the dead did rise. Yet beyond His miracles, *never man spake like this man* (Jno 7:46). *He taught them as one having authority* (Mt 7:29). The people flocked to Him, to experience His miracles, and to hear His words.

All was going very well, except this Jesus kept bringing up the idea that He was really God. *I and my Father are one* (Jno 10:30). *He that hath seen me hath seen the Father...* (Jno 14:9). *And he that seeth me seeth him that sent me* (Jno 12:45). The so-called religious men of the day hated Jesus for His claims that He was God. *Therefore the Jews sought the more to kill him, because he not only had broken the sabbath, but said also that God was his Father, making himself equal with God* (Jno 5:18).

As it turned out, Jesus confession to being the Son of God was the so-called crime for which He was crucified. *But he held his peace, and answered nothing. Again the high priest asked him, and said unto him, Art thou the Christ, the Son of the Blessed? And Jesus said, I am* (Mr 14:61-62). *And they said, What need we any further witness? for we ourselves have heard of his own mouth. And the whole multitude of them arose, and led him unto Pilate* (Luk 22:71-23:1). In their minds such a claim was blasphemy, and for the so-called crime that Jesus had claimed to be God, they crucified Him.

One of the strange things about Jesus' crucifixion is that Jesus had known about it all along. He had often spoken of it, repeatedly telling His followers that He would be crucified. In some ways Jesus even set the stage for His own crucifixion. As the time drew near, Jesus told His followers that He must go to Jerusalem, so that it would happen. Yet there was more to it than just being crucified. Jesus had also repeatedly told His followers that He would be buried for three days, and that He would raise Himself from the grave.

Remember the arrogant fool who claimed to be God. Remember how everybody had the last laugh when he was buried in a tomb of death, where the worms consumed his mortal flesh. Now what would you have thought of a man, who not only claimed to be God, but repeatedly declared that He would prove it by raising Himself from the dead? Common sense says that only a fool would make such claims. You might have assumed that Jesus was a fool, until He did it. A self-resurrection can change peoples' minds. When the one who had made such claims really did raise Himself from the grave, you would have been compelled to conclude that this man, Jesus, was not a fool at all. He must be what He claimed to be, even Whom He claimed to be. Jesus is God.

Jesus really did raise Himself from death. If not, the scoffers would have stopped it all by simply presenting His dead body. Nobody stole His body. First of all, His discouraged and fearful followers immediately went into hiding. Secondly, Roman soldiers stood guard at His sealed tomb. Finally, over five hundred witnesses testified to the fact that Jesus arose.

The reality of resurrection changed people. After seeing resurrection, Jesus' cowardly companions found new courage. They died as martyrs, because they refused to stop preaching the reality of Jesus' resurrection, and the truth that this Jesus was God. Resurrection turned the world upside-down.

When Jesus raised Himself from death, many began to believe. I believe too. I say that Jesus must be the God that He claimed to be.

If He got the raising Himself from the dead part right, I firmly believe that He must have been right about all His other claims. I believe Jesus' claim that He is God. I also believe His claim that He will give eternal life to His people. I believe in the God/man, Savior Jesus Christ. I cannot understand or explain how a man can be God, but I conclude that the man, Jesus, truly was, and is, God. Even though the idea of a God/man is more easily rejected as impossible, than accepted as truth, I choose to believe it, simply because the Bible says it is so. Since the Bible proves itself to be truth in so many ways, and since Jesus proved Himself to be God through His self-resurrection, I choose to believe what the Bible says (and what Jesus said) about Jesus truly being God.

Now let us further look at the Bible to determine what it declares about the idea of the God/man, Jesus Christ. Here is the most straightforward verse in all of scripture to express the truth that Jesus is God. *For there are three that bear record in heaven, the Father, the Word, and the Holy Ghost: and these three are one* (1 Jno 5:7). There is no doubt that Jesus is *the Word*. The Bible says: *In the beginning was the Word, and the Word was with God, and the Word was God* (Jno 1:1). There is no doubt that the Word became a man. *And the Word was made flesh, and dwelt among us* (Jno 1:14). There is no doubt that the Bible declares that Jesus is God.

The voice of the Father twice proclaimed that Jesus was His Very Son. This happened once at Jesus' baptism: *And lo a voice from heaven, saying, This is my beloved Son, in whom I am well pleased* (Mt 3:17). It happened again on the Mount of Transfiguration: *While he yet spake, behold, a bright cloud overshadowed them: and behold a voice out of the cloud, which said, This is my beloved Son, in whom I am well pleased; hear ye him* (Mat 17:5).

The Bible declares Jesus to be the Creator God. *All things were made by him; and without him was not any thing made that was made* (Jno 1:3). And in another place: *For by him were all things created, that are in heaven, and that are in earth* (Col 1:16). Jesus is God.

The Bible proclaims that '**God**' laid down His life for us. *Hereby perceive we the love of **God**, because he **laid down his life** for us* (1 Jno 3:16). Surely Jesus is the '**God**' who laid down His life. The Bible further says that God's people are **looking for** *that blessed hope, and the glorious* **appearing of the great God** *and our Saviour Jesus Christ* (Titus 2:13). The Savior Jesus Christ is who Christians are looking for to come back, and that Jesus is here called the great '**God**'. There is no doubt that these verses declare Jesus to be '**God**'.

The Bible even directly calls the Son, '**O God**'. *But unto the Son he saith, Thy throne, O God, is for ever and ever: a sceptre of righteousness is the sceptre of thy kingdom* (Heb 1:8). The Bible further proclaims Jesus to be 'God with us'. *Behold, a virgin shall be with child, and shall bring forth a son, and they shall call His name Emanuel which being interpreted is, God with us* (Mt 1:23). Jesus is God.

The Bible proclaims Jesus to be the mighty God, and even to be the Father. *For unto us a child is born, unto us a son is given: and the government shall be upon his shoulder: and his name shall be called Wonderful, Counselor, The mighty God, The everlasting Father, The Prince of Peace* (Is 9:6). Jesus is one with the Father. Jesus is God.

The Bible declares Jesus to be the exact likeness of God. *Who being the brightness of his glory, and the express image of his person...* (Heb 1:3). Thus Jesus did not take any glory from God by claiming to be God. *Who, being in the form of God, thought it not robbery to be equal with God...* (Phi 2:6). The Bible further says that in Jesus was everything that is God. *For in him dwelleth all the fulness of the Godhead bodily* (Col 2:9). If Jesus had all the fullness of God in Him, then there is no part of God that Jesus does not fully contain. Jesus is God.

God claimed the name, 'I Am'. *And God said unto Moses, I AM THAT I AM: and he said, Thus shalt thou say unto the children of Israel, I AM hath sent me unto you* (Ex 3:14). Jesus likewise took the name, 'I Am'. *Jesus said unto them, Verily, verily, I say unto you, Before Abraham was, I am* (Jno 8:58). Jesus is that I AM. Jesus is God.

Some might find it surprising that the Old Testament often used the Hebrew name, YHWH, to speak of the Jesus that was to come into the world. YHWH is equal to the name, Jehovah. YHWH is translated **LORD**, with all capital letters in our Bible. Here is one of many examples where Jesus is called Jehovah. *I the LORD am thy Saviour and thy Redeemer, the mighty One of Jacob* (Is 49:26).

Thus, the Bible considers Jesus to be one with God, equal with God, and even God. Jesus is called God, Emmanuel (God with us), and even Jehovah. There is no doubt that the Bible undeniably proclaims these things to be truth. We can choose to believe what God has revealed about Himself in His word, or we can choose to believe only what the finite mind can reason out. The Three-in-One God is no doubt past what a finite mind can comprehend. The idea of God being a man is likewise impossible to understand and explain. Yet by the gift of faith, we can believe what we cannot understand. I firmly believe that Jesus is God.

5
How Do Primitive Baptists Differ from Other Baptists?

At one time, most Baptists seemed to believe essentially the same things concerning the basic Bible doctrines, especially the doctrines that pertained to God's plan for eternal salvation. It would surprise most modern-day Baptists to know that our Baptist forefathers did not scoff at the Bible's teachings that God unconditionally elected particular individuals to be His children, and that God predestinated that these particular chosen people would eventually, and eternally, be conformed to the image of His Son, Jesus Christ. Historical Baptists did not reject these Bible truths, but defended the beliefs: that God chose particular people, that God gave those particular people to Christ, that Christ died for those particular people, and that Christ secured the eternal salvation for each of the particular individuals whom God had chosen.

Yet, in the late 1700's and the early 1800's, prominent men among the Baptists began to preach and promote new ideas. Around 1832, the differences in the old doctrines and the new ideas became so pronounced that a split in the Baptists occurred. One group would come to be called Primitive Baptist, while the other would come to be called Missionary Baptist.

Most of today's Baptists would be shocked, if they took the time to do a little research, even about their own local church. With a little searching, they should be able to locate and examine an old historical copy of the Articles of Faith, which would have been adopted when their church was constituted. In this historical document, which states the beliefs on which their church was founded, they will very likely find a statement declaring unquestioned belief in God's election of a God-chosen people. If their Baptist church is a rather newly constituted church, they might need to go to the history of the Baptist church from which they branched off. Or if their church is a longstanding Baptist church, and if they do not find such a statement of belief, a search of their own church history should show when their church changed its Articles of Faith, and adopted new statements of belief.

Now the statements in the Bible, on which historical Baptists based their Articles of Faith, have not changed. The Bible's statements continue to confirm that salvation is based in God's purposes, and not in man's decisions. God's perfect plan of salvation remains the same as it has always been. The word of God has not changed; nor has God changed. It is men who have changed. Preachers have changed.

Through the centuries, Baptist preachers defended God's doctrines, even to the point of being willing to burn at the stake. Modern day preachers have become men pleasers, preaching man-made doctrines that exalt men. The God of glory receives the glory that is due Him, only in the preaching of salvation that is by grace, and grace alone.

Primitive Baptists continue to hold to the original Baptist beliefs.[1] They still cling to the original New Testament doctrines, concerning God's successful and sufficient salvation of a vast host of particular, God-chosen individuals. Primitive Baptist preachers persist in proclaiming the old Baptist beliefs, even the Bible truth, that salvation is solely and completely by the grace of God.

Most other Baptists have come to believe in the Arminian version of eternal salvation. This much more popular Arminian explanation of salvation includes the idea of general atonement, or universal redemption, which claims that Christ died for every individual who has ever lived, or will ever live, through all history, and throughout the whole world. The Arminian explanation also includes the idea that the sinner must actively participate in his own new birth, and that the sinner's choice makes the difference, as opposed to God's choice.

---

[1] As a matter of interest, the word, *primitive*, was synonymous with the word, *original*, at the time of the Baptist split.

Primitive Baptists hold dear the age old doctrine of limited atonement, or particular redemption, which claims that Christ died for His people: a vast host of people from throughout history and throughout the world, even people from every nation and family under heaven. Yet Christ did not die for every individual, worldwide and throughout world history. In many places the Bible declares that God's salvation is for a defined group of people that God possessively claims to be His people.

The angel said: *Thou shalt call his name JESUS: for he shall save **his people** from their sins* (Mt 1:21). God said: *For the transgression of **my people** was he stricken* (Is 53:8). Jesus said: *I am the good shepherd: the good shepherd giveth his life for **the sheep*** (Jno 10:11). Then Jesus further explained that some people are not His sheep: *But ye believe not, because **ye are not of my sheep*** (Jno 10:26). Jesus finally declared that He gives eternal life only to His sheep. ***My sheep** hear my voice, and I know them, and they follow me: And **I give unto them eternal life**; and they shall never perish...* (Jno 10:27-28).

So did Jesus die for all people, or just for some defined group of people? And what did Jesus accomplish for whomever He died? I borrow from the teachings of the great Bible scholar, John Owen, in saying that there are only a few possible options, as to the answers to these questions. The first possibility is that Jesus might have died for all the sins of all the people. So if Jesus died for all the sins of all the people, then Jesus would have paid for all the sins of all the people (leaving none of the people owing anything). And if Jesus died for all the sins of all the people, then Jesus would have removed all the sins from all the people (leaving none of the people with any sins that could be charged against them). Thus, if none of the people owe any debt, and if all the people have all their sins removed, then all the people would be justified, and it would be certain that all the people must someday end up in heaven. Yet the Bible says that all people will not someday end up in heaven. So the conclusion to this possibility is that Jesus did not die for all the sins of all the people.

The second possibility is that Jesus might have died for some of the sins of all the people. So if Jesus died for some of the sins of all the people, then Jesus would not have paid for all the sins of any of the people, (leaving all the people still owing for some of their sins). And if Jesus died for some of the sins of all the people, then Jesus would not have removed all the sins from any of the people, (leaving all the people with some sins that could still be charged against them). Thus, if all the people still owe for some of their sins, and if none of the people have all their sins removed, then none would be justified, and it would be certain that none of the people will ever end up in heaven. Yet the Bible says that some people will someday end up in heaven. So the conclusion to this possibility is that Jesus did not die for some of the sins of all the people.

The third possibility is that Jesus might have died for all the sins of some of the people. So if Jesus died for all the sins of some of the people, then Jesus would have paid for all the sins of some of the people, even the people for whom He died, (leaving none of the people for whom He died owing anything). And if Jesus died for all the sins for some of the people, then Jesus would have removed all the sins from some of the people, even the people for whom He died, (leaving none of the people for whom He died with any sins that could be charged against them). Thus, if some of the people (that is all the ones for whom Jesus died) owe no debt, and if some of the people (that is all the ones for whom Jesus died) have all their sins removed, then some of the people (that is all the ones for whom Jesus died) would be justified, and it would be certain that all the people for whom Jesus died must someday end up in heaven. This possibility fits what the Bible says about some, but not all, people ending up in heaven. This possibility fits what the Bible says about salvation by grace, and grace alone. This possibility fits the scheme of historical Baptist beliefs. This possibility is not just possibility. This possibility is the Bible's reality about God's salvation.

Let us further pursue the idea that every individual for whom Jesus died must end up in heaven. Let us do this by examining what the Bible proclaims about what Jesus accomplished through His sacrificial death on the cross. First of all, the Bible declares that Jesus accomplished redemption (paid the debt in full) for every individual for whom He died. *Neither by the blood of goats and calves, but by his own blood he entered in once into the holy place, having obtained eternal redemption for us* (Heb 9:12). The statement is past tense. The redemption has been accomplished. The accomplished redemption is eternal redemption, even forever redemption. So there is no more debt to be paid, and no more debt can ever be owed, for any person for whom Jesus died.

Secondly, the Bible proclaims that Jesus removed the sins from all for whom He died. *As far as the east is from the west, so far hath he removed our transgressions from us* (Ps 103:12). Jesus not only removed the sins from those for whom He died, but He also made sure that the sins would never be remembered again. *I, even I, am he that blotteth out thy transgressions for mine own sake, and will not remember thy sins* (Is 43:25). Moreover, Jesus cleansed away the sins from every individual for whom He died. *Unto him that loved us, and washed us from our sins in his own blood* (Rev 1:5). If Jesus removed, blotted out, and washed away all the sins of all for whom He died, then there are no more sins left to the account of any person for whom Jesus died. So all the ones for whom Jesus died have become sinless in God's judgment.

Thirdly, the Bible says that Jesus reconciled to God every individual for whom He died. *And all things are of God, who hath reconciled us to himself by Jesus Christ...* (2 Cor 5:18). And in another place: *For if, when we were enemies, we were reconciled to God by the death of his Son, much more, being reconciled, we shall be saved by his life* (Rom 5:10). Both statements are past tense. God **hath reconciled** us to Himself by Jesus Christ. We **were reconciled** to God by the death of His Son. It is finished. The peace is made. So there can be no rejection of any person for whom Jesus died and for whom His death accomplished reconciliation.

Fourthly, Jesus took the wrath of God in the place of every person for whom He died. *Surely he hath borne our griefs, and carried our sorrows... But he was wounded for our transgressions, he was bruised for our iniquities: the chastisement of our peace was upon him; and with his stripes we are healed...the LORD hath laid on him the iniquity of us all...for the transgression of my people was he stricken* (Is 53:4-6). Jesus suffered in the stead of each one for whom He died. God poured out His wrath on His Son. So there is no more punishment due to any for whom Jesus died.

Fifthly, Jesus accomplished remission (the removal of the consequences of sin) for all for whom He died. *For this is my blood of the new testament, which is shed for many for the remission of sins* (Mt 26:28). Jesus has already suffered the consequences of the sins for His people. Jesus has thus eliminated the eternal consequences of sin for all for whom He died. So there can be no future consequences for sin placed on any for whom Jesus died.

Sixthly, Jesus has made to be righteous every person for whom He died. *For he hath made him to be sin for us, who knew no sin; that we might be made the righteousness of God in him* (2 Cor 5:21). All for whom Jesus died were made the righteousness of God. Nothing can be wrong with any for whom Jesus died and *made the righteousness of God.* So nothing can be held against anyone for whom Jesus died, in that He made them the righteousness of God.

Seventhly, Jesus made every person for whom He died to be perfect. *For by one offering he hath perfected for ever them that are sanctified* (Heb 10:14). Jesus has perfected (past tense) all who were sanctified (set apart) to salvation. It is further noted that the perfection is *for ever.* So Jesus has already accomplished an ever-existing perfection for all for whom He died.

Eighthly, Jesus successfully saved every individual for whom He died. The angel said: *Thou shalt call his name JESUS: for he shall save his people from their sins* (Mt 1:21). Paul said: *Who hath saved us…* (2 Tim 1:9). Jesus came *to save His people,* and He *hath saved* all He came to save. It is finished. So Jesus has saved all for whom He died.

Ninthly, Jesus' suffering satisfied God's justice. *He shall see of the travail of his soul, and shall be satisfied: by his knowledge shall my righteous servant justify many; for he shall bear their iniquities* (Is 53:11). When God looked upon the suffering of Jesus, God was satisfied that Jesus' salvation was successful in saving every person for whom Jesus died. So what can go wrong with a salvation that God is satisfied with?

Tenthly, God has justified every individual for whom Jesus died. The Bible says: *Being justified freely by his grace through the redemption that is in Christ Jesus* (Rom 3:24). The Bible further says: *Much more then, being now justified by his blood, we shall be saved from wrath through him* (Rom 5:9). The Bible still further says: *Who shall lay any thing to the charge of God's elect? It is God that justifieth* (Rom 8:33). To justify is to render the verdict of innocence. To justify is to legally declare to be righteous. God was satisfied that Jesus had saved all for whom He died. Thus God has justified (declared to be righteous and innocent) all for whom Jesus died. So if God has justified, what can condemn any for whom Jesus died?

Jesus completely and successfully accomplished eternal salvation for every individual for whom He died. If Jesus fully paid their debt, cleansed them from all sins, reconciled them to God, took God's wrath upon Himself in their place, removed the consequences of their sins from them, made them to have His righteousness, perfected them forever, successfully saved them, satisfied God in it all, and brought upon them God's eternal justification, what can keep a single one for whom Jesus died out of heaven?

The point is that every individual for whom Jesus died has been saved, and must finally be eternally saved. So if Jesus died for all people, then all people must finally get to heaven. Yet the Bible is clear that all people will not finally get to heaven. Thus, the Bible's answer is that Jesus did not die for all people. Jesus died for a particular people, for His people, for God's elect people, for the ones the Father had given Him in the Covenant of Grace before the world began. Moreover, Jesus' atonement is not universally offered to all people, but is limited to, and successfully applied to, the particular ones for whom He died.

Primitive Baptists believe in the age old doctrine that the choice for salvation is of God and not of the sinner. The Bible teaches that God foreknew, elected and predestinated His people before the world began, not according to any foreseen actions or thoughts in the people, but according to His own purpose and grace. *According as he hath chosen us in him before the foundation of the world, that we should be holy and without blame before him in love: Having predestinated us unto the adoption of children by Jesus Christ to himself, according to the good pleasure of his will, To the praise of the glory of his grace, wherein he hath made us accepted in the beloved* (Eph 1:4-6).

Primitive Baptists believe that God chose His elect people, and gave them to Jesus Christ in the Covenant of Grace before the beginning of the world. The Father gave His chosen elect people to Jesus, so that Jesus would save them from their sins. Jesus came into the world with this mission in mind. *Thou shalt call his name JESUS: for he shall save **his people** from their sins* (Mt 1:21).

The people, who are here called *his people*, had become Jesus' people when the Father gave His elect people to Jesus. *Thine they were, and thou gavest them me* (Jno 17:6). Jesus came to *give eternal life to as many as thou hast given him* (Jno 17:2). Jesus came into the world to do His Father's will in regards to the salvation of His Father's chosen people. *For I came down from heaven, not to do mine own will, but the will of him that sent me* (Jno 6:38). At the end of time, Jesus will have saved each and every one of the Father's elect people that the Father had given to Him before the world began. *And this is the Father's will which hath sent me, that of all which he hath given me I should lose nothing, but should raise it up again at the last day* (Jno 6:39).

All Baptists say they believe in the depravity of man, but most go on to tell how man has to help save himself. Primitive Baptists say that man is so depraved that he has no power, by his own free will and ability, to raise himself from the fallen state he is in by nature. Primitive Baptists read where Jesus said: *And ye will not come to me, that ye might have life* (Jno 5:40). So we hold to the truth that 'born again' is not by man's free will. Primitive Baptists read where Jesus said: *No man can come to me, except the Father which hath sent me draw him...* (Jno 6:44). So we hold to the truth that 'born again' is not by man's ability. Primitive Baptists read where Paul said: *But the natural man receiveth not the things of the Spirit of God: for they are foolishness unto him: neither can he know them, because they are spiritually discerned* (1 Cor 2:14). So since Paul said that spiritual things are foolishness to the natural man, we believe that it is unreasonable to think that 'born again' occurs by a natural, unborn again man strangely deciding to seek after what he thinks of as foolishness. And since Paul said that the natural man cannot know spiritual things, we logically believe that 'born again' cannot occur by man seeking that which he cannot know about. Primitive Baptists read where Jesus said: *Except a man be born again, he cannot see the kingdom of God* (Jno 3:3). So since Jesus said that unless a man is first born again, he cannot even see the kingdom of God, Primitive Baptists believe it would be unreasonable to think that 'born again' is by a man reversing Jesus' order, and seeing that which he cannot see.

Concerning the new birth, Primitive Baptists believe that the Bible proclaims a *'born again'* that cannot be accomplished by man for himself, or for his neighbor. The new birth is a miracle that only God can do. Jesus spoke of 'born again' as a sovereign act of God, the Holy Spirit. *The wind bloweth where it listeth...so is every one that is born of the Spirit* (Jno 3:8). Jesus spoke of 'born again' as a life giving command from His own voice. *The hour is coming, and now is, when the dead shall hear the voice of the Son of God: and they that hear shall live* (Jno 5:25). This resurrection from spiritual deadness to spiritual life is an ongoing process: *The hour is **coming**, and **now is**.* This life-giving act of 'born again' is not by the voice of the preacher, or by the sound of the gospel. It is by Jesus' command: *The dead shall hear the voice of the Son of God: and they that hear shall live.*

Jesus spoke of 'born again' as the drawing to Jesus of one who could not come on his own. *No man can come to me, except the Father which hath sent me draw him: and I will raise him up at the last day* (Jno 6:44). Of his own ability, man cannot come. Yet the Father draws the man to Jesus who would not, and could not, come on his own. Moreover, all who are born again by the Father's drawing power will be raised up by Jesus at the last day to be with God forever.

Baptists have historically held to a *'born again'* that goes beyond what man is able to do. Notice the following statement from the *1655 Midland Confession of Faith* (Article 8):

> *That all men until they be quickened by Christ are dead in trespasses (Eph 2:1); and therefore have no power of themselves to*

believe savingly (Jno 15:5). But faith is the free gift of God, and the mighty work of God in the soul, even like the rising of Christ from the dead (Eph 1:19). Therefore consent not with those who hold that God hath given power to all men to believe to salvation.

From this 1655 Baptist quote, we see that historical Baptists were determined to hold to the Bible-taught doctrine that God, and God alone, accomplishes 'born again', and that man cannot believe himself into such a miracle.

Today's Primitive Baptists feel the same sense of urgency about holding to these truths. Modern day Baptists are onboard the 'Born-Again-*Ism* Bandwagon'. This 'do-it-yourself-born-again' plan loses all sense of reasonableness. The Bible describes the miracle of regeneration, as being born. *The wind bloweth where it listeth...so is every one that is born of the Spirit* (Jno 3:8). Can the unborn do anything to bring about his own birth? (What did you do before you were you?) The Bible's *'born again'* is a resurrection from spiritual deadness. *And you hath he quickened, who were dead in trespasses and sins* (Eph 2:1). Can one who is dead in sin raise himself from his spiritual deadness? (How dead is dead?) The Bible describes the miracle of regeneration as a new creation. *If any man be in Christ, he is a new creature* (2 Cor 5:17). Can the yet-to-be-created do something to create himself? (Could Adam have helped God make Adam?) The idea of actively participating in our own regeneration is not only illogical, it is also unscriptural. Moreover, it robs God of His glory.

The Bible teaches that salvation is of the Lord. God planned it before time. God paid for it on the cross. God applies it to each of His children at the new birth. At the end of time, each of God's children will be with Him, and will be saved for all eternity. Unlike most modern day Baptists, today's Primitive Baptists believe (as historical Baptists believed) that salvation is of the Lord. We preach the successful Savior, who did save and will save each and every one He died for.

6

How Do Primitive Baptists Differ from Reformed Protestants?

Most people would assume that an explanation of the difference between Primitive Baptists and Protestants should begin with the details of when the Primitive Baptists split from the original Protestant churches. Many would imagine that since Primitive Baptists are not Catholics, they must be some branch of Protestantism. Yet this is not true. History proves that Baptists were in existence prior to the Reformation, even before the time when the Protestants broke from the Catholics. Thus a surprising difference between Primitive Baptists and Protestants is that they never were of the same group.

It should not surprise the Bible student that a church, which held to New Testament doctrines, would have been in existence somewhere in the world, prior to the time of the Reformation. Jesus declared that even hell itself could not destroy the church that He would establish. *I will build my church; and the gates of hell shall not prevail against it* (Mt 16:18). The Old Testament had prophesied that Jesus would set up a kingdom in this world in the days of the Roman Empire, and that Jesus' kingdom would never cease to exist, from the time that He set it up to the end. *In the days of these kings shall the God of heaven set up a kingdom, which shall never be destroyed...and it shall stand for ever* (Dan 2:44). So since Jesus' church is a key aspect of His kingdom, and since Jesus proclaimed that nothing could destroy His church, we can reasonably assume that the church that Jesus established has existed somewhere in this world from His day to now.

So where was Jesus' church prior to the Reformation? Many people would point to the Catholic Church, but this cannot be the case, because the Bible teaches that Jesus' church can be recognized by the truth that she maintains: *the church of the living God, the pillar and ground of the truth* (1 Tim 3:15). Since it is obvious that the Catholic Church has not maintained the truth of salvation by grace, she cannot be the world's never-ceasing *pillar and ground of the truth.* Yet the Catholic Church's failure to maintain the truth did not cause Jesus' words about the perpetuity of His church to become void. Scattered bits of history verify that Jesus' church, which preached the gospel of grace, has continued to exist throughout the centuries (oftentimes in hiding from the so-called church). Though the complete lineage is untraceable by man, Bible-based conjecture concludes that the true church, which held to the doctrines of Bible-based truth, surely has an unbroken lineage all the way back to Jesus' day. Primitive Baptists do not claim Protestant roots, but instead claim to be a part of an unbroken succession with apostolic roots.

As we return to our attempt to explain the difference between Primitive Baptist and Protestants, we acknowledge that the task is difficult, in that the term Protestant is not easy to define. In the first place, when the original Protestants broke from the Catholic Church, there was never a single body of beliefs that defined the early Protestants. Beyond that, many divisions have occurred in Protestant churches, and in Protestant beliefs, since the time of the Reformers, so that most Protestants today have little in common with their founders. Thus, I will not try to speak concerning the doctrines of today's Protestants, in that I would not know where to begin.

Yet I will say that, for the most part, modern day Protestants and modern day Baptists now seem to believe about the same things, in that the historical marked distinctions between 'Calvinist' and 'Arminian' doctrines have become blurred. Most of today's Christianity is obsessed with what might be called 'Born Again-Ism'. Unlike the original Reformers, and the historical Baptists, modern day Christianity is caught up in trying to 'born again' the entirety of humanity. In the thinking of today's Christians, the miracle of God is no longer necessary for a new birth. The wonder of being quickened by God from spiritual deadness to spiritual life has lost its wonder. The marvel of God creating a new creature in the act of regeneration has lost its marvel. The God-breathed phenomenon of His giving spiritual life (even eternal life) has become just another sinner that some preacher saved, just another star in some preacher's crown.

So let us confine our comparison between Primitive Baptists and the historical Protestant Reformers. The writings of the Reformers confirm their belief in many crucial doctrines concerning salvation by grace. Unlike most of today's Protestants, the Reformers held to the truths of election and predestination. They defended particular redemption (limited atonement) in a most scholarly manner, so that the most indisputable defenses of particular redemption since the days of the New Testament come through the pens of Protestants. Historical Protestants held to the truth that the elect would be finally saved. All these doctrines are common with Primitive Baptist beliefs. Yet the key distinction between the two groups lies in beliefs about the doctrines pertaining to regeneration.

Both groups believe in the necessity of the new birth for eternal life, but the two differ in their beliefs concerning the manner in which regeneration occurs. Primitive Baptists believe in Holy Spirit unassisted regeneration, even that regeneration is a sovereign act of God upon the sinner without any means. Most Protestant Reformers believed in Holy Spirit regeneration, but through the means of the gospel, and through faith in the gospel.

It would be impractical to try to lay out the specifics as to how the original Protestants explained regeneration. I will allow the hundreds of Protestant-written volumes to speak for themselves. I admit that the authors of these books were more intelligent than I shall ever hope to be; more scholarly than I have proved to be; better with words than I can possibly be; more skilled in teaching than I can dream of being. I look at the lives of these men and am ashamed of the life I have wasted. When I read their scholarly books, I invariably question my own beliefs. If so many men, with such apparent understanding and wisdom, claimed that faith was the means to regeneration, who am I to think that regeneration occurs solely and only by a sovereign act of God? This question has sent me back to 'ground zero' to re-assess the issue of regeneration many times. Yet each time I re-study the question, my belief in Holy Spirit unassisted regeneration becomes stronger.

As a Primitive Baptist preacher, I often feel like the sparrow alone on the rooftop. In the era in which I live, there are only a few like me. In the geographical area in which I live, there are only a few like me. Why do I not just give in and join the crowd? I cannot give in. I have been entrusted with the gospel. Paul marveled that the Galatians were so soon removed from the gospel of the grace of Christ. I wish to enlighten God's children to the gospel that is all of grace. I want to guide their feet to the way of peace. Jesus said: *The truth shall make you free* (Jno 8:32). I wish to free God's children from the bondage of trying to secure their own eternal salvation. I wish to preach that eternal salvation is by grace, and grace alone. I wish to preach that eternal salvation is by God and God alone. I wish to preach what gives glory to God and God alone. *He that glorieth, let him glory in the Lord* (1 Cor 1:31).

Primitive Baptists believe that regeneration ('born again') is totally and only by the grace of God. We believe that God solely and wholly accomplishes the new birth without any assistance from man, or without the use of any other means beyond Himself. We believe that man's part in the new birth is the part of a totally passive recipient of God's grace. The primary way that I shall defend these doctrines is to prove from the scriptures, both the unwillingness, and the inability, of unregenerate man to raise himself from the fallen state he is in by nature. In the process of showing man's absolute unwillingness, his complete impotency, and his utter helplessness in actively bringing to pass his own new birth, I hope to secondarily show the exceeding greatness of the power of God necessary for the miracle of regeneration.

So let us examine the Bible-based premise that the fallen sinner is unwilling to come to God that he might be born again. The line of reasoning is simple, yet profound. The assertion is that the unborn again man will not come to God, simply because he does not want to. Natural man has a free will, but his will follows his nature. A wolf has a wolf's nature. By nature, he kills: sometimes because he is hungry, but sometimes just because he is a wolf. Like wolves, men follow their nature. According to scripture the nature of fallen men makes them *haters of God* (Rom 1:30). Their carnal minds are at *enmity against God* (Rom 8:7). Moreover, *there is no fear of God before their eyes* (Rom 3:18). Will a free-willed man willfully choose to come to the God that he hates? Will a free-willed man willfully choose to come to the God that he thinks of as his enemy? Love will not move him to come, in that he hates God. Friendship will not move him to come, in that he sees God as his enemy. Fear will not move him to come, in that he does not fear God. It is agreeable to scriptural teaching that a man with this kind of thinking will never (according to his willful pleasure) desire the presence of God.

Let us see how God describes the thinking of the carnal mind. *The wicked, through the pride of his countenance, will not seek after God: God is not in all his thoughts* (Ps 10:4). It would seem strange indeed for this man to make a decision to seek the God that he never thinks about. If you were to force this man to listen to things about the God that he refuses to think about, he would reject it all. *The natural man receiveth not the things of the Spirit of God: for they are foolishness unto him: neither can he know them, because they are spiritually discerned* (1 Cor 2:14). The unborn again man will not accept spiritual concepts. He will have no part of the things of God's book. He wants nothing of Christianity. He scoffs at such foolishness, as a Christ on a cross. What could motivate this unborn again man to choose to be a part of something that is so utterly ridiculous to his way of thinking?

Jesus said: *Ye will not come to me, that ye might have life* (Jno 5:40). These straightforward Jesus-spoken words are not hard to understand, though many find them hard to accept. The carnal minds of these men that Jesus addressed were so against God that they were unwilling to come to Jesus, even so that they might have life and escape eternal doom. Just think about a hell-bound sinner, who could hate Jesus so much that he would refuse to come to Him for eternal life. What a picture of the extent of depravity! This is the nature of fallen man in a fallen world. This is where we are, who we are, and how we think according to our innate nature.

Fallen man has a 'free will', but not a 'willing will'. Sinful man's *'will'* is really a *'will not'*. Only God can cause the *'will not'* to say, "I *will*". So since man by nature will not choose to come to God, God must do the choosing in salvation. Beyond just choosing to save men in general, God must choose which men in particular to come to with salvation. God's choosing which sinners He would come to is election. Moreover, since man will not choose to come to God, God must at some point in time actually come to the sinner that He had previously chosen. God's coming to the sinner with the new birth is regeneration, even irresistible, effectual, unassisted, Holy Spirit regeneration upon an unwilling soul.

Yet the problem with natural man goes beyond an unwillingness to come. Even if the unwilling man willed to do that which Jesus said he will not do, there is still an insurmountable problem. The Bible repeatedly declares that natural man is not just unwilling, but also unable to come to God. He simply cannot come. Men are limited by their nature. A man may choose beans for breakfast, but a mentally deficient person may not choose to be smart. So past a *'will not'* come that is in fallen man, there is a *'cannot'* come in fallen man. If fallen man were to find the *'want to'*, he still does not have the *'can do'*.

So it is not just that the natural man **will not** receive spiritual things, in that they are foolishness to him. Paul's statement went on to say, *neither can he know them* (1 Cor 2:14). A natural (unborn again) man cannot know spiritual things. Without the Spirit of God in a man, he cannot understand the things of the spiritual realm. Since natural man cannot know spiritual things, and since God is a Spirit, it seems reasonable that natural man cannot know God. Surely, a man cannot come to that which he cannot know. God must first give the natural man spiritual life, before the man can know spiritual things, even before the man can know God and come to Him.

An unborn again man cannot seek after and come to the God that he cannot understand. *There is none that understandeth, there is none that seeketh after God* (Rom 3:11). Nor can a man see and come into the kingdom of God, unless he first is born again. *Except a man* *be born again, he **cannot see** the kingdom of God* (Jno 3:3). It also makes sense that this same unborn again man cannot enter into that which he cannot see. *Except a man be born of water and of the Spirit, he **cannot enter** into the kingdom of God* (Jno 3:5). So since an unborn again man has no ability to seek and come to the God that he cannot know and understand, and since an unborn again man has no ability to choose to enter the kingdom of God that he cannot see, the only hope, which an unborn again man has, is that God would choose him, seek him, find him, come to him, and 'born' him again.

That is exactly what happens at the new birth. According to God's sovereign will, God first chooses which man. According to God's eternal purpose, God seeks and finds the chosen man. According to God's amazing grace, God comes to and 'borns again' His chosen child. God does the choosing, the seeking, the finding, the coming, and last of all, God does 'born again'. The Spirit moves where He pleases, and so it is with everyone who is born again.

Jesus asked this question: *Why do ye not understand my speech?* He then answered His own question: *Even because you **cannot hear** my word* (Jno 8:43). Jesus did not say that these people were just unwilling to listen. He said that they could not hear. They were not naturally deaf. With natural ears, they heard Jesus' whole speech. Yet, spiritually, they understood nothing that Jesus said. The reason that they had no ability to hear and understand spiritual things was because they had no spiritual life. They had never been made to be spiritual creatures with spiritual ears to hear and understand spiritual things. They had not been born again.

Jesus said: *But ye **believe not, because ye are not of my sheep**, as I said unto you. My sheep hear my voice, and I know them, and they follow me* (Jno 10:26-27). These people had seen Jesus' works and had heard Jesus' words. It seems that they would have had no choice but to believe in Him. Yet they believed not. Why did they not believe? Jesus said they did not believe because they were not of His sheep. They were not of His shall-be-saved people. They could not believe, because the new birth gives the ability to believe, and God had not given them the new birth. So who can believe? *And as many as were ordained to eternal life believed* (Acts 13:48). The elect believe, because it is given to them to believe. The sheep believed, because God had given them the ability to believe. Faith is a gift of God (cf. Eph 2:8). Jesus is the author of our faith (cf. Heb 12:2). Faith is the fruit of the Spirit, even a result of the new birth (cf. Gal 5:22). It is given unto God's people to believe (cf. Phi 1:29). It takes the same exceeding great power of God to believe, which it took to raise Jesus from death (cf. Eph 1:19-20). The power of God must first give life to one who is dead to the spiritual realm before he can believe. People do not believe, and then receive the Spirit in the new birth. They receive the new birth, and then they can believe. So unless God first gives the ability to believe, the scriptures are clear that a man cannot believe. Those ordained to eternal life believed. Born again sheep believed. Yet these men that Jesus addressed could not believe, because they were not among the elect sheep, and had not received the gift of faith.

Even after Jesus raised Lazarus from the dead, there were many who did not believe. *But though he had done so many miracles before them, yet they believed not on him* (Jno 12:37). It is not just that they did not believe. The passage goes on to say that *they could not believe...* (Jno 12:39). Even beyond the idea that these could not believe, it is further stated that they could not *be converted* (Jno 12:40). The ones who were born of God believed. The ones with the gift of faith believed. Without God's divine intervention by the life giving new birth, these were not only unbelievers, but unconvertible unbelievers.

The Bible states: *But **without faith it is impossible to please him*** (Heb 11:6). If it takes faith to please God, many say that men just first need to believe in God. Then God will be pleased to give the new birth. This is their proposed plan for eternal salvation. Yet their plan has a real 'Catch 22'. We have just seen from God's word that natural man cannot believe in God. So if man has to believe in God, in order to please God and be born again, and if the truth is that unborn again man cannot believe in God, then none can ever be saved by this plan. If it is impossible to please God without faith, and if a natural man is without faith, then a 'without-faith' natural man can never please God. Yet in spite of this clear Bible teaching, many still claim that faith in Christ is the secret to man's coming to God. Even in the face of teachings that man cannot know, cannot see, cannot enter, cannot understand, cannot hear, cannot believe, and cannot be converted, many still declare that faith is the first-move factor that allows a sinner to come to God and please Him. Let us hear the scriptures and not our man-devised schemes, whereby we claim to be able to do that which the Bible labels as impossible.

Peter declared that the natural man *cannot cease from sin* (2 Pet 2:14). Paul declared that *the carnal mind...is not subject to the law of God,* **neither indeed can be** (Rom 8:7). Many scriptures speak of the sinfulness of fallen man. Paul said: *There is none righteous...there is none that doeth good* (Rom 3:10-12). James said: *Whosoever shall keep the whole law, and yet offend in one point, he is guilty of all* (Jas 2:10). John said: *If we say that we have no sin ...the truth is not in us* (1 Jno 1:8). Thus to think that the way to come to God is to become sinless is to deny these, and many other passages that declare the sinfulness of man. Not only is man sinful, but the depth of the problem is that man *cannot cease from sin.*

At least these ten places in scripture declare that man lacks the ability to come to God. Natural man cannot know, cannot see, cannot enter, cannot understand, cannot hear, cannot believe, cannot be converted, cannot please God, cannot cease from sin, and cannot be subject to the law of God. Yet just in case you think that natural man might do something to change all his 'cannots', let us yet go to an eleventh place, and find one more thing that natural man cannot do. A 'cannot' cannot become a 'can'. *Can the Ethiopian change his skin, or the leopard his spots? then may ye also do good, that are accustomed to do evil* (Jer 13:23). By nature, man is what man is. Just as the Ethiopian is what he is, so natural man is what he is. Just as the leopard is what he is, so natural man is what he is. A 'cannot-do-good' man cannot become a 'can-do-good' man. *There is none that doeth good, no not one* (Rom 3:12). Carnal man cannot do 'good', and he cannot change the 'cannot-do-good' that is within him. He is what he is, and he cannot change his case.

The most powerful truth is yet a twelfth statement, even direct words from Jesus. **No man can come to me**, *except the Father which hath sent me draw him* (Jno 6:44). This simple statement of truth is not hard to understand, just hard to swallow. The idea that **natural man will not come to God** is hard to accept. The statement that **no man can come to God** is equally hard to accept. Yet truth is truth. Jesus said: *No man can come to me.*

At this point someone might ask, "Do you really believe that nobody has ever come to Christ?" I am not saying that nobody has ever come to Christ. I am saying that nobody has ever come to Christ, unless the Father first drew that particular 'nobody' to Christ. I realize that many have come to Christ. Yet I also realize that no one has ever come, being led by his natural will: *Ye will not come to me that ye might have life.* No one has ever come of his own ability: *No man can come to me.* No unborn again person has ever had the *'want to'* or the *'can do'* that would be necessary to come to Christ. There has never been a *'will not'* who (of his own natural free will) suddenly said, "*I will*". There has never been a *'cannot'* who (of his own natural abilities) mustered up the strength to become a *'can'*. So since man will not come and cannot come, God must be the one to come. God can come. God will come. God does come to the unborn again. The Father draws to Jesus whomever He chooses. Jesus finds whomever He seeks. The Spirit moves as He pleases upon everyone that is born of the Spirit.

No man could, and no man would, and no man did. Yet God could, and God would, and God did. Man does not choose God, and come to God. God chooses man, and comes to man. God decided to save according to His sovereign will and pleasure. God chose people to save according to His election. God paid for the chosen through the redemption that is by the blood of Christ. God applied the spiritual life by regeneration in the new birth. God will finally deliver the whole chosen family to glory at the last day. Every step in the plan is of God, and every step is essential for salvation.

In conclusion, the Reformed Protestants were probably the finest Bible scholars in history. They discovered and defended much of what is involved in salvation by God's sovereign grace. Yet, I do not believe that their 'born again grace' was equal to God's 'born again grace', in that they believed that sinful man had the will and ability to come to God, in order to be born again. Primitive Baptists believe in Holy Spirit unassisted 'born again', even that God's grace has to do this part, too. We believe that every step in God's eternal salvation of His children is *to the praise of the glory of his grace.*

7
Do Primitive Baptists Believe in 'Born Again'?

Primitive Baptists most certainly believe in the Bible-taught concept of 'born again'. Jesus taught that the new birth is an absolute necessity for salvation. He told Nicodemus: *Except a man be born again, he cannot see the kingdom of God* (Jno 3:3). Jesus further stated: *Ye must be born again* (Jno 3:7). Yes, indeed, the Bible teaches 'born again'. Yes, indeed, Primitive Baptists believe in 'born again'.

Yet Primitive Baptists are not on the 'Born-Again Bandwagon' with most other Baptists. Primitive Baptists have not converted to 'Born-Again-*Ism*'. Over the last few decades there has been a rapid growth of many non-Christian religions and *isms*: Mormonism, Jehovah's Witnesses, Islam, Wicca and Christian Science. America has many new relevant *isms*, such as: narcissism, hedonism, earth worship and self-defined morality. Yet 'Born-Again-*Ism*' is perhaps the fastest growing American '*Ism*'. It includes over 30% of the US population. It has permeated 'Bible-based' congregations like leaven in dough. 'Born again' has become the American Christian catch phrase. Politicians campaign by claiming it. Businesses capitalize by professing it. Preachers fixate on preaching it. Churches grow '*mega*' by pushing it. It has become the driving force for so-called 'Christianity'.

Christians cannot blame the atheists, or the news media, or the far-left for this one. 'Born-Again-*Ism*' did not come from the Muslims. So-called Bible believers are the source of this '*Ism*'. In most cases, it is the blind leading the blind. In some cases, preachers who know better continue to perpetuate Satan's lie. Underneath it all is a Satan-based conspiracy of deception. Error is being preached as truth. Cult-like zeal drives intense recruitment. The obsession infiltrates funeral messages. The passion assaults hospital deathbeds. 'Born-Again-*Ism*' has become the sole-goal of Christianity.

You might say, "But doesn't the Bible teach that men must be born again?" Indeed, it does. Without the new birth, there are no Christians. Without the new birth, there is no Christianity. Yet without God, there can be no new birth. God alone gives the new birth, without means or help. Modern day Christianity takes the miracle out of the birth. In 'Born-Again-*Ism*' the impossible becomes doable. The wonder becomes commonplace. 'Born-Again-*Ism*' says that men are born again as a result of something they do: 'going forward', 'making a decision', 'accepting', 'believing', 'receiving'. Whatever the requirement, the idea is that sinful man brings about his own regeneration. The whole premise is unreasonable, unbiblical and dishonoring to God. Oh, the heresy in begging sinners to help poor, weak, 'beggar-man', 'wanna-be-savior' Jesus!

Jesus began a conversation with Nicodemus with the words: *Verily, verily, I say unto thee, except a man be born again, he cannot see the kingdom of God* (Jno 3:3). This statement is not hard to understand. Jesus plainly said that except something first happens, something else could never happen. Jesus said that the new birth comes first; then comes seeing the kingdom.

Though Jesus' statement is not hard to understand, most seem to find it hard to accept. Most so-called Bible teachers declare that you must first hear of Jesus and His kingdom. Then you come to the point where you see and understand what you have heard. Then you need to believe that this King is your personal Savior. Then you need to confess that Jesus is your Savior. After you do all this, Jesus will finally 'born' you again. All this might be okay, except it is not what Jesus said. All this is what 'Born-Again-*Ism*' says.

Jesus did not say that you need to see and understand the kingdom, in order to be born into it. Jesus said that you need to be born into the kingdom, before you can see and understand it. Before the new birth there is no awareness of a spiritual kingdom, or of any spiritual things. The words of the Apostle Paul echo the same thing that Jesus here declares. *But the natural man receiveth not the things of the Spirit of God: for they are foolishness unto him: neither can he know them, because they are spiritually discerned* (1 Cor 2:14). Except a man first have spiritual life by the new birth, he cannot see and understand the things of Christ, or the things of Christ's kingdom. If a man cannot see and understand the things of the kingdom, how could he cherish and desire what he cannot even see? Furthermore, why would a man seek that which is 'foolishness' to him?

Paul further said that *there is none that understandeth, there is none that seeketh after God* (Rom 3:11). Again speaking of the natural, unborn again individual, Paul declared that none in that state of spiritual deadness can understand the things of the kingdom. A person does not first understand it, and then come and get it. A person does not first see it, and then seek it. A natural, carnal individual will never seek for such things, except he first be born again. Jesus said that a man must first receive the eternal life. Then the man can see the things pertaining to that life.

Nicodemus responded to the words of Jesus with these words: *How can a man be born when he is old? Can he enter the second time into his mother's womb, and be born?* (Jno 3:4). Oh how confused Nicodemus seemed to be! Yet in reality, Nicodemus is closer to understanding what Jesus said than most are today. In a sense, Nicodemus' questions make a profound statement. In so many words, Nicodemus stated, "Jesus, I cannot do what you just said must occur in order for me to see this kingdom. I cannot 'birth' myself again. It is impossible for me to accomplish such a thing as this."

That is just exactly the point Jesus was making when He described a new birth. By using the concept of a birth, Jesus showed Nicodemus that this was not something that man could accomplish for himself. Surely Jesus intends for us to understand that we cannot have any control or power concerning our own new births. Instead of man coming up with a 'how to do it' scheme, he should come to the logical question that Nicodemus came to, "*How can a man?*"

Jesus might have said to Nicodemus at this point in the conversation, "Aha, you understand my point. You did not cause your natural birth. You have sense enough to know that you cannot go back now and do it again. Furthermore, if you are so helpless in the lesser natural birth, surely you must see that you certainly cannot do anything to bring the greater spiritual birth to pass. Yes, Nicodemus, from the standpoint of man's strength and abilities, a new birth is absolutely impossible."

Yet Jesus did not give Nicodemus this explanation. Instead, it seems that Jesus would have brought Nicodemus further distress with the later words: *Ye must be born again* (Jno 3:7). Do you see the dilemma that Nicodemus was in? Can you sense the entrapment the poor man must have felt? My friend, do you see the impossibility of your own case? Look at the catch-22 situation that is developed in the conversation. Jesus stated a first truth: You cannot now see and be aware of, nor will you ever see the concept of Jesus' kingdom, unless you are first born again. Nicodemus' questions imply a second truth. His queries acknowledge the fact that since you have no ability to cause your own birth, it would be quite impossible for you to accomplish this act of 'born again'. Jesus stated a third truth with the haunting words, "*Ye must be born again.*" How can you do that which you cannot do?

How can Jesus tell us that we must do something that He has just taught us that we cannot do? With man it is impossible. At this point in the conversation, this is just exactly the idea Jesus has led Nicodemus (and you and me) to understand. The impossibility of the whole scenario is the lesson thus far. Yet, never fail to remember that what is impossible for man can be certain and sure in the hands of an Almighty God.

Jesus' next words are by far the most wonderful words of the whole conversation. At this point, Jesus told Nicodemus (and you and me): *The wind bloweth where it listeth, and thou hearest the sound thereof, but canst not tell whence it cometh, and whither it goeth: so is every one that is born of the Spirit* (Jno 3:8). In these words, we find a sovereign God doing for man, that which man could never do for himself. We find the wind blowing where the wind is pleased to blow. This is not a description of weather controlling itself. It is a depiction of the sovereign Holy Spirit moving as He pleases, and giving the new birth to men as He pleases. In this verse, the word, *wind*, is translated from the Greek word, *pneuma*. In many places in the New Testament this word, *pneuma*, is translated as *Spirit*.

There is no doubt that the verse refers to the work of the Holy Spirit (even the breath of God), as He breathes upon a man. This life-giving breath of God imparts eternal spiritual life to the man. It is by the power and will of God, the Holy Spirit, that the man becomes a born again, spiritually living soul.

This verse declares the solution to the dilemma, and it declares the only solution to the dilemma. There is only one way of being born again. It is by the will of the wind, even by the will and the power of the Spirit of God. So it is with everyone who is born again. It makes no difference whether young or old, whether infant or ancient, whether idiot or intellectual, whether BC or AD, whether Jew or Gentile, whether modern American with all the opportunities to hear the gospel, or extinct Mayan with never a chance to hear. There is only one way to enter the kingdom: the new birth. There is only one way to see the kingdom: the new birth. There is only one power sufficient for the new birth: the Holy Spirit.

Perhaps you are still puzzled by the words: *Ye must be born again.* Do not be confused. Before you twist these words into something Jesus never meant, please consider the exact way He said the words. Jesus did not say in the active voice, "You *must 'born' yourself* again." Jesus did not tell you that you had to actively do something in order to be born again. Jesus stated the requirement in the passive voice. He said, "*Ye must **be born** again.*" There is much difference in the idea of *'birthing' yourself* and the idea of *being born*. In order for you to *'birth yourself'*, you would have to be active as the agent causing the birth. The very thought is absurd. Yet, you may rest easy, for Jesus never said you should *'birth yourself'*. He said, "*Ye must **be born** again.*" In the idea of **being born**, you are passive, as the beneficiary receiving the birth. This is very plausible, and it is what Jesus said.

Yet you still might emphasize the word, *must*, and question why Jesus said: *you must be born again*. You may say, "If we cannot actively cause ourselves to be born again, why did Jesus say, '*ye must be born again*'?" The simple answer lies in the following explanation. Jesus said these words, not indicating that you **must** actively do it yourself, but indicating that it **must** occur, according to God's sovereign will and purpose. What God has purposed to occur **must** occur. God is always capable of actively causing His purposes to come to pass. Moreover, God's purposes **must** always come to pass. The new birth **must** occur to each of God's children. It **must** occur when God chooses to cause it to occur, and God's Spirit (the Wind) is the active cause.

This identical concept is presented in Paul's great teachings about a final resurrection of the bodies. Consider the statement: *For this corruptible **must** put on incorruption, and this mortal **must** put on immortality* (1 Cor 15:53). Paul declared that an earthly body **must** become a heavenly body. The teaching is that a carnal, natural body **must** become a spiritual body at the final resurrection. Can you bring that to pass? Can you actively cause yourself to have that new body? Of course you cannot. You cannot resurrect yourself, nor can you cause an earthly body to become heavenly, but it **must** happen. You cannot change your mortal body into an immortal body, but according to God's word, it **must** happen. It **must** happen, in order to fulfill all things according to God's unchangeable plan. Yet you have nothing to do with it, other than to passively receive it when it is given to you. According to God's purpose, the corruptible body **must** be changed at the resurrection, but God **must** do it, because He is the only one capable of doing it.

In the same way, you cannot 'birth' yourself into a spiritual existence, but it **must** happen. It **must** happen, in order to fulfill all things according to God's unchangeable plan. Yet you have nothing to do with it, other than to receive it when it is given to you. Moreover, even this reception of the new birth is out of your control. You do not choose to receive it, nor can you reject it. As you did not cause your natural birth, you cannot cause your spiritual birth. As you cannot cause your final resurrection, you cannot cause your new birth. According to God's purpose, all His children will at some time in their natural lives be breathed upon by the Holy Spirit, and be given the new birth, even eternal life. The Holy Spirit **must** do it. He is the only one capable. So it is with everyone who is born again.

So if you are a child of God, the new birth **must** happen to you, according to God's unalterable purpose. Yet it is not something that you actively do. This is consistent with your natural birth. Did you actively do anything to bring that to pass? No, you did not! You were very much a part of it, but you were only a passive recipient. Someone before you took an action that caused you to be born. A power that was greater than you, and that existed prior to you, acted in such a way as to result in you being born. You could not have caused it. Nor could you have prevented it. You did not accept it, agree to it, or request it. Nor could you have rejected or refused it. You did not consider the idea and decide that it would be okay. You did not do anything in order to help you to become you.

Jesus did not choose His words carelessly. His name is the Word. Surely the Word knows how to communicate a concept efficiently. He chose the analogy of a birth because our understanding of the natural process should give us a clear understanding of the spiritual process. We did not actively 'birth' ourselves the first time. Nor can we 'birth' ourselves the second. We are in no way the cause of our receiving the new birth. Someone before us and greater than us, even the Spirit/Wind/God, brought upon us something we could neither cause nor prevent. We were a part of it, but only in the capacity of being a passive recipient. The Spirit moves upon a person as He pleases, and so it is with every one that is born again.

We can further notice that in Jesus' conversation with Nicodemus, He taught just the opposite of what the 'soul-winners' teach. Jesus used no manipulative techniques. He made no emotional tug at the heart. Jesus said nothing to intimidate Nicodemus with fear. Jesus said nothing of any action or decision on the part of Nicodemus. Jesus said nothing of repenting, coming, accepting, praying, receiving and signing. Jesus said nothing of Nicodemus 'borning' himself. Nicodemus knew from the start that he could not do that. Jesus said, "*Ye must be born again.*" Yet, Jesus said it as a matter of fact, not as a command. Jesus just matter-of-fact-like taught Nicodemus what God does for His children. Jesus said that the Spirit does the doing: as He pleases, when He pleases, every time. Jesus emphasized that being born again is a miraculous work of God.

The Bible proclaims a 'born again' that goes beyond the capabilities of man to accomplish for himself, or for his neighbor. The Bible's 'born again' is equivalent to being resurrected from spiritual deadness. Jesus said: *The hour is coming, and now is, when the dead shall hear the voice of the Son of God: and they that hear shall live* (Jno 5:25). Jesus said nothing about words from the sinner's voice. The power is in Jesus' voice. Only Jesus has the power to speak the words that will raise the dead sinner to a life in the spiritual realm of existence. Paul said: *And you hath he quickened, who were dead in trespasses and sins* (Eph 2:1). Here again, it is God who quickens (makes alive) those who are dead in trespasses and sins.

The Bible's 'born again' requires a power equivalent to raising Jesus from the dead. Paul prayed that we might know *what is the exceeding greatness of his power to us-ward who believe, according to the working of his mighty power, which he wrought in Christ, when he raised him from the dead...* (Eph 1:19-20). The passage teaches that it takes the same exceeding great power of God to cause somebody to be able to believe, as it took to cause Jesus to come out of His grave. Now it should not surprise anybody that a great power was involved in raising Jesus from the dead. Yet many seem to be surprised that an unborn again man cannot just decide to believe. The problem with the unborn again man deciding to believe is that he is dead. So since Jesus and the dead sinner were both dead, it took the same power in each case.

Furthermore, the Bible's 'born again' is equivalent to God creating a new creature. *For we are **his workmanship, created in Christ Jesus** unto good works, which God hath before ordained that we should walk in them* (Eph 2:10). As God breathed life into Adam at the first creation, only God can breathe life into the new creature that He enlivens with each new birth.

The Bible-taught doctrine is that God, and God alone has the power to accomplish the new birth. Moreover, man cannot believe himself into such a miracle. These truths are God honoring. These truths demand that the glory and praise for 'born again' be given to God and not to the preacher. God is a jealous God. He will share His glory with nobody. These truths really matter. To get on board the 'Born-Again-*Ism* Bandwagon' is to rob God of His glory. The 'do-it-yourself-born-again' plan of today's Christianity loses all sense of reasonableness. The 'faith-yourself-to-heaven' plan of salvation loses all sense of being Bible-based.

The Bible describes the miracle of regeneration as being born. Can the unborn do anything to help bring about his own birth? What did you do before you were you? You could not do before you were you, simply because you were not yet you. It seems silly to say such a thing, because it is so obvious. Yet today's Christianity, with its '*Born-Again-Ism*' mentality, totally misses the obvious. The Bible describes the miracle of regeneration as being raised from the dead. Can the dead in sin raise himself from his spiritual deadness? What can a dead man do? How dead is dead? The Bible describes the miracle of regeneration as a new creation. Can the yet-to-be-created do something in order to help create himself? Did Adam help God create Adam? The idea of actively participating in your own regeneration is not only illogical, it is also unscriptural, and it so much robs God of His glory.

'Born-Again-*Ism*' (in its zeal to do what it cannot do) causes Christianity to lose its sense of honesty and integrity. Any and every kind of emotional, psychological, pressure-filled inducement is used in order to accomplish 'born again'. If the appeal to faith fails, the '*born-againers*' appeal to fears. They threaten their victims with fears about the certainty of future fire. They tug at broken hearts through fears about never seeing departed loved ones again. They play on never-ending fears about the insufficiency of past professions of too-feeble faith.

The 'Born-Again-*Ism*' scheme includes highly emotional meetings, prolonged appeals and repeated choruses. It incorporates peer-pressure manipulation so the '*lost*' will move forward to the altar. They even stoop to the deceit of staging '*counselors*' to begin the migration to the kneeling bench. The urgency is to get the masses to sign a card, raise a hand, recite a prayer, say the words and 'get saved' one more time. Ill-based fervor coaches and coaxes sinners to believe that God has come into their lives, even if there is a deep down sense that nothing really happened.

This so-called 'Christianity' (in its zeal to do what it cannot do) loses its separateness from the world. It is okay to bring the ways of the world into the church. The end justifies the means. It is okay to cease to be the pillar and ground of truth. The end justifies the means. It is okay to cease to stand on God's standards. The end justifies the means. Whatever it takes to help save a soul! Sacrifice all for the cause of 'Born-Again-*Ism*'!!

'Born-Again-*Ism*' is the '*Faith in my Faith*' plan of salvation. Yet, if I have put my faith in my faith, I cannot help but question whether my faith was good-enough faith. Was all that I did, and all that I said, and all that I prayed, enough? Did I do it right enough, say it right enough, and believe it right enough? Was I sincere enough? Was it real faith or the devil's faith? Oh, if I could only be sure!

Now with some it is real. Yet the system's 'un-real-ness' leaves both the 'soul-winner' and the 'soul-won' in doubt. The preacher is never sure whether the Lord worked, or the tactics worked. The sinner tries to rejoice in it all. Yet, after the show, he is unsure if anything really happened. If we are honest about 'Born-Again-*Ism*', it cries: *Peace, peace, when there is no peace* (Jer 6:14).

True peace for the sinner comes in knowing that salvation is of the Lord. The Bible states that salvation is of the Lord. God planned it before the world began. God paid for it on the cross. God applies it to each of His children at the new birth. At the end, God will have each of His children with Him for all of eternity. Historical Baptists, and today's Primitive Baptists, believe that salvation is of the Lord.

8
How Do Primitive Baptists Explain John 3:16?

"For God so loved the world, that he gave his only begotten Son, that whosoever believeth in him should not perish, but have everlasting life."

We live in strange times. Our Bible-believing fathers would be amazed by what is now proclaimed. A brief study of Christian history shows that salvation was not always considered to be so man-centered. Bible believing Baptists once proclaimed a God, mighty to save. They believed in a Jesus who **shall** save His people, even a Jesus who **did** save His people. They declared a God who came down to His people and saved them, not a people able to rise up to God of their own initiative and strength.

An objective, honest study of God's word finds that the Bible's salvation is not centered on what man does. Yet today's Christianity has predominantly left the teachings of the Bible about God's salvation. Error is whole-heartedly accepted, while feebly presented truth is for the most part totally rejected. Yet, truth remains truth, even if no one preaches it or accepts it. The truth is that the Bible's salvation is centered solely on Jesus Christ, the Savior. He has always been, and shall forever remain, the Savior. Salvation is of the Lord. God alone shall save, has saved, and does eternally save His people from their sins.

It is amazing that the most recognizable verse in the Bible is also the most misunderstood verse. It is uncanny how a misapplication of the verse has led to its widespread fame. Modern day Christianity presents John 3:16 as an invitation for the new birth. It may shock you, but there are serious problems with this view. As you ponder the idea of a different view of John 3:16, please consider which view is more agreeable to common sense, more agreeable to the Bible's entire teaching on salvation, and more agreeable to the context of the passage.

First of all, the generally accepted view that John 3:16 is an invitation for you to be born again disagrees with logic. The idea of having to accept an invitation to your own birth defies common sense. It is absurd to think that you can do something to bring about your own birth. Did you do anything to cause your natural birth? Neither can you do anything to cause your spiritual birth. The scriptures describe the miracle of regeneration as a birth, as a raising from the dead, and as a new creation. Reasonable thinkers must conclude that it is beyond the individual to bring to pass his own birth, to raise himself from the state of deadness, or to create himself. It disregards all reasoning to view John 3:16 as an invitation to accomplish that which is logically absurd. Surely basic good sense and simple logic must conclude that John 3:16 cannot be an invitation to cause your own spiritual birth.

Next, the idea of self-instigated born-again does not fit into the Bible's general scheme of salvation. The Bible presents the unborn again as a person who has no desire for God, as a hater of God, and as one who is at enmity against God. The Bible says that spiritual things are foolishness to the natural, unborn again person. What could motivate a man to come to the God that he hates? Does this man desire to be with his enemy? Will he seek things that are to him ridiculous? No, no, no. According to an abundance of Bible teaching, it is wrong to think that an unborn again person will (or can) believe in Jesus. Some may say, "Whosoever will, let him come." Yet Jesus said that an unborn again man is a 'will not'. Jesus said: *Ye will not come to me that ye might have life* (Jno 5:40). A natural, carnal person will never come to Jesus by an invitation. If he comes, God must irresistibly compel his coming. Jesus said: *No man can come to me, except the Father which hath sent me draw him...* (Jno 6:44). The Father must do the drawing. The Holy Spirit must move, as He pleases. 'Born again' is a miracle of God. A preponderance of Bible teachings proves that John 3:16 cannot be an invitation to be born again.

Finally, a proposition for man to come and be born again does not fit into the context of Jesus' teachings in John 3. In the third verse, Jesus put first things first. Here Jesus said that the first thing is 'born again'. *Except a man be born again, he cannot see the kingdom...* In the fourth verse, Nicodemus questioned: *How can a man...?* Here he acknowledged that a man cannot do such a thing as 'born again'. In the seventh verse, Jesus further complicated the conversation with the words: *Ye must be born again.* (Notice that Jesus did not say in the active voice, "Ye must *'born yourself'* **again**." Jesus said in the passive voice, "Ye must **be born again**." God does the 'borning'. You are the passive recipient. Furthermore, God **must** 'born again', because it is His immutable purpose to give eternal life to each of His children.) In the eighth verse, Jesus proclaimed God's action of giving the eternal life, where He described the sovereign moving of the Holy Spirit, as the sole and only means to the new birth. The Holy Spirit does 'born again', and so it is with everyone who is born of the Spirit.

Now consider the sixteenth verse. Does it fit the context of this conversation that John 3:16 is an invitation to believe and be born again? Jesus has already taught that the sole and only means of the new birth is the moving of God upon the individual, as God pleases. Why would Jesus now change His whole teaching, and invite individuals to be born again of their own will, initiative and decision? If Jesus gave an invitation for sinners to do what He had already said that God alone does, then He interjected an intolerable strain on the context of the entire passage. The context will not allow John 3:16 to be an invitation to be born again.

Now I admit that at first glance John 3:16 does appear to be an invitation to be born again, but logic and the context demand otherwise. Common sense says that you cannot believe before you are born. Scriptural sense says the same thing. Jesus did not say that seeing and believing are the requirements for being born again. Jesus said that being born again is the requirement for seeing and believing. Jesus said that 'born again' is the essential prerequisite that enables you to see. Jesus did not invite you to be born again by believing, when He had just taught that you could not believe unless you had first been born again. Faith is not the means to being born again. Faith is the result of already having been born again. The Holy Spirit is the means to the new birth. Faith is the fruit of the Holy Spirit (Gal 5:22), even the result of the Holy Spirit having indwelled the child of God at the new birth.

John 3:16 is not an invitation for a natural man to do what he cannot do, to see what he cannot see, to desire what is foolishness to him, to enter into what he has no interest in, or to take hold of what he has no strength to attain. John 3:16 does not stand against the consistent New Testament teachings that man will not come to God, and that man cannot come to God. John 3:16 does not contradict Jesus' previous teaching in the passage. John 3:16 is not directing you to do that which only the Holy Ghost can do. John 3:16 is not the means for you to do what Jesus said you cannot do. John 3:16 is not the plan for you to get eternal life. John 3:16 cannot be an invitation to be born again.

So if John 3:16 is not an invitation, what is it? If you understand that you must be born again before you can ever see or enter the kingdom, and if you understand the impossibility of 'birthing' yourself by your own power or initiative, and if you further understand that only the Holy Spirit can accomplish this miraculous thing with such eternal ramifications, then a very pertinent and personal question might be, "Has the Holy Spirit done it for me?" If you understand Jesus' teachings in John 3:3-8, you might say, "Jesus, you said it was a necessity. Jesus, I cannot do it for myself. Jesus, you said the Holy Spirit does it for some. Jesus, am I one of the ones? Have I been born again? How can I know if I have eternal life?"

The context of the third chapter of John does not allow an invitation to the unborn, but it screams for an assurance to the reborn. John 3:16 is that proclamation of assurance, so that you can know that you are born again. The answer to your doubts lies in the words: *For God so loved the world, that he gave his only begotten Son, that whosoever believeth in him should not perish, but have everlasting life* (Jno 3:16). The bottom line is: if you believe in Jesus, then you are already born again. If you believe in Jesus, you already have eternal life, for Jesus has already taught you that without having already been born again, you would not be able to see and believe in Jesus. Thus, John 3:16 gives confident assurance to the questioning child of God.

The teaching is not 'if you believe, you will get everlasting life'. The teaching is 'if you now believe, you already have everlasting life'. John 3:16 is not an impossible proposition for you to attain life. It is a reliable proclamation that you already have life. John 3:16 does not offer the new birth to one who cannot 'birth' himself. John 3:16 offers the already born again evidence of his prior new birth. Jesus did not tell those without life how to get it. Jesus told those who have life how to know it. John 3:16 is not an invitation to be born again. John 3:16 is an assurance to the already born again.

Belief is not what gives life. Belief is an evidence that life exists. First comes eternal life by the breath of the Holy Spirit; then comes belief in Jesus. Thus, if you believe, then you must already have eternal life. Oh, what comfort and consolation are in the teachings of Jesus! He does not ask the impossible of the unborn. Instead, He reassures the born again who may be a doubter. Which idea fits into the passage better?

Much of the misunderstanding of John 3:16 comes from the word, *world.* Let the scriptures interpret the scriptures. John seldom (if ever) used the word, *world,* to refer to every individual in all humanity. John used the Greek word, *kosmos,* which simply means 'an orderly arrangement'. The word can describe any such concept. John used *kosmos* to speak of God's created earth. *And there are also many other things which Jesus did, the which, if they should be written every one, I suppose that even the **world** (kosmos) itself could not contain the books that should be written. Amen* (Jno 21:25). Here *world* seems to be the volume of all the space on the earth (or maybe even in all creation). Surely God's earth, God's universe, God's creation is an 'orderly arrangement'. Yet this *kosmos* is not the same as the John 3:16 *kosmos*. So *world* can mean different things in John's writings.

Jesus used the word, *world,* to speak of an 'orderly arrangement' that is against God, even a *world* that hates God. *The **world** cannot hate you; but me it hateth...* (Jno 7:7). Jesus talked of a *world* that rejoiced at His death. *Ye shall weep and lament, but the* **world** *shall rejoice...* (Jno 16:20). Jesus spoke of Satan as the leader of this *world*. *For the prince of this* **world** *cometh, and hath nothing in me* (Jno 14:30). There is an 'orderly arrangement' that is led by Satan, that hates God, and that laughed at the death of Jesus. Is this Satan-ordered *kosmos* the *world* that God so loves? Did God give His Son for this *world* and its prince? Certainly not! This is a *world* much different to the *world* of John 3:16.

Jesus said to His Father: *I have manifested thy name unto the men which thou gavest me out of the* **world**: *thine they were, and thou gavest them me...* (Jno 17:6). Jesus further said: *I pray for them: I pray not for the* **world**, *but for them which thou hast given me; for they are thine* (Jno 17:9). Jesus said, "I pray for them," signifying a particular group, which had been given to Him "out of the **world**." Jesus said, "*I pray not for the* **world**." If the *world* of John 3:16 is the entirety of humanity, then it is strange that Jesus would not pray for the *world* that God so loved. If God loves a *world* that Jesus refused to pray for, then there is disunity in the oneness of the Godhead. Are Jesus and the Father one, or are they at odds? They are not at all at odds! Jesus made the same distinction between two groups that is seen throughout scriptures. There is a *world* that Jesus was not praying for, and there was a group that had been given to Jesus out of that *world*. Jesus was praying for the ones that had been given to Him *out of the world*. Jesus is not wooing, and begging, and pleading with a *world* that He refuses to even pray for. Jesus is not wishing that this 'un-prayed-for' *world* would come to Him and get salvation. (By the way, the Father does not love this 'un-prayed-for' *kosmos*.)

You may think that these are hard sayings, but the Bible is clear that Jesus did not pray for the whole *world*. He only prayed for the ones that the Father had given to Him out of the *world*. It can be further noted that the Bible is clear that Jesus did not die for the whole *world*. He only died for the ones that the Father had given to Him out of the *world*. Jesus spoke of more than one *world*, and neither *world* included all people in the *world*.

In these teachings, we can see that God does not love the whole *world*. We can see a choice, even God's choice. The Bible teaches election, where God chose a people out of this *world*. God gave the elect to Jesus. Jesus prayed for the ones who were taken out, but not for the *world* from which they were taken. Jesus prayed for a *world*, which was taken out of a *world* and given to Him. Jesus died for a *world*, which was taken out of a *world* and given to Him. These are two distinct and different *worlds*. On one hand, there is an unloved, and 'un-prayed-for', and 'un-died-for' *world*. On the other hand, there is a so-loved, prayed for, and died for *world*, even a vast host that no man can number from every nation, family, tribe and tongue of people in the *world*.

So there is a *world* of space where books can be stored, even an 'orderly arrangement' created and maintained by God. There is another Satan-led *world*, even an 'orderly arrangement' that Jesus does not pray for, that He did not die for, that He is not after, and that He does not want. There is yet another *world* chosen out of this *worldly world*, even an 'orderly arrangement' that is made up of those given to Jesus. God took them out of one *world*, and placed them into another *world*. For this 'taken-out-of-the-world' *world* Jesus fervently prayed. For the *world* from which they were taken, Jesus refused to pray. Do you see the teachings of God's word? Do you see a *world* of this *world*? Do you see another *world* of the Father?

Jesus further said: *If ye were of the* **world***, the* **world** *would love his own: but because ye are not of the* **world***, but I have chosen you out of the* **world***, therefore the* **world** *hateth you* (Jno 15:19). '**You**' are not of the *world*. '**You**' are chosen out of the *world*. The *world* hates '**you**'. Do you see the two groups, '**you**' and the *world*? There is a *world*, not prayed for and not chosen. Then, there is the '**you**' of this verse. This '**you**' group makes up a different *world* than the *world* of this verse. The '**you**' *world* is prayed for and much loved. The '**you**' *world* is the so loved *world* that God gave His Son to die for.

Jesus yet further said: *Even the Spirit of truth; whom the* **world** *cannot receive, because it seeth him not, neither knoweth him: but ye know him; for he dwelleth with you, and shall be in you* (Jno 14:17). Jesus spoke of a Spirit whom the *world* cannot receive. Why could this *world* not receive the Spirit? Jesus said this *world* could not see the

Spirit, and that it could not receive what it could not see. Do you remember how Jesus said in John 3:3 that except you first be born again, you cannot see the kingdom? Here in John 14:17, Jesus similarly taught that except the Spirit dwell in you, you cannot see Him or know Him. Again we have two distinct groups. There is a *world* that cannot see, cannot receive, and cannot know. Then there is the other *world*, the *'ye'*, that know Him, see Him, and believe in Him because He dwells in **'you'**.

So who is it that can see and believe? The ones who are in the Father's *world* believe. *As many as were ordained to eternal life believed* (Acts 13:48). The 'orderly arrangement' of the foreknown, elected, predestinated, given-to-Jesus, died for, prayed-for and so-loved can see and believe. Each child in the Father's *world* is born again by the will and power of the Holy Spirit. God orders it. God arranges it. *The wind bloweth where it listeth...so is every one that is born of the Spirit* (Jno 3:8). With the new birth comes the ability to see and believe. **You** can see and believe, because of the Father's 'orderly arrangement'. This is the Father's *kosmos*. Those in the Father's 'orderly arrangement', even the Father's *world*, even the *world* of John 3:16, can see and believe. **You** see and believe because the Father orders His *world* in such a way as to equip His children to see and believe in Jesus.

John said: *Love not the* **world**, *neither the things that are in the world* (1 Jno 2:15). Concerning this verse, a lady once asked me the question, "How can God so love the world, and then tell His children not to love the world?" She had two problems. First of all, she did not know that the Bible speaks of more than one *world*. Secondly, she took *world* to mean the entirety of humanity. Comparing John 3:16 to 1 John 2:15 does not prove an inconsistent God. Nor does it prove a contradictory Bible, if we simply understand that there is more than one *world* in the Bible, and that *world* does not include every individual. There is the *world* of John 3:16 that God so loved. There is another Satan-led *world* that Jesus refused to pray for, and that we are not to love. The invariable God of the infallible Bible loves the *world* that consists of the ones He chose and ordained to eternal life. The Father's so-loved *world* are the ones in His 'orderly arrangement' unto salvation. What a *kosmos* is the Father's *world*!

Oh, that the Spirit of God would grant His children to understand that the Bible speaks of more than one *world*. On the one hand, there is the *world* that is under the leadership of Satan, the *world* that Jesus did not pray for, the *world* that cannot see and believe in Jesus, the *world* that we are not to love, the *world* that Jesus will one day judge. On the other hand, there is the *world* that God so loved, the *world* that God chose and gave to Jesus, the *world* that Jesus came to save, the *world* that the Lamb of God took from them their sins, the *world* that God justified, the *world* that the Holy Spirit regenerates, the *world* that is saved eternally by the grace of God. This last *world* is the *world* of John 3:16.

So if there are two distinct *worlds*, how can you know which *world* you are in? John 3:16 gives you your answer. If you believe in Jesus Christ, then you can rest assured that you are already in (and shall ever remain in) the Father's *world*. Your belief is not how you got into the Father's *world*. Your belief is your certain evidence that you have forever been a part of the Father's *world*. Your belief in Jesus comes way down the list of the chain of events that occurs for those in the Father's *world*.

If you now believe, then you must be one of the ones that God foreknew and loved before creation. If you now believe, then you must be one that God elected before time. If you now believe, then you must be one that God gave to Jesus in the Covenant of Grace. If you now believe, then Jesus has already given His life to take away your sins. If you now believe, then the Spirit must have already born you again, for it is impossible to see and believe, except you first are born again. If you now believe, then you will never perish, for you already have everlasting life.

Be reminded of some simple Bible truths about your belief, even truths that give assurance as to the fact of a prior new birth. Belief does not precede the new birth in the chain of salvation. Belief follows the new birth. Belief does not cause the new birth. Belief is the result of the new birth. The ability to believe spiritual things comes as a result of having already received spiritual life. Belief is impossible prior to being born again. So if you now believe, then you can be sure that you must already have been born again. If you now believe, then rest assured, for you have already been given everlasting life.

Jesus never intended John 3:16 to be the means to being born again. Jesus meant for John 3:16 to be an assurance to the already born again. John 3:16 is not an invitation to the unborn to be born again. It is an assurance to the already reborn of the certainty of his new birth. John 3:16 does not tell the spiritually dead how to get life. John 3:16 proclaims to the spiritually alive (yet doubting child of God) that he already has everlasting life. John 3:16 is not a proposition for you to do, but a proclamation of what God has already done.

John 3:16 is a proclamation about God's love, about God's Son, and about God's *world*. John 3:16 does not proclaim a feeble, failing, futile love. The love of John 3:16 is a 'mighty-to-save' love, which refuses to lose any who are so loved. John 3:16 is a proclamation of the greatest love in existence, even a love that gave a Beloved Son. John 3:16 does not proclaim a feeble, failing, begging, 'wanna-be-savior' Son of God. The Son of God in John 3:16 is a 'mighty-to-save' Savior. Call His name Jesus, for He shall save His people from their sins. John 3:16 does not proclaim anything about the *world* that Jesus refused to pray for, or the *world* that we are not to love. John 3:16 proclaims no love for the prince of this *world's world*. John 3:16 is a proclamation about God's so-loved *world*, even God's *kosmos*, that Jesus shall save. John 3:16 proclaims the greatest of loves for the *world* that the Lamb of God died for.

Yet, above a proclamation about God's love, about God's Son, and about God's *world*, John 3:16 is a proclamation about assurance. John 3:16 is the doubter's answer. John 3:16 is your answer. If you now believe, that is your greatest evidence that you have always been in the Father's *world*. If you now believe, you have already been born again. The fact of your present belief proves the fact of your previous new birth. Do you believe in Jesus Christ? If you do, then you will never perish, because you already have everlasting life.

9
How Do Primitive Baptists Explain the *Worlds, Alls & Everys?*

Many people claim to believe in salvation by grace, but then add this or that to their proposed plan of salvation. It is common to hear such things as, "I believe in grace, but..." Or "I believe in grace, if..." Yet, the Bible makes the case for:

- Amazing grace (and grace alone) that saves God's people from their sins.
- Election, not based on foreseen works or cooperation in the one chosen.
- Particular redemption, not offered to everybody, but certain for some.
- Holy Spirit unassisted regeneration, not based upon the consent of man.
- A plan of salvation, based on God's control, and not man's.
- A plan of salvation, perfect in the way the parts of the plan fit together.
- A totally successful plan of salvation, in that none in the plan can be lost.

An honest Bible study reveals a cohesive plan of salvation for a particular God-chosen people. Yet, if taken at first glance, a few *worlds, alls,* and *everys* seem to contradict this consistent set of teachings.

Taken by themselves, these isolated *world, all,* and *every* statements seem to offer universal redemption to all humanity, as opposed to finished redemption for particular God-chosen people. So should we discard the bulk of the Bible, which makes the case for salvation by grace, and then use a few *worlds, alls,* and *everys* to make the case for salvation by man's cooperation? Or should we hold to the bulk of the Bible, and throw out the *worlds, alls,* and *everys*? Neither! We simply need to fit the *worlds, alls,* and *everys* into the consistent Bible-based foundation of salvation by grace. We need to get beyond thinking of just one verse out of the context of its passage. We must put passages in the context of the bulk of the Bible. We must first fit the big pieces of the puzzle together to get the right foundation. Then we will be able to put a few little (seemingly hard to fit) pieces into the big puzzle.

So let us first lay the foundation for salvation by grace. The Bible is clear that God has a particular people that He possessively claims to be His. God calls them my people: *For the transgression of my people was he stricken* (Is 53:8). Jesus saved His people: *He shall save his people from their sins* (Mt 1:21). Jesus said of some: *My sheep hear my voice,* while at the same time, Jesus said to others: *Ye are not of my sheep* (Jno 10:26-27). So we see a foundational truth: Some people, **but not all** people, are His people.

God chose particular, individual people to be His people. *According as he hath chosen us in him before the foundation of the world* (Eph 1:4). Some try to explain election away by saying that God looked into the future, and based His choice of individuals on some foreseen merit in the ones chosen. Yet the scriptures clearly state that election is not of works. *For the children being not yet born, neither having done any good or evil, that the purpose of God according to election might stand, not of works, but of him that calleth...* (Rom 9:11). Moreover, election is *to the praise of the glory of his grace* (Eph 1:6). If God's choice was based on His foreseeing the works or the choices that men would make, then election was not based on grace, but in what men did, and God is a liar. God's election is not conditioned on anything beyond God's own sovereign will.

The Father gave His elect people to Jesus before the world began. Jesus prayed *not for the world, but for them which thou hast given me* (Jno 17:9). Jesus promised to eternally save all that the Father had given Him. *Of all which he hath given me I should lose nothing, but should raise it up again at the last day* (Jno 6:39). Jesus is the successful Savior. On the cross Jesus saved each and every one of

God's elect from their sins. By His life-giving voice Jesus speaks eternal life into each one that the Father gave to Him.

What began with election and predestination, ends in salvation! *Moreover* **whom** *he did* **predestinate**, **them** *he also called: and* **whom** *he called,* **them** *he also justified: and* **whom** *he justified,* **them** *he also* **glorified** (Rom 8:30). Trace it through this chain of salvation. In each link of the chain the *'whoms'* become *'thems'*. In the end, every *'whom'* that God predestinated ends up a *'them'* that God glorifies. Praise God! Salvation is of the Lord!

The Bible's plan of salvation is a plan of God's grace, not of man's cooperation. God's salvation is exact and precise. It involves no guesswork. It has no loopholes. God chose whom to save. Jesus died for the chosen. The Holy Spirit gives life to the chosen. Those predestinated by God are called by the Spirit, justified by the blood, and glorified in the end. God's plan is for His particular people. The only plan of salvation that will agree with the Bible is:

- Unconditional election by the Father, not based on foreseen works.
- Particular redemption, only for those chosen by God and given to Jesus.
- Unassisted Holy Spirit regeneration, for those who cannot and will not come.
- Final successful salvation, for all that God initially chose to salvation.

Taken as a whole, the Bible declares that God saves His elect people by grace, and grace alone. Yet, people grab a few isolated *worlds, alls,* and *everys,* in order to make a case for the offer of universal redemption, as opposed to the successful salvation accomplished in particular redemption. I admit that on the surface the *worlds, alls,* and *everys* seem to apply to every individual everywhere. Yet, we must go beyond the surface. We must take the scripture as a whole. The Bible is its own interpreter. When it is rightly divided, it all makes sense. When you start with the right foundation, it all fits together.

The Bible taught truth of total depravity will not stand on a foundation that is built on a few *worlds, alls,* and *everys*. A vast host of Bible teachings declare that fallen man is impotent by his own will and ability to save himself. Fallen man cannot come. He will not come. A plan of salvation that requires fallen man to come and accept the universal offer of redemption will not tie together with a man who will not and cannot come. Truth and error will not mix.

The Bible consistently and repeatedly proclaims that God chose a people to be His people. The Bible taught truth of God's election of a particular people based on God's choice will not tie together with the universal offer of salvation to all men based on man's choice. Truth and error will not mix.

The Bible taught truth concerning regeneration declares that a natural man is spiritually dead, and that God has to raise him from that state of deadness. The universal offer of redemption demands that this dead man must make a decision. The dead cannot make a choice to be alive. Neither can the unborn choose to be born. Nor can the 'yet-to-be-created' participate in his becoming a 'new creature'. Absurdities! The universal offer of redemption, based on a dead man's decision, or somebody causing his own birth, or a creature creating himself, will not tie together with the scriptures. Nor will it agree with common sense. The universal offer of salvation is untruth. Untruth and truth will not mix.

If our foundation is based on error, the whole building quickly collapses. The Bible has no errors or contradictions. *Thy word is truth* (Jno 17:17). When rightly divided, the Bible will agree with itself. The foundation of truth will support the word of truth. Instead of trying to build on error, we need to start with the right foundation. Then the Bible will interpret itself.

So let us start with the word *world*, even start with the best known of the Bible's *worlds*.

> John 3:16 *For God so loved the **world**, that he gave his only begotten Son, that whosoever believeth in him should not perish, but have everlasting life.*

This verse is truth. The part about God so loving the *world* is absolute truth. Yet if the word, *world*, is taken to mean every individual that has ever lived in the world, then this verse comes into great conflict with other verses, such as *Jacob have I loved, but* **Esau have I hated** (Rom 9:13). If God hated Esau, then He does not love everybody. Does the Bible really say that God '*so loves*' everybody? *Then shall he say also unto them on the left hand,* **Depart from me, ye cursed, into everlasting fire,** *prepared for the devil and his angels* (Mt 25:41). Does this casting away sound like '*so loved*' love? *What if* **God, willing to shew his wrath,** *and to make his power known, endured with much longsuffering the* **vessels of wrath** *fitted to destruction* (Rom 9:22)? Can a consistent God really be willing to show such wrath to someone that He '*so loves*'?

The Bible declares that God has a chosen people that He loves with an everlasting love. Yet God does not love all people. God is not unfair in not loving all. No sinner deserves God's love. No sinner deserves the death of God's Son. The shock is not that God could hate Esau. The shock is that God could love the conniving Jacob. The shock is that God would love any sinner to the extent of sending His Son to die for that sinner. Whomever God loves, He loves them with a great and everlasting love. No one, whom God loves, can ever be separated from God's love, or from the God Who loved him.

God loved, and ever loves, the *world* of John 3:16, but what is that *world*? Is it the *world* that Jesus refused to pray for? *I pray for them: I pray not for the* **world,** *but for them which thou hast given me* (Jno 17:9). If God so loved the *world*, such that He gave His Son to die for it, how can the Son's feelings toward that *world* be such that He refused to pray for it? Is the Trinity in disunity? How could Jesus love the *world* enough to die for it, and then refuse to pray for it, even to intercede for it? Is Jesus that fickle?

All this makes no sense, unless you realize that these are two different *worlds*. Jesus said: *I pray for them: I pray not for the world.* These are two different groups. Jesus prayed for the ones God gave Him, but not for the rest of the *world*. Jesus died for the ones God gave Him, but not for the rest of the *world*. The *world* of John 3:16

and the *world* of John 17:9 are two different, and opposing *worlds*, neither of which contains all humanity. The John 3:16 *world* is the chosen *world* of people God gave to Jesus out of the *world*.

Look at yet another verse: *Love not the world, neither the things that are in the world* (1 Jno 2:15). Did *God so love the world that He gave His only Begotten Son?* Absolutely! Are we then told not to love the ones God so loved? Not at all! Again these are two different *worlds*. Jesus spoke of a *world*, ruled by the prince of this *world*, even Satan himself. We are not to love **that** *world*, and God does not love **that** *world* either. Moreover, Jesus did not pray for **that** *world*. Jesus did not die for **that** *world*. God does not love every *world* in the Bible. God will eternally destroy the *world* of Satan and his followers. On the contrary, God will eternally save the *world* of God and His children. This is the *world* that God so loved, even so-loved this *world* enough to send His Son to die for it.

I am not twisting the scriptures to make them say what I want them to say. I am fitting an individual verse into the foundation of truth that ties the whole Bible together. If we start with God loving every individual in all humanity, nothing fits together, and the Bible remains a huge unsolvable puzzle. On the contrary, if we put the big pieces of the puzzle in their right places, then the individual verses can be fitted in. If we first fit total depravity, unconditional election, particular redemption, Holy Spirit unassisted regeneration, and the certain final salvation of the saints into their right places, then the little pieces of the puzzle can be properly fit into the big pieces. This is called rightly dividing the word of truth. If we start with a foundation of truth, then we can end with a building of truth, which will fit together and stand.

Sometimes the Bible says the *whole world*. So let us look at a *whole world* passage.

> 1 John 2:1 *My little children, these things write I unto you, that ye sin not. And if any man sin, we have an advocate with the Father, Jesus Christ the righteous:*
>
> 1 John 2:2 *And he is the propitiation for our sins: and not for ours only, but also for the sins of the whole world.*

Many would argue that this verse, by itself, proves universal redemption. They say that the *'whole world'* has to be everybody. Now this verse states truth, but does the Bible phrase, *whole world,* mean every individual in the world? Paul said of the church at Rome: *Your faith is spoken of throughout the whole world* (Rom 1:8). Were native American Indians speaking of the faith of the Romans? If *whole world* means every individual in the world, then we have caught the Bible in a lie. Luke said that Caesar taxed *all the world*: *There went out a decree from Caesar Augustus, that all the world should be taxed* (Lk 2:1). Do you suppose any Siberians paid Rome's *'all the world'* tax? We see that it is easy to prove that phrases like *all the world* and *whole world* do not refer to every individual in the world.

So what did John mean by *whole world*? John wrote to *my little children.* Writing in second person, John cautioned against sin: *These things write I unto you, that ye sin not.* Switching to first person, John reassured them (and himself) that *if any man sin, we have an advocate with the Father, Jesus Christ the righteous.* Staying in the first person, John said that Jesus *is the propitiation for our sins.* Who are the *'we'* and *'our'*? John was a Jew writing to *'my little children'* (his family). The *'we'* are John and the Jews. Yet, what about all of *'them'*, the Gentiles? As Gentiles, we can rejoice in John's next words: *and not for ours only, but also for the sins of the whole world.* Here is the *'them'*. Jesus' propitiation is not for the Jews' sins only, but also for the Gentiles' sins. John did not mean that Jesus is the propitiation for every sin of every individual in the *whole world.* John meant that Jesus' propitiation extends beyond Jew sins, even to Gentile sins. Jesus is the propitiation for the sins of His people from all families in the *whole world.* How do we know that this is what the verse means? This interpretation fits into the teachings of the whole Bible. This interpretation allows us to put this piece of the puzzle into the well-fitted foundation. Truth and truth can be fitted together, but truth and error will not mix.

Now let us look at the word, *all.*

> *1 Timothy 2:1 I exhort therefore, that, first of all, supplications, prayers, intercessions, and giving of thanks, be made for **all men**;*
>
> *1 Timothy 2:2 For kings, and for **all** that are in authority; that we may lead a quiet and peaceable life in all godliness and honesty.*
>
> *1 Timothy 2:3 For this is good and acceptable in the sight of God our Saviour;*
>
> *1 Timothy 2:4 Who will have **all men to be saved**, and to come unto the knowledge of the truth.*
>
> *1 Timothy 2:5 For there is one God, and one mediator between God and men, the man Christ Jesus;*
>
> *1 Timothy 2:6 Who gave himself a ransom **for all**, to be testified in due time.*

These words are true words. *Thy word is truth.* Yet these words must fit into the entirety of the word of truth. So let us first see that the words, *all men*, do not necessarily mean every individual in all humanity. John stated that *all men* came to Jesus to be baptized: *the same baptizeth, and all men come to him* (Jno 3:26). Did any Australian Aborigines come to be baptized? Did even all the Pharisees consent to be baptized? So the words, *all men*, do not necessarily mean every individual in the world. Moreover, *all men* in our passage does not mean every individual in the world. If we attempt to fit our passage into the rest of the scriptures, it makes about as much sense to think that the Aborigines came to Jesus' baptism, as it does to think that Jesus died for every individual in the world.

In the context of the Bible, and in the context of our passage, *all men*, must mean all sorts of men, kings and servants, those in authority and those under authority. Salvation is for all sorts of men, Jews and Gentiles, kings and paupers. Salvation is for men from all nations, all families, all tribes and all tongues under heaven, indeed all sorts of men. Again I am not trying to distort the scriptures. I am just trying to fit little isolated pieces of the puzzle into the huge foundational truths that perfectly fit together.

Finally let us look at the word, *every*.

> *Hebrews 2:9 But we see Jesus, who was made a little lower than the angels for the suffering of death, crowned with glory and honour; that he by the grace of God should taste death for* **every man.**

By itself, this verse sounds like universal redemption. By itself, so does John 3:16. The challenge before us is to look at a verse, not by itself, but in its context. The bulk of the Bible will not allow the *world* of John 3:16, or the *'every man'* here, to mean all humanity. Neither will the context of this passage allow *every man* that Jesus tasted death for, to be every man that has ever existed. So let us continue reading.

> *Hebrews 2:9 ...that he by the grace of God should taste death for* **every man.**
> *Hebrews 2:10 For it became him, for whom are all things, and by whom are all things, in bringing* **many sons** *unto glory, to make the captain of* **their** *salvation perfect through sufferings.*
> *Hebrews 2:11 For both he that* **sanctifieth** *and they* **who are sanctified** *are all of one: for which cause he is not ashamed to call them* **brethren**...
> *Hebrews 2:12 Saying, I will declare thy name unto my brethren, in the midst of the church will I sing praise unto thee.*
> *Hebrews 2:13 And again, I will put my trust in him. And again, Behold I and* **the children which God hath given me.**

Surely the words, **many sons**, restrict the meaning of the words, **every man.** **Every man** is not **every man** imaginable, but **every man** in the group described as, **many sons**, who will be brought to glory. **Their** salvation (even the **many sons'** salvation) is what is being considered. The captain did not bring **every man** in history to glory, but He brought **many sons** to glory, and the salvation is **their** salvation. Furthermore, the word, sanctify, means to set apart to be holy. Now He that **sanctifieth** is God, and the ones **who are sanctified** are the ones that the sanctifier set apart to be holy. **Every man** is not everyone who has ever lived, but **every man** is **every** *man* that God chose and set apart to be eventually made holy. Next, we find that *every man* is defined as the men Jesus calls His *brethren*. The familial words, *many sons* and *brethren,* limit the words *every man* to mean *every man* that is in the family of God. Finally, the words, *the children which God hath given me*, take us all the way back to the Covenant of Grace. The '*every man*' in this passage is the '*every man*' that God gave to Jesus before time began, and the '*every man*' that God gave to Jesus will be the '*every man*' who will be with Jesus when time ends. So Jesus did not taste death for *every man* in all history. Jesus tasted death for *every man* in the context, even *every man* in God's plan.

We have tried to explain a few of the *worlds, alls,* and *everys*. We have not covered all the *alls*, or every *every*, or the *whole* of the *worlds* of the Bible. Yet we have laid out a pattern for fitting the *alls*, the *everys*, and the *worlds* into the Biblical foundation of salvation totally by the sovereign grace of God. Only by fitting the *worlds, alls,* and *everys* into this foundation, and into their context, can we find the Bible's truth.

I admit that I do not understand all the Bible. Yet the right foundation is the key to best understanding God's word, and the right foundation is based upon salvation by the sovereign grace of God. Any proposed plan of salvation that is based on the works or cooperation of fallen man will not hold up when compared to the bulk of Bible teaching. God's plan of salvation by grace passes the test of scriptural comparison. It all fits together. God's plan of salvation by grace passes the test of reason. It all makes sense. He that worships, must worship in truth. God's word is truth. Truth and errors will not mix. May God bless us to find the perfectly fitting foundation of truth, and then to fit the little pieces into God's mosaic of God-honoring truth.

10
How Does Faith Fit In?

Faith can be defined in many ways, but one scripture defines it as *the substance of things hoped for, the evidence of things not seen* (Heb 11:1). Consider the words: *the substance of things hoped for.* Something with substance has realness to it. It can be taken hold of. Faith allows the regenerate mind of a child of God to actually take hold of the real substance of that which literally exists out of his reach. Next, consider the words: *the evidence of things not seen.* Evidence bears witness to truth. Evidence that bears witness to truth (even truth that has not been seen) causes truth to become known as a reality. Faith bears witness and gives evidence of unseen things to the mind. Faith allows the truth that lies in the realm of the invisible to be seen. Thus, one who possesses God's marvelous gift of faith has abilities beyond the realm of natural possibilities. He can hold to things that cannot be held. He can see things that cannot be seen. Through faith, unreachable things are in full grip. Invisible things are in full view.

Perhaps no one fully comprehends the wonder of the miracle of faith. It is not surprising that the natural man does not understand faith. There is no way to know, or even imagine, the concept of faith, unless you first have faith. Yet, it is surprising that most people who have faith take for granted their ability to hold the unreachable, to see the invisible, and to know the eternal. They look at faith as if it is something that they just decided to have on their own. They think that they just had it within themselves to work up a little faith, and to begin to see invisible things in the spiritual realm. Today's Christianity greatly underestimates, and grossly unappreciates, the miracle of faith. Most have no idea of the wonder of the event that must take place before a child of God can actually believe in God.

The scriptures repeatedly state that God is the source and origin of our faith. Faith *is the gift of God* (Eph 2:8). Faith is a *fruit of the Spirit* (Gal 5:22). Jesus is the *author of our faith* (Heb 12:2). God even gives us the ability to believe. *It is given…to believe on him* (Phi 1:29). The scriptures are likewise clear as to the miracle and wonder of faith. In order for us to be able to believe, God must do a work in us, which is on the level of the exceeding great work of His mighty power involved in raising Jesus from the dead. Listen to these words about the extent of power involved in bringing us to a point where we would be able to believe: *And what is the exceeding greatness of his power to us-ward who believe, according to the working of his mighty power, which he wrought in Christ, when he raised him from the dead* (Eph 1:19-20). An unborn-again, spiritually dead person cannot just formulate a little faith, and begin to see the invisible realm of eternity. God must first execute the power involved in resurrection, even give spiritual life to the spiritually dead, before belief is possible. Belief in Jesus is not just something that we do. Belief in Jesus is a miracle that God gives us. The faith that is in us is not of us. It is a wonderful and miraculous gift from God to us.

The same modern Christianity that tends to underestimate the miracle of faith, also tends to overestimate the role of faith. First of all, the scriptures are clear that faith is not the means to being born again. God independently 'borns again' His children, without means, and without help from man. Secondly, the best of faith is so unfaithful that nobody can really have faith that his faith has secured his eternal life. Man's faith is as inadequate as anything else he thinks or does. As all works and thoughts of man are lacking, so is man's faith. Jesus declared that the apostles' faith was *little faith* (Mt 8:26). If Jesus said that these notable men's faith was 'little', what could describe the tiny faith of other, more common believers?

Jesus said that the faith of a grain of mustard seed could move mountains. Has your faith moved many mountains? How adequate is the best of men's faith? Can a failing, doubting, faltering, unbelieving faith, which cannot perform the comparatively simple task of moving mountains on earth in time, be depended on to move a person to heaven eternally? Is this weak, inadequate, unbelieving belief the basis for declaring the salvation of sinners? If so, who then can be saved? If so, who can ever be assured about his salvation?

Though faith is not the means through which man has eternal life, faith is the means through which man can know that he has eternal life. Though faith does not give eternal life to a man, faith gives to a man the assurance that he has eternal life. Though faith is not the means to being born again, faith is the means to knowing we have been born again. Instead of faith being the means for us to enter into a state of regeneration, or into the realm of eternal life, faith is the means to our awareness that we already exist in such a state.

There is a difference in having eternal life, and having the assurance of knowing that we have eternal life. There is a distinction in being eternally saved, and having the peace that comes from realizing that we are eternally saved. There is a difference in being in the state of having eternal salvation, and being in the state of mind of knowing that we have eternal salvation.

Now the sole, and only, cause and basis of our having eternal life is Jesus Christ. Yet the means to our understanding that Christ is the cause and basis of these things is faith. This makes faith to be of extreme value to us.

Furthermore, there is a big distinction between falsely believing self to be the means to eternal life, and truly believing Christ to be the means to eternal life. There is much difference in mistakenly believing in our own works (or faith) as the source of our eternal salvation, compared to accurately believing that Jesus is the sole source of our eternal salvation. There is great contrast in believing that our faith is sufficient, as opposed to believing that Jesus is sufficient.

To believe that salvation is based in self, leaves us with many doubts. We find little assurance in basing our eternal salvation on ourselves. Yet by the means of faith, we can know that Christ is the basis for our salvation, and we can find much comfort and confidence in knowing that. Faith is not essential for eternal salvation. Yet faith is essential for assurance and peace in the inner beings of the ones who have the eternal salvation. Faith is not essential for the possession of eternal life. Yet faith is essential for the peace that we enjoy about having the eternal life.

Both the eternal life, and the faith, are gifts of God by grace. First God gives the life. Then He gives the faith, in order that we can know that we have the life. With the gift of faith, we can begin to experience and live the life that we possess. By faith, we can know spiritual things. By faith, we can know the God who is our Father, the God who is our Savior, and the God who is our life-giving (and faith-giving) Comforter.

So God gives faith in order that His child can somewhat understand and know God. God gives faith in order that His child can understand spiritual things. God gives faith in order that His child can have a sense of reality in things hoped for. God gives faith in order that His child can see things that are unseen by natural eyes. God gives faith in order that His child can know things that the natural mind cannot know.

To illustrate the purpose of faith, we can consider how faith is connected to Jesus' work on the cross. God does not give faith to a child of God, so that the child might help Jesus finish His work of saving that child. Jesus accomplished salvation, and even declared: *It is finished* (Jno 19:30). Jesus does not need the sinner's help to finish what is already finished. So God does not give faith to His child, so that the child might help Jesus finish His work of saving that child.

Instead, God gives faith to His child, so that the child might know that Jesus has finished His work of saving that child. By faith, the child of God can know that his sins were placed on Jesus at the cross. By faith, the child of God can even see Jesus' blood applied to himself. By faith, the sinner can sense the removal of his own sins by that blood. By faith, the sinner can know that God will never remember those sins again.

God gives faith to His child, so the child can know that no charge can ever be placed against him. By faith, the child of God can know that the blood of Jesus has made even a sinner like himself to be righteous. By faith, the child can (in his own mind) declare himself to be in a state of righteousness.[1] So, by faith, the child of God can (in his own mind) be justified.

Let us further pursue this idea of being justified by faith. Eternal justification is not based on our faith. Eternal justification is based on God's grace, and the blood of Jesus. By grace we were justified in God's mind, when God judged us based on the blood of Jesus, and the finished work of Jesus. So where does faith fit in? By faith, we are justified in our own minds, as we judge ourselves based on the blood of Jesus and His finished work.

How does this justification by faith work? A man who is justified by faith must, first of all, be a man who has been made to be in a state of righteousness by the blood of Jesus and the finished work of Jesus on the cross. Secondly, a man who is justified by faith must be a man who has already been born again, and has been given the gift of faith that is a result of the new birth. Once this man has been given spiritual life, and the resulting gift of faith, he is enabled to know the things of the mysterious, invisible, spiritual realm. By the faith that has been given to this man, he is able to know that he has been made to be in a state of righteousness by the blood of Jesus, and by the finished work of Jesus on the cross. By faith, he can declare himself to be in a state of righteousness by the blood of Jesus, and by the finished work of Jesus. This declaration of righteousness is by definition justification. So by faith, the man is justified, as he judges himself, based on the blood of Jesus, and the finished work of Jesus.

In other words, faith in the finished work of Christ leads a man to declare to himself that he is what Christ has already made him to be. God gives faith to His child, so that the child can (in his own mind) declare himself to be what he has already become in Christ. The faith did not make the man righteous. Christ did that. The gift of faith only declared to the man what Christ had already done for the man, in order that the man might declare himself to be what he already is. By faith, a man can see that Jesus has made him righteous, even in the sight of God. By faith in Jesus, a man can

---

[1] To declare to be in a state of righteousness is by definition justification.

declare himself to be what he sees that he is. I say again that this declaration of righteousness is by definition justification. So by faith in Jesus, a man can justify himself in his own view of self. This is what it is to be justified by faith.

These things that man knows by faith, God has known all along. God does not need man's faith, so God can know what He already knows. Neither can a man's lack of faith undo what God has already done. A man's unbelief cannot make God's faithfulness to His plan of salvation fall apart. *For what if some did not believe? shall their unbelief make the faith of God without effect? God forbid* (Rom 3:3-4).

Christ accomplished what He accomplished, whether we know it or not. God knows what Christ accomplished, whether we believe it or not. God cannot deny the work of Christ. *If we believe not, yet he abideth faithful:* **he cannot deny himself** (2 Tim 2:13). What was accomplished is accomplished. Jesus came to save His people from their sins. Jesus did save His people from there sins. Moreover, God knows that Jesus saved His people from their sins. The eternal salvation of all that Jesus died for remains an unchangeable eternal reality, even if nobody ever believes it. God can never deny Himself.

The truth about God's salvation does not cease to be truth, just because it is not believed. The truth is that Jesus removed all the sins from all His people. The truth is that all the sins, which were removed, are forever removed. The truth is that Jesus made all that He died for to be righteous. The truth is that Jesus finished His work, and that He accomplished salvation for each one He died for. God knows that all these things about the finished work of Christ are truth, whether anybody believes these things or not. God has declared all these things about the finished work of Christ to be true, whether anybody else declares them or not. God legitimately and eternally justified all that Jesus made to be righteous, whether anybody knows it or not. God's eternal justification remains eternal reality, whether anybody believes it or not.

So God can, and does, save His children without them having to believe in His finished salvation. Yet, by God's grace, God has devised the means for His children to be able to believe in His finished salvation. That means is God's gift of faith that results from having been born again. The born again child of God has the ability to know the things that God knows. Ears of faith are able to hear the gospel of the finished work of Christ. Eyes of faith are enlightened to see that Jesus finished the work of salvation. By faith, the mind can know and understand that Jesus totally accomplished salvation for all of God's children. By faith, the sinner sees that the blood of Christ has made him righteous. Now God in His eternal plan saw the sinner righteous through Christ before time began. God likewise saw the sinner righteous when Jesus accomplished God's purpose on the cross. Yet God enabled the sinner to see all this through faith. Faith even declares it to the sinner. Faith did not cause the righteousness. Christ did that. Faith does not cause God to see the righteousness. Faith simply allows the sinner to see himself as righteous, and having seen himself righteous, the sinner can declare himself to be thus.

At this point, the sinner is justified by faith. By faith in the finished work of Christ, the sinner can declare himself to be righteous in his judgment of his own case, even in his own mind. Faith is the wonderful means by which a man can see himself to be justified.

Faith has nothing to do with how God looks at and eternally judges a sinner. Faith has to do with how the sinner looks at and judges himself. God saw Christ die for the sinner. God saw it all, and knows that it is so. By faith, the sinner can see himself in the same way that God already sees him. By faith, the sinner can know what God already knows. God declared the sinner to be righteous by the blood of Christ, because God saw that the blood of Christ had made the sinner righteous. The sinner declares himself to be righteous by the blood of Christ, because, by faith, the sinner sees that the blood of Christ has made the sinner righteous.

By definition, justification is the declaration of righteousness. So God justified the sinner by the blood of Christ, because God saw that the blood of Christ had made the sinner righteous. The sinner justifies himself by the blood of Christ (in his own mind), because by faith the sinner sees that the blood of Christ has made the sinner righteous.

The faith-gifted mind sees that the righteousness is not of self, but is by the work of Christ. The faith-gifted mind knows that the declaration of righteousness concerning self is not based on self, but is based on the work of Christ. Works did not make the sinner righteous. Faith did not make the sinner righteous. Christ made the sinner righteous.

Christ is the only basis by which a sinner can be righteous. Christ is the only basis by which a sinner can be declared righteous. Any declaration of righteousness based on anything else is a false declaration. The declaration of righteousness is not based on the deeds of the law. The declaration of righteousness is not based on the act of faith. Neither the deeds of law, nor the acts of faith, are sufficient to bring a man into a state of righteousness. There is no righteousness in, or of, the self. Any righteousness that is in man is the result of Christ's righteousness having been put in the man. Any faith that man has is a result of the Holy Spirit dwelling in the man.

So a man is not, and cannot be, declared righteous by looking to self. To attempt to base righteousness upon self is wrong. Yet to declare a man to be righteous based on the work of Christ is correct. For a man to believe himself to be righteous based on anything of self is wrong. For a man, by faith, to believe himself to be righteous based on the finished work of Christ is correct. A man can declare himself to be righteous only when he considers himself from the vantage point of what Christ accomplished for him on the cross.

Real faith in Jesus is total trust in His finished work. By definition, total faith in Christ eliminates self. The very notion of complete faith totally eliminates all boasting of self. *Where is boasting then? It is excluded. By what law? of works? Nay: but by the law of faith* (Rom 3:27). Prior to this verse, Paul had already totally excluded boasting by proving the universal failure of all men to keep God's law. *What things soever the law saith, it saith to them who are under the law: that every mouth may be stopped, and all the world may become guilty before God* (Rom 3:19). Surely it would seem that above all things our unrighteous works would 'stop every mouth' from boasting. Yet, Paul said that the '*law of faith*' (the very principle of scriptural faith) eliminates boasting, even more than the law of works.

This statement is true, because true faith in Jesus is the belief that Jesus has totally accomplished salvation. Bible-based faith incorporates the idea that nothing from self can help save self. Faith is neither the sinner's righteousness, nor his claim to righteousness. Jesus is the sinner's righteousness, and the sinner's claim to righteousness. Bible faith is the exact opposite of man becoming righteous of self. Scriptural faith denies any merit in man. Faith in Jesus destroys the idea that man can contribute. True faith in Jesus is totally self-eliminating, and in no way self-promoting. True faith demands elimination of trust and confidence in self. Bible faith is an unqualified looking to Christ as the sufficient righteousness of God for us. God-given faith takes self out of the plan, and gives all the glory to the Savior. So if the very principle of Biblical faith acknowledges that Jesus is the absolute and total Savior, then where is there any room for self in the plan of salvation? If faith gives the understanding that salvation is of the Lord, how can anybody boast of self in any way?

So what is faith, and what is it for? From an eternal perspective, the sinner realizes the hopelessness of salvation through his own righteousness. By faith, he hears and understands that God provides the righteousness. Upon understanding this God-given revelation about God-given righteousness, the sinner's manner of thinking is changed. He now lives with full realization of the insufficiency of self. Yet, he lives with full confidence that his salvation is certain in Jesus. To the faithful the thing hoped for, even his eternal salvation, has a present reality.

Faith is the God-given means, whereby sinners can hold to the reality of the substance of the truth of salvation. Faith is the Spirit-given evidence that lets sinners see and know these unseen things. Eternal salvation is totally of the Lord, even without means. Yet the understanding of the Lord's eternal salvation is by the means of God-given faith. Praise God for the grace of salvation, and praise

God for the grace of faith, which gives the understanding of the grace of salvation.

Yet, beyond faith letting us know that the certain hope of eternal life is real, faith is also what gets us through the day to day life, in which we now exist. God told Habakkuk, *the just shall live by his faith* (Hab 2:4). These words do not tell the just how to become spiritually alive. They tell the just how to live the spiritual life that they have been given. Habakkuk's problem was how to get through life, even how to live life in this world that we are stuck in. Habakkuk had come to the end of self. He was in great despair of life. In the words, *the just shall live by his faith*, God taught Habakkuk a new lifestyle, a new way of looking at things.

The lesson was to quit focusing on the hopeless situation, and to have faith in God. Quit living by sight, and start living by faith. The just (one whose life is conformed to the will of God) will live his life by his faith. Faith is not the one-time event whereby eternal life is acquired. Faith is a constant lifestyle that is necessary for getting through life. Faith is not for getting life. Faith is for living life. Faith is not for getting things. Faith is for facing things. Faith is a continual realization of the need for Christ. Faith is knowing the sufficiency of Christ for every situation we face. True faith passes through hopelessness to confidence.

So faith empowers us to know that the certain hope of eternal life is real, and faith also enables us to get through the day to day struggles of life. Yet there is still a deeper meaning in the words, *the just shall live by his faith*. The God-given gift of faith allows us to see Jesus hanging on a cross. By faith, we see Jesus suffering in our place, even dying because of our sins (What wondrous love is this, that Jesus would give His life for the likes of me!). By faith, we can see that Jesus saved even sinners like us.

Once faith lets us see Jesus in this way, we will never be the same. We will live the rest of our lives differently. If we are thinking in a right manner, we will never get over what faith has shown us. If we are just and right in the way we live, we will live our lives saying, "Lord, what wilt thou have me to do?" The just (those who are right in their manner of thinking and living) shall live their lives by their faith, not just believing in Jesus as their Savior, but also believing in Jesus in their times of troubles, and even believing Jesus, as to the right way to live life.

Let those who have faith in the power of God unto salvation live their lives looking to that powerful God. Let those who have believed in the righteousness of God, even Jesus Christ, always be looking to that righteous Jesus. Let those, who by faith know eternal truths, live by that faith through the remainder of their days. Let that God-given faith abound to God's glory, as we live out our lives.

11
What is the Purpose of Preaching the Gospel?

M any declare that faith in the gospel is the means to being born again. Yet that is not what the Bible really teaches. The Bible proclaims that God alone is the sole and only cause of the new birth. The Bible does not say that faith is the requirement for being born again. The Bible instead says that faith is the consequence of having been born again. The Bible says that faith is a *fruit of the Spirit* (Gal 5:22).

If faith is the fruit of the Spirit, it cannot be the means to receiving the Spirit. If faith is the result of the Spirit having already moved into the heart, then faith cannot be something that we do in order to become spiritually alive. The Bible does not say that faith is something that we present to God in order to have eternal life. The Bible instead says that faith is something that God gives to us at the new birth, so that we can be able to believe. *It is given..to believe on him* (Phi 1:29). The Bible declares it plain and simple when it says that faith is the *gift of God* (Eph 2:8).

Jesus said: *The wind bloweth where it listeth...so is every one that is born of the Spirit* (Jno 3:8). Jesus said: *...The hour is coming, and now is, when the dead shall hear the voice of the Son of God: and they that hear shall live* (Jno 5:25). Jesus said: *No man can come to me, except the Father which hath sent me draw him* (Jno 6:44). From these three statements, we can see that Jesus taught that regeneration is a sovereign act of Father, Son and Holy Spirit. It is not something that the sinner helps do.

Jesus said: *Ye will not come to me that ye might have life.* (Joh 5:40) Jesus said: *No man can come to me, except the Father which hath sent me draw him* (Jno 6:44). Jesus said: *No man can come unto me, except it were given unto him of my Father* (Jno 6:65). From these three statements, we can see that Jesus taught that the unborn again man is not the one who comes to God. God is instead the One who must come to the unborn again man.

Paul said: *But the natural man receiveth not the things of the Spirit of God: for they are foolishness unto him: neither can he know them, because they are spiritually discerned* (1 Cor 2:14). Jesus said: *Except a man be born again, he cannot see the kingdom of God* (Jno 3:3). Jesus said: *Why do ye not understand my speech? even because ye cannot hear my word* (Jno 8:43). Paul said: *There is none that understandeth, there is none that seeketh after God* (Rom 3:11). From these, and a host of other statements that could be cited, we can see that the Bible declares that carnal sinful man is both unable and unwilling to raise himself (or even help raise himself) from the state he is in by nature.

Come, let us reason together. It is both unscriptural, and unreasonable, to surmise that the yet-to-be-born can, or will, actively participate in bringing to pass his own birth. It is both unscriptural, and unreasonable, to surmise that the spiritually dead can, or will, actively participate in bringing to pass his own spiritual resurrection. It is both unscriptural, and unreasonable, to surmise that the yet-to-be-created new creature can, or will, actively participate in bringing to pass his own creation. Thus, it is both unscriptural, and unreasonable, to surmise that faith in the gospel is the means to regeneration.

God, and God alone, is the sole and only means to eternal life. God elected His people and gave them to Jesus before time began. At God's appointed time, Jesus came to save, and did save, God's elect people from their sins. The Holy Spirit moves as He pleases, and through His sovereign power He 'borns again' each and every one of God's elect that Jesus died for. At the end of time, none will be lost. All who were ever in God's plan of salvation will be with God in heaven forever. *Moreover whom he did predestinate, them he also called: and whom he called, them he also justified: and whom he justified, them he also glorified* (Rom 8:30). Every step is of the Lord. Every '*whom*' ends up a '*them*'. From start to finish, salvation is totally and completely of the Lord.

So, if salvation is totally of the Lord, and without the means of the gospel, why do we bother to preach? Though the gospel is not the means to eternal life, the gospel is the means to peace of mind when we think about eternal life. God's children need the peace in knowing that God has already saved them. They need to know about the successful Savior. They need to have the assurance of knowing that salvation is of the Lord, and not of the sinner. They need to know the certainty of the eternal life that waits for them. They need the gospel of peace, so that they might have peace.

The following passage teaches us two distinct and important aspects about the gospel, even about the good news of our salvation. First of all, the passage proclaims the gospel of the good news of what God has accomplished in our salvation. Secondly, the passage explains what the minister is to accomplish in preaching the gospel, even the good news of what God has accomplished in our salvation.

> 2 Corinthians 5:18 *And all things are of God, who hath reconciled us to himself by Jesus Christ, and hath given to us the ministry of reconciliation;*
>
> 2 Corinthians 5:19 *To wit, that God was in Christ, reconciling the world unto himself, not imputing their trespasses unto them; and hath committed unto us the word of reconciliation.*
>
> 2 Corinthians 5:20 *Now then we are ambassadors for Christ, as though God did beseech you by us: we pray you in Christ's stead, be ye reconciled to God.*

Let us first look at the good news of what God has accomplished. *God...hath reconciled us to himself by Jesus Christ.* To reconcile is to make peace. The statement is in the past tense. God has already made peace. God purposed the reconciling. Jesus Christ did the reconciling. God saw Jesus do the reconciling. God recorded the reconciling in His word. The reconciling is completed. Surely God knows that He has reconciled us to Himself by Jesus Christ. In the mind of God there is no doubt, as to the peace that Jesus accomplished on the cross. God's mind is at peace toward all Jesus died for. God knows for certain that the result of this peace is that all that God reconciled by Jesus will be with God forever in heaven.

From 'God-accomplished reconciliation', the passage moves on to what preachers are to accomplish. God gives His ministers *the ministry of reconciliation*. They are *to wit, that God was in Christ, reconciling the world unto himself, not imputing their trespasses unto them*. To them is committed the *word of reconciliation*. They are Christ's ambassadors, beseeching God's people with the plea, '*be ye reconciled to God*'. In these things, the passage seems to be in conflict with itself. If the gospel message is that God has already reconciled us to Himself by Jesus Christ, why did God give His ministers the *ministry of reconciliation*? Why did God commit to preachers the *word of reconciliation*? Most of all, why should the gospel preacher beseech God's people with the entreaty, '*be ye reconciled to God*'?

We begin to answer these questions by acknowledging that there is no contradiction in God's word. *Thy word is truth* (Jno 17:17). It has to tie together. We just need to rightly divide the word of truth.

The passage clearly states that God has already reconciled us to Himself by Jesus Christ. So it makes no sense for the passage to be telling the preacher to do something, so that God will be able to do what He has already done. The preacher's work does not help God do what God has already done. The preacher's work does not redo God's work, nor does it deny God's work. The preacher's work must be a different work. The preacher has nothing to do with God being eternally at peace with us. The preacher's work has nothing to do with our being eternally saved and getting to heaven. God has already accomplished these things by Jesus Christ.

God does not need the *ministry of reconciliation*, nor the *word of reconciliation*, so that God can finally have a sense of peace toward His sinful children. God does not need His children to be reconciled to Him, so that He can be reconciled to them. God does not need His children to be satisfied with the work of Christ, in order for God to be satisfied with it. God was satisfied with Christ's work long before we ever thought about these things. God remains satisfied that He has reconciled us to Himself by Jesus Christ, whether we are reconciled toward Him or not. God is at peace with us, whether we feel to be at peace toward God or not. Moreover, if God is at peace toward us, we are going to heaven, whether we know it or not, whether we feel peace toward God or not.

So what is the preacher's work? What is the *ministry of reconciliation*? What is the *word of reconciliation*? Why should preachers be pleading, *'be ye reconciled to God'*? For a sinner to feel any peace of mind, his mind needs to be reconciled to the fact that God's mind has been reconciled. If you can know that God has made peace through Jesus Christ, then you can have peace. When you come to know that God is reconciled toward you, then you can feel to be reconciled toward God. When you come to know that God feels peace toward you, then you can feel peace toward God. Peace comes to you when you come to know what God already knows about peace. When you come to know what God's mind knows, you can know peace of mind about the certainty of your eternal salvation.

So by God's grace God has given to His gospel ministers the *word of reconciliation*. The true gospel minister preaches the gospel of peace, which declares that God has already made peace between God and the troubled sinner. By the gift of faith, and by the means of the gospel, the sinner hears and understands the good news that God has already made eternal peace. This understanding of the gospel brings peace to the burdened sinner's soul. This truth will set a sinner free.

The preacher of the true gospel of peace tells anybody that will listen that God has already *reconciled us to Himself by Jesus Christ*. When God's children come to know that God has reconciled them to Himself by Himself, they can become reconciled to God in their minds. If you believe God-accomplished reconciliation to be true, and if you know this reconciliation to be a finished work, then you can be reconciled to what God is already reconciled to. This is what is meant by the entreaty, *be ye reconciled to God.*

There is a difference in God reconciling you to Himself by Jesus Christ, and you being reconciled to God through the gospel message of peace. God reconciling you to Himself by Jesus Christ gives you eternal life. Your being reconciled to God through the message of peace gives you the assurance of eternal life. The first satisfies God's mind, while the second satisfies your mind. The first makes you acceptable to God, while the second makes you know that you are acceptable to God. The gospel does not give spiritual life. It gives enlightenment to those to whom God has already given spiritual life. The message of reconciliation does not make you right with God. Jesus made you right with God. The message of reconciliation lets you know that you have been made right with God.

Peace exists in the mind of the sinner, who knows that the mind of God is at peace with him. To know that God is at peace with the sinner allows the sinner to know that he is going to heaven. So the sinner has peace of mind about his eternal destiny, when he comes to know that God's mind feels peace toward him. Moreover, the sinner is reconciled to God, when he becomes sure that God is reconciled to him. This feeling of peace comes only through the preaching of the true gospel of peace. If you have this peace with God in your mind, you have something that very few children of God have ever experienced.

Many think that man has to believe that God did what He did, in order for it to become real. God did what He did, whether we believe it or not. God has *reconciled us to Himself by Jesus Christ,* whether we believe it or not. God knows that He has *reconciled us to Himself by Jesus Christ,* whether we know it or not. Our not knowing what we do not know, cannot make God not know what He already knows. Our not believing in what God has accomplished, cannot undo what God has already done. The truth about 'God-accomplished reconciliation' does not hinge upon anybody knowing it to be the truth.

Truth is truth, because it is truth, and not because it is believed to be truth. The truth is that God has made peace with His people, whether they believe it or not. The truth is that faith in the gospel has nothing to do with God being eternally reconciled to each of His children. Whether we believe it or not, the truth is that each one of God's children has to end up in heaven, because God *hath reconciled us to Himself by Jesus Christ.*

The word *gospel* means 'good news'. God-accomplished reconciliation is good news. The truth of the gospel is that God has already made peace with His sinful children. Jesus said *the truth shall make you free* (Jno 8:32). The truth that God is at peace with the sinner is a soul-freeing truth. Yet, most of today's preachers miss the 'good news' in the good news, in that they preach that man has to make his own peace with God.

This 'so-called gospel' brings bondage. Where is the soul-freeing good news in believing that you are responsible for saving yourself (and all humanity) from a burning hell? The Bible calls the true gospel, *the gospel of peace*. Today's 'another gospel' gives no peace, but instead gives its believers vexation and turmoil. Where is the peace in believing the eternal destiny of the multitudes rests on your shoulders? That 'non-good news gospel' brings no rest. It brings unrest. That 'supposed gospel' cries *peace, peace, when there is no peace* (Jer 6:14), That 'gospel' is not '**the gospel**'. The true gospel trumpet makes no uncertain sound. The true gospel preacher preaches that God has *reconciled us to Himself by Jesus Christ*. To know that God has made eternal peace with a sinner like me, sure brings peace to this sinner's soul.

So there is much assurance in knowing that God has *reconciled us to Himself by Jesus Christ*. Yet in a backwards way of thinking, there is also much assurance in understanding that if we have no knowledge that God has *reconciled us to Himself by Jesus Christ*, then our lack of knowledge cannot 'un-reconcile' God's reconciling. This simple understanding certainly takes away the burden of trying to save souls from a burning hell. Yet, in spite of not having the responsibility of eternally saving souls, the gospel minister still has the great responsibility to enlighten God's people to the truth that their souls have been saved. To know that your soul is eternally saved gives a peace that passes understanding.

So do you know that you are saved? Do you know that God has reconciled you to Himself by Jesus Christ? Do you know that peace has been made? God's mind is at peace concerning what Jesus accomplished. God is at peace with you. Do you have peace of mind that God is at peace with you? Are you at peace with God?

There is a difference in having eternal life, and having the peace that comes in knowing that you have eternal life. Many people exist in an eternally secure state of having eternal salvation, but still exist in a fearfully insecure state of mind of not knowing that their eternal salvation is secure.

There is great peace in knowing that our salvation is totally of the Lord. Yet, most modern day Christians believe in a combination plan of eternal salvation. They think that God started the process of reconciling the sinner to Himself by Jesus, but the sinner must finish the process of reconciling himself to God by something of himself. This combination plan leaves the sinner with many doubts and fears. He wonders if he has completed his part to God's satisfaction. He can never have true peace.

To understand the gospel of salvation by grace, and grace alone, is to know that God is not seeking satisfaction in the sinner's part. God is totally satisfied with the finished work of Christ. To know the gospel of grace, is to know that God is at peace with you, because of the finished work of Christ. To know the gospel of God's grace gives you peace about your eternal salvation. In salvation by grace, and grace alone, the sinner has no part. Jesus does it all. If you know the gospel of grace, then you know that you are saved by grace without adding any *ifs*, *ands* or *buts* to the plan. If you know, without doubt and without disclaimer, that Jesus has reconciled you to God, then you can have a peace of mind that few Christians have ever experienced.

So God is satisfied with Christ, but are you satisfied with the finished work of Jesus Christ? You should be, but so many Christians are not. Many people do not believe that Jesus finished what He said He finished. Jesus said: *It is finished* (Jno 19:30). Yet many believe there is still something left to do. Jesus came to redeem. *God sent forth his Son, made of a woman, made under the law, to redeem...* (Gal 4:4-5). The Bible says that Jesus accomplished eternal redemption. *...by his own blood he entered in once into the holy place, having obtained eternal redemption for us* (Heb 9:12). Jesus came to redeem. Jesus has redeemed. Redemption is accomplished.

Do you believe Jesus has saved you from your sins, or do you believe you must still do something in addition to what Jesus has done? The angel said: *He **shall save** his people from their sins* (Mt 1:21). Paul said: *God who **hath saved**...* (2 Tim 1:8-9). Jesus came to save. Jesus has saved. Salvation is accomplished. God is satisfied that Jesus has redeemed His people, and has saved His people, but are you satisfied? God is satisfied that you are going to heaven, but are you satisfied?

Do you believe that God has reconciled you to Himself by Jesus Christ? Or do you believe that you must reconcile yourself to God by something you do? Do you believe that God made you accepted in His Beloved Son? *He hath made us accepted in the beloved* (Eph 1:6). Or do you believe that God will accept you, only if you first accept Him? By God's grace, God has *reconciled us to Himself by Jesus Christ*. By God's grace, God has *made us accepted*. Jesus has made sinners to be acceptable to God. Our acceptance is not based on our accepting God's Son. Our acceptance is based on our having already been made acceptable to God by that Beloved Son. God knows that He has reconciled His children to Himself by Jesus Christ. God knows that He made His children accepted in the Beloved. Yet do you know these things?

God's children need to be satisfied with Jesus, and with Jesus' finished work, not so we can go to heaven, but so we can know we are going. If we understand the good news of the finished work of Christ in salvation, then we have the truth that will make us free. If we are persuaded of the 'past-tense accomplishments' of our salvation by Jesus, then we can rest in peace. If we know that God has *reconciled us to Himself by Jesus Christ*, then we, like God, can be satisfied with the eternal reconciliation that God accomplished by Jesus Christ. God hath reconciled us to Himself by Jesus Christ. So be ye reconciled to God.

There is peace of mind when a child of God understands salvation by grace. It is a relief to know that God's plan to save me does not hinge on my works. Instead of being based on my works, God's plan of salvation is totally based on Jesus' finished work. There is a big difference between trying to find peace in thinking that my works must get me to heaven, and experiencing the peace of knowing that Jesus' finished work gets me to heaven.

It is a further relief to know that God's plan to get me to heaven does not depend upon my believing in the plan. My faith is weak. If I believe in my belief to get me there, I have no peace. If I have faith in my weak faith to make the difference, then I fear I will burn in hell. We are not to have faith in our faith, but to have faith in our Savior.

Some would say that there is no difference, but there is a big difference. Faith in weak faith gives no real peace. Yet, faith in a mighty Jesus to save by His grace gives a great peace of mind, which is based in Him, and not me. God did not give us the gift of faith, so that we might have faith in our faith to save us. God gave us faith so that we might believe that our Savior has saved us. Jesus has saved His children, whether they believe it or not. God has *reconciled us to Himself by Jesus Christ,* whether we know it or not. Yet when we by faith believe what God already knows, then we have peace that assures our souls of our eternal destinies. There is little peace in trying to do good enough, or in having faith in my faith. Yet, there is great peace in trusting in my Savior to have accomplished my salvation for me.

Some men say, "Peace, peace when there is no peace." The teaching that interjects man into God's way of reconciling sinners unto Himself will give little, if any, peace. There is no peace in thinking that your failure to do good works will save you. There is no peace in thinking that your weak faith will save you. Real mind-settling peace can only be found in knowing that God, and God alone, saves you. Real peace is found in knowing that God has already reconciled you to Himself by Jesus Christ. If and when you come to know this, you can, in your mind, be reconciled to the God who is already very much reconciled to you.

So what is the gospel for? It is not for getting eternal life. Jesus has already done that for us. Jesus has already saved us. The gospel of salvation by grace is to be preached, so that we can know that God has already saved us. The gospel is *to guide our feet into the way of peace* (Lk 1:79). If we can know that God has made peace, then we can have peace. Hearing and believing the gospel of peace does not give us life. It gives us peace.

There is a ministry of peace, even a *word of reconciliation*. We need the assurance of knowing that our salvation has been accomplished for us. We need to know that God has reconciled us to Himself by Himself, so that we can in our minds be reconciled to God. We need the peace of mind that can only come by believing the gospel of peace about God's salvation by grace.

12
Is Eternal Salvation Based on Good Works?

The Bible declares that eternal salvation occurs, not by works, but by grace, and grace alone. The Bible says that *by the deeds of the law there shall no flesh be justified in his sight* (Rom 3:20). The Bible says that eternal salvation is *not of works, lest any man should boast* (Eph 2:9). The Bible says that *the purpose of God according to election…(is) not of works, but of him that calleth* (Rom 9:11). The Bible says that *it is not of him that willeth, nor of him that runneth, but of God that sheweth mercy* (Rom 9:16). The Bible says that God *hath saved us, and called us with an holy calling, not according to our works* (2 Tim 1:9). The Bible says that *if by grace, then is it no more of works: otherwise grace is no more grace* (Rom 11:6). The Bible does not teach a combination plan of salvation. The Bible does not say that salvation comes through a combination of God's grace and man's works. The Bible does not even say that salvation comes through a combination of God's grace and man's faith. The Bible declares salvation by grace, and grace alone.

We begin with Holy Spirit inspired summation statements. These are God's assessments of both the innate and enacted sinfulness, which He sees in each person in all humanity.

> Romans 3:9 *What then? are we better than they? No, in no wise: for we have before proved both Jews and Gentiles, that they are all under sin;*
>
> Romans 3:10 *As it is written, There is none righteous, no, not one:*
>
> Romans 3:11 *There is none that understandeth, there is none that seeketh after God.*

Romans 3:12 They are all gone out of the way, they are together become unprofitable; there is none that doeth good, no, not one.

These words come near the end of an extended teaching on the sinfulness of man. The case against man has been made. Man's depravity has been proved. So we face a Holy Spirit inspired question: *What then?* God challenges us to answer in our own behalf. Are we better than this description God has given of all mankind? *What then? Are we better than they?* Are any of us better than any of the rest of us?

You may think that you are better than me. I may think that I am better than you. Surely neither of us is the worst person in the world. So if we are not the worst, we must be better than somebody somewhere. Right? God's answer, *No, in no wise.* In our sinfulness, none is any better than any other. All are equal, in that we all fall short of God's holy standards that require perfection. *Jews and Gentiles,* anybody and everybody, *are all under sin* (under sin's dominion and under God's condemnation of sin).

There is none righteous, no not one. These are severe words against all mankind. Most say, "Surely, man is not that bad. There are lots of basically good people." God says: *There is none that doeth good, no not one.* No one is excluded. When God looks at the vast host of all humanity, He sees universal unrighteousness. He sees failure of goodness. Both collectively and individually, God condemns everybody, everywhere.

What does it take to be guilty before God? *For whosoever shall keep the whole law, and yet offend in one point, he is guilty of all* (Jas 2:10). So breaking one part of God's law, only one time, renders the same guilty verdict, as breaking all God's law, all the time. God's judgment is unlike man's judgment. Men judge by comparison. A little under the average is not that bad. Yet God does not compare man to man. Our peers are not our standard. God's perfection is the standard. God's only passing grade is to totally keep His law, in all its details, and in its entirety. With God there are two options: law keepers and lawbreakers. There are two classes: guilty and not guilty. Hitler broke God's law by killing millions. I broke God's law by coveting, and not being content with what I had. Hitler and I are both lawbreakers. We both are guilty. Neither of us is righteous. Both of us deserve to burn in hell. God does not judge us, as to whether we have been better than someone else. God watches to see if we have maintained perfection. There are two verdicts: perfect and unrighteous. In case we have forgotten: *There is none righteous, no not one. There is none that doeth good, no not one.* Nobody makes the grade.

Some claim that they have not broken even one point of the law. God says that they are lying to themselves. *If we say that we have no sin, we deceive ourselves, and the truth is not in us* (1 Jno 1:8). Yet, they are not just lying to themselves. The Bible goes on to say that *if we say that we have not sinned, we make him a liar* (1 Jno 1:10). To say that we have no sin is to call God a liar, because God says that *all have sinned, and come short of the glory of God* (Rom 3:23).

In our self-righteousness, we tend to think that we must have a little righteousness that ought to count for something. The Bible replies: *But we are all as an unclean thing, and all our righteousnesses are as filthy rags* (Is 64:6). If we think that God looks favorably on fallen man's righteousness, we should think again.

Assume we gather together *all our righteousnesses*. You bring yours. I will bring mine. Be sure to bring all you can remember from the past. Have everybody bring some. Pile them up together. Present them to God. God says the whole pile is *as filthy rags* (literal translation—soiled menstrual cloths). Think of used toilet tissue. What is filthy toilet paper worth? How about a whole pile of it? The more the pile grows, the worse the situation becomes. Likewise, the more *righteousnesses* we pile before God, the worse the situation becomes. As it is appropriate to burn the soiled toilet tissue, so it is fitting to burn the unclean things with all their so-called *righteousnesses.* Soiled menstrual rags are God's illustration of all the good works of all unclean men added together. This is the Holy God's view of the goodness of men! Ouch! That hurts!

All that appears to be righteousness to men is not righteousness to God. Supposed good works without the Holy Spirit's driving influence in the heart are not really good works in God's eyes. Men see the outside. God views the heart. Men do good to be seen of men. Men do good to receive good in return. Men do good in fear of consequences for doing bad. Many so-called good works come from selfish motives. God's righteous judgment condemns self-interest driven deeds to be nothing more than unrighteous hypocrisy. True righteousness begins and ends with God. All else falls short. It is doubtful that a born-again man is capable of pure righteousness. How much more is it impossible for the unregenerate man to do a good work!

In early history, *God saw that the wickedness of man was great in the earth, and that every imagination of the thoughts of his heart was only evil continually* (Gen 6:5). If every imagination is only evil, then no imagination is not evil. Moreover, these evil imaginations are not just occasional. They are said to be continual. From near the beginning, there was none righteous.

There is still none righteous, for *who can bring a clean thing out of an unclean? Not one* (Job 14:4). Sinful fathers father children in their own carnal image. *Behold I was shapen in iniquity; and in sin did my mother conceive me* (Ps 51:5). From birth, we are innately wicked. *The wicked are estranged from the womb: they go astray as soon as they be born, speaking lies* (Ps 58:3). We enter the world *by nature the children of wrath, even as others* (Eph 2:3). A clean thing cannot come from an unclean thing. A pure child cannot come from a sinful father. We are formed in sinfulness. We are sinners by nature and by inheritance. No scriptural teaching supports purity in infancy. A child does not become sinful when he commits his first sin. A child commits sin, because he is sinful. We do not have to learn to be sinners. We do not have to wait to become sinners. We arrive as sinners. We are what we are by nature.[1]

---

[1] Perhaps I should insert a thought regarding the eternal state of those who die as babes. Let me reassure you that there is good hope for these infants, but their hope is not in their purity. They had no purity to present to God. Yet, though they lack a presentable sinless nature, their hope is in something much better than supposed infant purity. Their hope is in their Savior, who took their inherited impurity from them, and gave to them His perfect purity. Their hope is the same as your hope. Their hope is the sinner's only hope. Yet it is the sinner's sufficient hope. Their hope is Jesus, their Savior. They need no other plan.

The depraved little child does not improve with age, but soon proves his sinful nature by his actions. *The imagination of man's heart is evil from his youth* (Gen 8:21). Playgrounds are places where older kids train the younger to bully the youngest. Inappropriate behavior does not need to be reinforced. The child is a natural at perfecting his imperfections. Selfishness does not have to be taught, but sharing with others is most difficult to swallow. Curbing the naturally bad behavior is the challenge in parenting. So does the child finally mature and outgrow all this sin? If you think the 'terrible twos' are rough, just wait for the 'sweet sixteens'. Aging only brings smarter sinners, who are better at hiding their bigger sins. By nature, man starts bad, and gets worse.

If you have a problem with God judging infants to be sinners, then you may really have a problem with God judging all men through Adam. *By one man, sin entered into the world, and death by sin; and death passed upon all men, for all have sinned* (Rom 5:12). God universally condemned all men, because of one man's sin. God did not wait until we committed our first sin to condemn us. God did not wait until we reached a contrived age of accountability to condemn us. God did not even wait until we were born with a sin nature to condemn us. God universally condemned us, and all men, to death when Adam sinned. When Adam sinned, God judged all men to have sinned. As human beings in the loins of Adam, waiting for our lives to begin, God had already judged us to be sinners.

So God's word declares man's sinfulness in three ways. We are sinners by representation, in that we were in Adam when he sinned. We are sinners by nature, in that we inherit sinfulness from our carnal fathers. We are sinners by practice, in that we do wicked things.

Moreover, our practice of sin is not limited to what we do. We also sin in what we say. Some have said, "Sticks and stones can break my bones, but words can never hurt me." The first part of the saying is certain, but what of the last? Though sinful words may not directly break bones, they surely can still cause great harm, even destroy lives. James said that *the tongue is a little member*. Yet he went on to *behold, how great a matter a little fire kindleth!* That little tongue can be *a fire, a world of iniquity.* The vile tongue *defileth the whole body.* The fiery tongue receives its fire from hell itself, in that *it is set on fire of hell.* The flaming tongue *setteth on fire the course of nature.* The snake-like tongue *is an unruly evil, full of deadly poison* (Jas 3:5-8). Surely we can discount the old saying that declares no hurt in words. Great raging fires, whole bodies destroyed, nature ablaze, the igniting of the fire of hell on earth, uncontrollable evil, and deadly poison—that sounds like a lot of hurt to me. All this hurt started from a few words. That ought to shut our mouths.

Oh but sinners seem to keep talking! The Bible shames *slanderers, talebearers, tattlers and busybodies.* It condemns *whisperers.* These are not people who speak softly in a library. These are gossips who slander other people. *Whisperers* and *backbiters* are included with those who are filled with *all unrighteousness* (Rom 1:29-30). Some say, "It's not gossip, if it's the truth." Yet, where is the Christian spirit in telling everything you know about somebody? Where is *The Golden Rule* in speaking the truth, the whole truth, and nothing but the truth, when sharing that truth destroys your neighbor? It is hard to keep juicy gossip a secret. If you *whisper*, they will strain to hear. You are center stage. It is your little 'gossip moment in the sun'. Then, they all run to enjoy their little gossip moments in the sun. A life is destroyed; a reputation is ruined; but oh how fun it was to have that little moment! Is this Christianity? Was it worth it? Words really matter.

Paul said: *Let no corrupt communication proceed out of your mouth, but that which is good to the use of edifying, that it may minister grace unto the hearers* (Eph 4:29). Think of how much hurt could be eliminated if nobody spoke harmful words. Think of how much happiness could be spread if we only spoke words that would build up others.

Paul continued: *But fornication, and all uncleanness, or covetousness, let it not be once named among you, as becometh saints; Neither filthiness, nor foolish talking, nor jesting, which are not convenient: but rather giving of thanks* (Eph 5:3-4). The same sentence lumps *foolish talk* and *jesting* with such sins as: *fornication, uncleanness, covetousness and filthiness*. Surely God did not mean to have joking and sexual impurity on the same list.

A bit of honest self-examination reveals to us that we are not very good judges of God's right and wrong. Today's America has come to look softly even on the 'big' sins in this list. *Fornication* has become the norm (and we all tend to be influenced by the norm). We have come to sense very little conviction about *covetousness*. Our capitalism admires the covetous spirit. It is the motivation to success. What is more important to Christian parents these days? Bringing up our children with the Lord's admonition against covetousness? Or inspiring and preparing our children to compete in the covetous world of capitalism? As we continue with the list, we are unsure what *uncleanness* and *filthiness* even refer to. So let us not even trouble our minds with God's view of sin on these two. (We probably would not agree with Him anyway.)

So we finally come to the God-defined sins of *foolish talk* and *jesting*. It truly speaks to man's corruption, when we respond to the sins of *foolish talk* and *jesting*, with *foolish talk* and *jesting*. When confronted with God's word, men casually joke, "Surely God does not really think *foolish talk* and *jesting* are wrong. God has a sense of humor. Otherwise, why would He have put stripes on zebras?" Everybody laughs. Nobody repents. Nobody confesses that man's words should rather be spent in *giving of thanks*. Who does Paul think he is anyway? What gives him the right to tell us what is wrong and right?

Surely Jesus has the authority to tell us wrong and right. Here are Jesus' words about our words. *But I say unto you, That every idle word that men shall speak, they shall give account thereof in the day of judgment* (Mt 12:36). The Greek word that was translated *idle* has the meaning of lazy, useless or barren. Barren words are empty words, even small talk and chitchat. Useless words serve no useful purpose. Lazy words refuse to work. One scholar defines *idle* as: "shunning the labor which one ought to perform." God calls us to a work of faith and a labor of love. Slothfulness in good works is condemned. Laziness is unacceptable, even in lazy words that refuse to be about the Father's business. Even our words should be put to work in our service to our King. As opposed to useless and barren words, our words should be useful in praising God, and in encouraging others. Oh, the dreadful thought of having to give account for all my words that have not been to the purpose of God's work!

So the idea of *none good, no not one* goes beyond our deeds, and even to our words. Yet this is not the end. There are sins of the mind and of the heart. Jesus equated angry thoughts to murderous hands. Surely covetousness takes place in the mind. Lusts originate in the heart. *Whosoever looketh on a woman to lust after her hath committed adultery with her already in his heart* (Mt 5:28). Cruel words arise from a vile heart. *Out of the abundance of the heart the mouth speaketh* (Mt 12:34). We tend to think of a 'spark of goodness' that lies in the human heart. God sees into the human heart and says: *The heart is deceitful above all things, and desperately wicked: who can know it?* (Jer 17:9). Our wicked hearts deceive us about the true condition of our own hearts, and we do not even know it is happening. When we dig deep into the heart of man, we find that the 'spark of goodness' is not even a smoking flax. Our hearts are not the source of our good. Our carnal hearts and minds are the source of our problem. God sees and judges the mind, the heart, and even the inner thoughts and feelings.

Yet the Bible says more about sin. God goes beyond judging us according to the wrong that we do. God also judges us according to the right that we do not do. *Therefore to him that knoweth to do good, and doeth it not, to him it is sin* (Jas 4:19). This might be called the 'sin of the recliner'. It is the sin of doing nothing, when there is potential good to be done. The world is full of people who need help. There is always a stranger in a ditch, and there is usually a priest passing by on the other side. It is not okay to not get involved. It is not okay to deny that you realized that somebody needed you. *If thou forbear to deliver them that are drawn unto death, and those that are ready to be slain; If thou sayest, Behold, we knew it not; doth not he that pondereth the heart consider it? and he that keepeth thy soul, doth not he know it? and shall not he render to every man according to his works?* (Pro 24:11-12).

When Jesus condemned the goats to everlasting fire, He never mentioned their sins of idolatry, blasphemy, murder and stealing. Jesus did not list what they had done wrong. He instead spoke of what they had failed to do that would have been right. *Then shall he say also unto them on the left hand, Depart from me, ye cursed, into everlasting fire, prepared for the devil and his angels: For I was an hungred, and ye gave me no meat: I was thirsty, and ye gave me no drink: I was a stranger, and ye took me not in: naked, and ye clothed me not: sick, and in prison, and ye visited me not* (Mt 25:41-42). Sins of omission! These are hard sayings!

Jesus' standard goes beyond just doing good to loved ones and friends. Jesus said: *Love your enemies, do good to them which hate you* (Lk 6:27). It is not good enough just to walk away from a fight. Jesus said to do good to your enemy. Jesus set a high standard for doing good. Paul confessed that he had not attained to God's standard of goodness. He knew that his best good was still tainted with bad. *For the good that I would I do not: but the evil which I would not, that I do* (Rom 7:19). We never do all the good that we could do. Nor do we ever cease from the bad that we should not do. *There is none that doeth good, no not one.*

Paul concluded his extended teaching on sin in Romans with these words: *Now we know that what things soever the law saith, it saith to them who are under the law: that every mouth may be stopped, and all the world may become guilty before God. Therefore by the deeds of the law there shall no flesh be justified in his sight: for by the law is the knowledge of sin* (Rom 3:19-20). God's law says something to all who are under it, and all are under it. The law stops every mouth: no excuses, no alibis, no more arguing your case. The law eliminates all attempts of self-justification. The law does not declare righteousness in the sinner. The law defines righteousness for the sinner. The law does not declare righteousness in the sinner. The law instead proves guilt in the sinner. The law proves that all the world is guilty before God.

Keeping the law has never justified a sinner before God, because no one has ever kept the law. The law is what condemns the lawbreaker, and that which condemns cannot be what justifies. By the law's defining of righteousness comes the knowledge of sin to the sinner. The law proves to the sinner that he is a sinner. The law proves universal condemnation of all men. The law proves the need of a Savior!

This concludes our discussion of what Primitive Baptists believe about eternal salvation based on good works. Yet, how can a preacher of the gospel leave God's people here. Paul did not stop with his proof of the universal condemnation of all humanity. Paul's next word was *"But"*. *But now the righteousness of God without the law is manifested, being witnessed by the law and the prophets* (Rom 3:21). Paul spoke of a newly revealed righteousness of God apart from man keeping God's law, even a righteousness that the Old Testament had spoken of. Jesus said that the Old Testament testified of Jesus (Jno 5:39). This righteousness that is of God is none other than Jesus Christ Himself.

This righteousness is said to be without the law. It is based on something other than the sinner keeping God's law. This righteousness is not of man, but of God for man. This righteousness that is of God makes the man to be righteous. In God's plan of salvation by grace, God made Jesus *to be sin for us, who knew no sin; that we might be made the righteousness of God in him* (2 Cor 5:21). God imputes Jesus' righteousness to man. At the cross Jesus took all the sins of all His people upon Himself. The blood of Jesus washed away every sin of all the ones He died for. God remembers those sins no more. The sins are as though they never existed. Blood washed sinners stand before God, as if they never had sinned. Yet beyond standing sinless, they stand with Jesus' righteousness having been imputed to their account. When God sees Jesus' righteousness, God is satisfied. God has legitimately declared all that Christ died for to be legally justified. Christ made them righteous, and God declared them to be so.

Now that is good news to sinners, of whom *there is none that doeth good, no not one.*

13

If Salvation is by Grace, Why Bother to do Good Works?

Eternal salvation is not by good works. The Bible says: *not of works, lest any man should boast*. The Bible says: *there is none that doeth good, no not one*. The Bible says: *all have sinned, and come short of the glory of God*. The Bible says that God *hath saved us... not according to our works, but according to his purpose and grace*. The Bible says: *if by grace, then is it no more of works: otherwise grace is no more grace*. Salvation is not through a combination of God's grace and man's works. God's salvation is by grace, and grace alone.

Yet scoffers line up with objections to salvation that is totally by God's grace. They argue, "If I believed that, I would just go out and do whatever I wanted to do. You people turn grace into a license to sin. If it is all by grace, why would anybody even bother to do any good works?"

God anticipated that men would sneer at His grace. He surely knew that His plan of salvation, which is by grace alone, would lay itself open to the challenge that the plan promoted acceptable lawlessness. So God answered the mockers objections, even before they could raise their protests: *What shall we say then? Shall we continue in sin, that grace may abound? God forbid* (Rom 6:1-2). The main point here is that God forbids anybody from using His amazing grace as permission to continue in a life of sin.[1]

As we begin our discussion as to whether men should bother to do good works, I invite you to go back in time to a mount called Sinai. There God defined His 'good works', but He did it in a way that seems very serious. Listen closely. *Moses brought forth the people*

---

[1] As a side note, a plan of salvation based on man's efforts would never have been accused of excusing licentious living. So the fact that God defended His plan in such a way is proof that salvation must truly be by grace.

out of the camp to meet with God; and they stood at the nether part of the mount (Ex 19:17). *And if so much as a beast touch the mountain, it shall be stoned, or thrust through with a dart* (Heb 12:20). *And the LORD came down upon mount Sinai, on the top of the mount* (Ex 19:20). *And mount Sinai was altogether on a smoke, because the LORD descended upon it in fire: and the smoke thereof ascended as the smoke of a furnace, and the whole mount quaked greatly* (Ex 19:18). *There were thunders and lightnings, and a thick cloud upon the mount* (Ex 19:6). *...blackness, and darkness, and tempest* (Heb 12:18). *And all the people saw the thunderings, and the lightnings, and the noise of the trumpet, and the mountain smoking* (Ex 20:18). *...the sound of a trumpet* (Heb 12:18). *...exceeding loud; so that all the people that was in the camp trembled* (Ex 19:16). *And so terrible was the sight, that Moses said, I exceedingly fear and quake* (Heb 12:21). *And when the people saw it, they removed, and stood afar off* (Ex 20:18). *...the voice of words; which voice they that heard intreated that the word should not be spoken to them any more* (Heb 12:19). *They could not endure that which was commanded* (Heb 12:20). *And they said unto Moses, Speak thou with us, and we will hear: but let not God speak with us, lest we die* (Ex 20:19). *For this great fire will consume us: if we hear the voice of the LORD our God any more, then we shall die* (Deut 5:25). *Let me not hear again the voice of the LORD my God, neither let me see this great fire any more, that I die not* (Deut 18:16).

What a scene! Visualize this fiery black trembling mountain. Sense God's anger and wrath against sin and sinners. Feel the fear. We may run with the people, but there is no place to hide. God's mountain still thunders. The trumpet still blares. God's voice still roars. We beg God to leave, but His mountain stands firm. We try sewing fig leaves, but God's law sees right through. We cry for mercy, but Sinai cries justice. We plead for God's pardon; God's mountain screams vengeance. We try to look up, but the mountain stares down. We repent with our tears, but the blackness still frowns. Our eyes turn to Moses, but Moses is quaking. We look to our preacher; yet he too is shaking. There is no place to turn. There is no place of cover. God's mount is never satisfied. God's law is never kept. So how do we feel as we shake under Sinai's shadow?

Do we feel that God does not really care about good works? I feel a sense of shame that I even posed the question: *If salvation is not by good works, why even bother to do good works?*

Good works matter to God. God declared *there is none that doeth good, no, not one.* That is not an inconsequential observation. Sinai was not just fireworks. Men are judged by Sinai's fierce wrath. All men have failed Sinai's test. Every mouth is stopped. All the world is guilty. By the deeds of the law no flesh is justified in God's sight.

God dares men to scoff that doing good does not really matter! Every iniquity is marked. God judges every sin. None are swept under the proverbial rug. Every crime must be punished. Sinai's rituals offer no cure. *For it is not possible that the blood of bulls and of goats should take away sins* (Heb 10:4). Animal sacrifice will not suffice. God's wrath is not appeased with goat blood. Man must pay, and the payment is excruciating.

God's great white throne judgment is inevitable. All men will be judged out of some book. *The books were opened: and another book was opened, which is the book of life: and the dead were judged out of those things which were written in the books, according to their works* (Rev 20:12). Men will be judged out of *the books*, even the books that mark all iniquities according to Sinai's fierce law.

Yet John said: *And another book was opened.* This is the *Lamb's book of life.* This is God's book, wherein are written the names of God's people. This book is God's record of His elect that God gave to Jesus in the Covenant of Grace before the foundation of the world. This book contains the list of *His people* that Jesus died for and saved. This book has the list of God's children that the Holy Spirit 'borns again'. This book defines the *'whoms'* and *'thems'*. *Moreover whom he did predestinate, them he also called: and whom he called, them he also justified: and whom he justified, them he also glorified* (Rom 8:30).

And whosoever was not found written in the book of life was cast into the lake of fire (Rev 20:15). Everybody will be judged out of some book: either the book of sins that the sinner has written throughout his life, or the Lamb's book of life that God has written. So were the sins of those in the Lamb's book of life not recorded? God forbid. God marked all their sins in His book of judgment. Their books were full. According to God's judgment, man must pay. Yet, which man? There was a Man sent from God. There was a substitute, an intercessor, a daysman. Moses' lambs had not been sufficient. The Lamb of God would suffice. The Man, Christ Jesus, took the sinner's place. God thrust those books of the sins of all His vast host of people at Jesus. Jesus despised the shame, but gladly opened the books. Jesus read every recorded name. Jesus read every recorded sin beside each name. Jesus took each person, whose name had been written in the Lamb's book of life, into His very being. Jesus took each sin to be His own. God made Jesus to be sin, who knew no sin of His own. Jesus felt Sinai's terror. From Calvary's hill, Jesus suffered Sinai's blackness. God's judgment blared down, while Jesus looked up and cried: *My God, my God, why hast thou forsaken me?* (Mat 27:46). Every sin was punished. None was ignored. Jesus experienced hell in our place. Jesus took God's wrath that should have been ours to take. God looked upon the suffering of Jesus' soul, and God was satisfied. And *they which are written in the Lamb's book of life* will dwell with the Lamb forever.

Well there it is! Salvation is of the Lord. Jesus will lose nothing of all which the Father had given Him. No one can be plucked out of His hand. All God's children must end up in heaven. So why should we be the least bit concerned about doing good works? Furthermore, God has already said: *there is none that doeth good, no not one* (Rom 3:12). Besides that, any good that we try to do, still has bad in it: *When I would do good, evil is present with me* (Rom 7:21). So if there is no such thing as doing good anyway, and if we are going to heaven anyway, then why should we even bother to do good works?

It is certain that all Jesus died for are going to heaven, but it is just as certain that we are not there yet. Do you suppose that there could be negative consequences while still in this world for the child of God who willingly ignores God's right and wrong? From an eternal perspective, Jesus has suffered the consequences for the sins of His children. Yet God says: *If we sin willfully after that we have received the knowledge of the truth, there remaineth no more sacrifice for sins, but a certain fearful looking for of judgment and fiery indignation, which shall devour the adversaries* (Heb 10:26-27).

These words do not mean that God will disregard the finished work of Jesus and condemn His children to hell, if they willfully sin. Yet, eternal hell is not God's only option. God personally deals with our willful sins in the here and now. The passage reminds us that Jesus is not going to come back and suffer the consequences, as it pertains to a Father dealing with a rebellious child. We have to take this chastisement ourselves. It is indeed fearful to know that God can bring judgment and fiery anger upon His children, as if He were devouring His adversaries. That sounds a lot like living hell on earth.

Yet God's warnings do not stop here. The passage continues with a reference back to Sinai's fierce law, and it makes a comparison: *He that despised Moses' law died without mercy under two or three witnesses: Of how much sorer punishment, suppose ye, shall he be thought worthy, who hath trodden under foot the Son of God, and hath counted the blood of the covenant, wherewith he was sanctified, an unholy thing, and hath done despite unto the Spirit of grace?* (Heb 10:28-29). Here God reminds us that Sinai's law showed no mercy. Lawbreakers were stoned. Then God speaks of *sorer punishment*, which a believer in Jesus would be worthy of, if he mocks the understanding of the gospel of grace, by continuing to live in disregard towards God's holy law.

This comparison is then followed with more frightful statements toward the willfully disobedient: *Vengeance belongeth unto me, I will recompense, saith the Lord...The Lord shall judge his people* (Heb 10:30). These are the same *'His people'* that the angel spoke of when he said: *for he shall save his people from their sins* (Mt 1:21). These are the ones that Jesus died for. They are going to heaven, but things do not look so rosy for them for the right now. The passage finally states: *It is a fearful thing to fall into the hands of the living God* (Heb 10:31).

There is perhaps yet another negative motivation that should encourage doing good. God does not just judge individuals. He also judges nations. God destroyed Sodom, Gomorrah, and all the land of the plain. Babylon is fallen. Where is the mighty Roman Empire?

Even God's chosen nations of Israel and Judah were not exempt. God wrote of Judah: *Were they ashamed when they had committed abomination? nay, they were not at all ashamed, neither could they blush: therefore they shall fall among them that fall: at the time that I visit them they shall be cast down, saith the LORD* (Jer 6:15).

At least Adam and Eve attempted to hide their shame. Judah was ashamed of nothing. She had forgotten how to blush. For this, she fell among them that fell. If God's chosen nation suffered God's wrath, who does America think she is? Like Judah of old, America no longer blushes at her sins. We taunt God with the sins of Sodom. We sacrifice our babies for our own convenience. We are ashamed of none of our sins. The only thing that we seem to be ashamed of is Jesus Christ. Jesus said: *For whosoever shall be ashamed of me and of my words, of him shall the Son of man be ashamed, when he shall come in his own glory, and in his Father's, and of the holy angels* (Lk 9:26). Isaiah said of the nation of Israel: *Woe unto them that call evil good, and good evil* (Is 5:20).

God always sends warnings before sending destruction. He did with Israel. He did with Judah. Perhaps, He has with America. Jesus called for repentance by referring to a tower that had fallen, killing eighteen (Lk 13:4-5). Is it unrelated that our towers have fallen, killing so many? It is sometimes uncanny how the warnings, even the initial phases of judgment, seem to match the sins. A new disease has come in our lifetime, called AIDS. The disease is undeniably linked with the sins of homosexuality, promiscuity, and illegal drug use. Perhaps we should connect the dots and ponder the possibility that God has sent us warnings. A new policy has come in our lifetime. Prayer and God's Law have been taken from our schools. It is eerie that these schools became the primary sites of mass shootings. The generations of the parents and grandparents have sinned, and countless innocent children and grandchildren have been killed. We made it legal to kill babies long before the mass shootings began. Our sin is the destruction of our children. Perhaps it is in judgment that we see our children destroyed.

America has lost her morality. We have no shame. Neither can we blush. We are a people taught by television, instead of the Bible.

Television has taken away our sense of shame. We watch shows with our grandchildren, that we would turn off if Jesus walked into the room. From the television, we receive our new standards. We become more and more politically correct, while becoming less and less Biblically correct.

Yet television may serve a useful purpose. From television, we see vivid warnings: the fall of the towers, the mass shootings, civil unrest, riots in our streets, cops shooting, cops being shot, 100 year storms, 1000 year storms, overwhelming floods, devastating droughts, out-of-control fires. It should be enough to bring a nation to its knees, but instead of responding to God's warnings with repentance, we counter as Israel of old. *The bricks are fallen down, but we will build with hewn stones: the sycomores are cut down, but we will change them into cedars* (Is 9:10). When our towers are fallen down, we vow to build them back stronger. When our cities are underwater, our leaders invariably speak of the strength and resiliency of Americans to rebuild. We may be knocked down, but we refuse to be brought down. We refuse to fall to our knees in repentance. We heed not God's warnings. We will not be humbled. We are strong. We shall rise and rebuild.

Is there any hope for America? God would have spared Sodom for the sake of ten. God spared wicked Nineveh, when she repented. We find hope in the long ago words: *...if I send pestilence among my people; if my people, which are called by my name, shall humble themselves, and pray, and seek my face, and turn from their wicked ways; then will I hear from heaven, and will forgive their sin, and will heal their land* (2 Chr 7:13-14).

God's threats of vengeance are indeed a motivation to good works. Sinai's *'Thou shalt nots'* are still serious. Yet the New Testament approaches righteous living in a totally different way to the Old Testament. The Old Testament presented the fear of Sinai. The New Testament presents the love of Calvary. The law promised justice against sin. Grace promises mercy to sinners. The Old drove men to hiding. The New invites men to come. Let us briefly look at four New Testament approaches for teaching God's children to live their lives in the doing of good works.

The first approach is: *'Now You Know Grace—Therefore...'* This was Paul's favorite. Through several chapters in Romans, Paul brilliantly laid out salvation by amazing grace. Then he came to his *'therefore'*. *I beseech you therefore, brethren, by the mercies of God, that ye present your bodies a living sacrifice, holy, acceptable unto God, which is your reasonable service* (Rom 12:1). *Now you know grace, therefore* sacrifice your old way of living, and live a holy life that God would find acceptable. *Now you know grace, therefore* it is only reasonable that you serve God.

Paul used the same approach in Ephesians. Through three chapters he nailed down God's plan of salvation by grace. Then he came to his *'therefore'*. *I therefore, the prisoner of the Lord, beseech you that ye walk worthy of the vocation wherewith ye are called* (Eph 4:1). *Now you know grace, therefore* do what God has called you to do. Walk in a worthy way that would honor the God who has saved you by His amazing grace. No fear here. Just love for God. Love for His Son. Love for His grace. *Now you know grace, therefore...*

Secondly, Jesus' approach to teaching right living was: *'The Kingdom of Heaven Is at Hand'*. Jesus preached: *Repent: for the kingdom of heaven is at hand* (Mt 4:17). *Repent*, that is change your way of living, because *the kingdom of heaven is at hand*. If something is *at hand*, it is within reach. You can take hold of it. Jesus said, *'Come follow me'* into a new way of living life, even a life where you can take hold of something akin to heaven, while you are still on the earth. Jesus said this *kingdom of God is within you* (Luk 17:21) It is not something that the world can see. It is something on the inside of a servant of the King. It is even a fellowship and closeness with the King, that occurs when a servant submits to live his life serving his King. The kingdom of heaven is *righteousness, and peace, and joy in the Holy Ghost* (Rom 14:17). To experience the *kingdom of heaven at hand*, you begin with righteousness, even living life doing good works. Then comes a life filled with *peace and joy*. *The kingdom of heaven is at hand*. What a New Testament motivation for the righteous doing of good works!

The third New Testament approach to teaching good works is: *'New Covenant'*. The new covenant is not the everlasting covenant.

The everlasting covenant predates creation, while the new covenant began in New Testament days. *New Covenant* is not a new plan of salvation. There has always been only one plan of salvation. It is based on the everlasting covenant between Father, Son and Holy Spirit, wherein each in the Godhead committed to His part in God's one plan of salvation. Whether BC or AD, there is only one plan of salvation. Old Testament saints were not saved by the law, while New Testament saints are saved by grace. Sinai never saved anybody in any era. Sinai condemns everybody in every era. Grace is God's one and only plan to save sinners. There is one plan, one way, one Savior, Jesus Christ.

So *New Covenant* was not a new plan of salvation. Instead, it was a new revelation about God's age old plan of salvation. God had been saving people through the everlasting covenant plan since the beginning, but nobody really understood that plan until God revealed it through the teachings of the New Testament. *New Covenant* was a new revelation that would start a new religion, even the religion of Christianity. *New Covenant* is '*The Religion of Understood Forgiveness*'. In '*The Religion of Understood Forgiveness*' God first writes His law on the sinner's mind and heart, thus giving the sinner a keen sense of guilt concerning his own sinfulness. This goes beyond man teaching man. *New Covenant* is based on God's direct revelation to the sinner, in such a way that the sinner can never forget what God has shown him.

After showing the sinner his sinfulness, God reveals to the sinner that He (God) is merciful, in regard to the law that He wrote on the sinner's heart and mind. God reveals to the sinner, that He (God) no longer remembers the sins that He had made the sinner so aware of. This '*Religion of Understood Forgiveness*' nurtures a close relationship between God and His people. Thus, the God who forgives shall be to them their God, and the forgiven people shall be unto that God, His people. Upon understanding God's forgiveness, the sinner covenants with God to be as one of His people, even to serve God with good works. Thus, we have the *New Covenant* approach to good works.

The fourth approach is: **'*Faith in Grace to Works*'**. This is the overall lesson of the book of Romans. Paul stated the purpose for writing Romans with the words: *The just shall live by faith* (Rom 1:17). Here we need to realize that faith is not for getting life. Faith is for living life. God first gives spiritual life (and its resulting faith), then we are to live our lives by faith.

After stating his purpose for writing, Paul proved that our salvation can be in nothing of self. Paul then spent chapters explaining God's plan of salvation that is totally by grace, so as to firmly and completely establish our faith in God and His grace. Once we come to see salvation by grace, it is only reasonable that we would desire to serve this God of grace. So after establishing our faith in God's grace, Paul lays out principles of living, which pertain to living a life by faith. In other words, Paul lays out good works for good living. To live by faith is to believe that God has saved us by His grace, and then to resolve to live our lives doing good works that honor God. Thus, we have the approach: *faith in grace to works*.

So why bother to do good works? From the negative, it is fearful to face God's vengeance, even if it is just for this life. Good works can spare us, as well as our nation. From the positive, **now you know grace, therefore** you should respond with good works. The **kingdom of heaven is at hand**, so serve the King with your good works, and enjoy His fellowship, even now.

In the **New Covenant** ('*The Religion of Understood Forgiveness*') God tells us that He does not remember our sins. That is not our license to sin, but our motive to do good, as one of His people. Finally, *faith in grace to works* declares that if we believe in God's grace, then respond with good works.

We know that we will never reach perfection, in that *there is none that doeth good, no not one*. Yet, our love for the God who saved us should move us to muster all the good that we can. God deserves our best!

14
Do Primitive Baptists Believe in Helping Others?

Primitive Baptists have a very high regard for Bible truth. Jesus said: *Thy word is truth* (Jno 17:17). Paul said: *preach the word* (2 Tim 4:2). Jesus said: *The truth will make you free* (Jno 8:32). Paul said that the *church of the living God* is the *pillar and ground of truth* (1 Tim 3:15). Truth really matters.

Yet most of today's Christians have no idea what truth is, and seem to care less about it. Today's false idea is that truth separates, while love unites. The modern trend is to say that it really does not matter what we all believe; we just need to all love each other. Most seem to be okay with sacrificing truth for the sake of love.

So Primitive Baptists oftentimes are critical of those who diminish the importance of truth. We sometimes seem to hold 'truth' above anything and everything. It is as if our quest is to find truth, to explain truth, and perhaps even to worship the very idea of truth. We sometimes seem to hold the idea of truth in higher regard, than the God of truth. Is it possible to worship the truth of God, even above the God of truth? Can the quest to know the word of God hinder our knowing the God of the word? There surely must be a balance that lies somewhere between truth and love.

Jesus surely taught that we should love each other and prove that love by helping each other. Jesus said: *For I was an hungred, and ye gave me meat: I was thirsty, and ye gave me drink: I was a stranger, and ye took me in: Naked, and ye clothed me: I was sick, and ye visited me: I was in prison, and ye came unto me* (Mt 25:35-36).

I doubt that you could find a Primitive Baptist anywhere who would argue with Jesus about the truth in these words. I dare say that no Primitive Baptist anywhere would declare that it is not right to help others. Yet observation tells me that the same Primitive

Baptist who holds such a high view of doctrinal truth may hold the Jesus-taught truth of helping others with little regard. Do Primitive Baptists believe in helping others? Or do we prefer to mock the church that holds little truth, but greatly focuses on helping others? Surely there must be a straight and narrow way that incorporates and combines both the truth and the love that the Bible teaches.

To know the words of Christ, without the ways of Christ and the walk of Christ, is nothing more than **egotistical intellectualism**. The point of Christianity is not *'to stand tall in our own understanding'*. To love God with the head (comprehension), but not with the heart (passion) and the hands (action), is not Christianity.

To have the ways of Christ, without the words of Christ and walk of Christ, is nothing more than **vulnerable emotionalism**. The point of Christianity is not *'to stand for nothing and to fall for anything'*. To love God with the heart (feeling), but not with the head (thinking) and the hands (doing), is not Christianity.

To have the walk of Christ, without the words and the ways of Christ, is nothing more than **hypocritical Pharisee-*ism***. The point of Christianity is not *'to stand by the rules in order to be admired by those standing by'*. To love God with the hands (motions), but not with the head (notions) and the heart (emotions), is not Christianity.

Real Christianity is to know the words of Christ, to have the ways of Christ, and to follow the walk of Christ. Real Christianity is to love God with the head, with the heart, and with the hands.

So as we come back to our question, I do not know how serious all Primitive Baptists are about helping others, but I know of some who are. Let me share with you my story of a particular Primitive Baptist preacher named Travis Housley. I was just a young man when Travis came into my life as my pastor at the Dawson Springs Primitive Baptist Church. Over the years, I came to realize that he had a deep understanding of the principles of the scriptures, even such as to surpass most preachers anywhere. (A well-respected minister once said to me that Travis Housley was 'the best kept secret that the Primitive Baptists have'.) God blessed me to sit under this man's preaching, his teachings, and his influence for several years. Not only did I hear this man's direct teaching of the written word, but I also saw his indirect teaching of how to walk with God in this world. He taught me God's principles of doctrine, and he taught me God's principles of living. It was by his guidance that I learned not only the words of Christ, and what they mean, but I also learned the ways of Christ, and what they mean. It was under his teaching that I experienced the call to preach the gospel, and it was through his influence, that God prepared even me to preach. I thank my God for such a servant of God, who has lived his life following his God-influenced heart, and accomplishing God-honoring things.

I begin my story in the Philippines in 1998. Travis Housley was the one with the zeal for evangelism, not me. He had had a burning in his bones for many years. The deception of Satan, and the discouragements of men, had caused him to miss what might have been an open door to China twenty-plus years earlier. So when Travis heard of efforts to take the gospel of grace to the Philippines, he began to ask questions, find out details, and make plans.

Though Travis was the driving force, I still sensed that the Lord was sending the two of us out together on the spiritual trip of a lifetime. This time God had opened a door for Travis, that no man would shut, and I was blessed to slip through that open door on a God-led journey. Travis would be the one that was more like Paul. Yet I was to be his 'Silas'.

God blessed us abundantly on that first trip to the Philippines, but my greatest blessing was the privilege of spending two weeks under the continual influence of Travis Housley, who was very much under the influence of the Holy Ghost. I could give many evidences of the Spirit's presence on Travis, and through him, on both of us. Yet for the moment, I want to tell the story that has to do with the question of whether Primitive Baptists believe in helping others.

Travis and I were in the little town of Nabunturan on the island of Mindanao. We were standing in front of the home of a Filipino preacher named Levi Sabuala. Another Filipino preacher, Ricardo Tabanyag, Jr. (Junio), approached Travis with not these exact words, but words very close to these, "I hear you are an electrical engineer. Is that true?" Travis responded that in addition to being a preacher of the gospel, he was also an electrical engineer, and that he worked in the office of an electric utility company back in Kentucky.

To these words Junio said something like, "I am a preacher, but also a civil engineer. I have a dream. The place where I pastor is a poor village named Matanao. The people have very little. The men know no trades to make money. The tribes in the mountains raid our village at night. The situation is bad. Yet, there is a river that comes out of the mountains. If we had electricity, we could see to defend ourselves at night. If we had electricity, I could teach the men to weld, so they could support their families. Surely, with what you know as an electrical engineer, and with what I know as a civil engineer, we could build a power plant on the river. The lives of my people could very much be improved."

At this point, Travis was fighting back tears. He normally hides his deep feelings, but for some reason, he had obviously become emotionally overwhelmed with Junio's request. I did not realize it at the time, but Travis would later share with me that for an extended time, he had been specifically praying concerning the Jesus-spoken words:

> *For I was an hungred, and ye gave me meat: I was thirsty,*
> *and ye gave me drink: I was a stranger, and ye took me in:*
> *Naked, and ye clothed me: I was sick, and ye visited me: I*
> *was in prison, and ye came unto me. (Matthew 25:35-36)*

Travis' prayers had been for God to show him how these words of Jesus should be personally applied to his own life. Upon hearing Junio's dream, Travis had the answer to his prayers. By the grace of God, and with the help of God, Travis would get electricity to an impoverished remote village in the Philippines, called Matanao.

Upon regaining his composure, Travis responded to Junio's request with words similar to these, "Let me see the river. You have to take me to the river, so that I can see if we can do it." The wheels were turning in the engineer's mind. The heart was stirring in the servant's chest. The prayers were being answered. This praying preacher would soon be blessed with his opportunity to serve his Jesus by serving others. There would soon be a light in Matanao.

Arrangements were made, and a day or two later, we stood by the river that runs beside that far-away village. The "river" did not look so good to me. We had creeks back home that would outdo that little '*riverlet*'. I felt like the Bible character, Naaman, when he said: *Are not Abana and Pharpar, rivers of Damascus, better than all the waters of Israel? may I not wash in them, and be clean? So he turned and went away in a rage* (2 Kings 5:12).

My thoughts were not thoughts of rage, like Naaman. My thoughts were more of disappointment. I was thinking about our rivers in Kentucky, where we made electricity. They were so, so very, much bigger than this little stream. I felt sorrow for Travis, and for Junio. They had both been so excited at the thought of a hydroelectric dam. Yet, I said nothing. I just watched and waited.

At first, Travis stood silent. Maybe he was trying to figure how to break the bad news to Junio. Travis finally looked toward Junio, and asked, "Does the river flow all the time?" Junio assured him that there was a continuous supply of water from the mountains high above.

The rest of us could not see the action under the surface, but the engineer's mind was computing. Travis looked toward the mountains silhouetted against the Filipino sky. He turned and gazed back toward the tropical valley that lay well below us. Finally, he turned again to Junio, and proclaimed, "We can do it! The lack of volume can easily be overcome by the fast flow, due to the steepness of the terrain." The Lord had provided a sufficient source of energy. The potential power in the stream could be converted to plenty of electrical power to light up the little village of Matanao.

For the remainder of our two weeks in the Philippines we preached, we prayed and we planned for the future. Roads were terrible. Places were far distant. Time was short. Yet the need was great, and the opportunities were real. It was oftentimes after midnight when we would finally get to bed, and depending on the next day's agenda, sometimes Junio would be knocking on our door at two in the morning. We pushed ourselves day and night to the physical limit, and by the end of our trip, I was exhausted. We finally boarded the plane for the long flight home. I slept most of the way.

A few men have the true burning in their bones, while others just go along for the ride. Some men have spirits that might be willing, but flesh that prefers to snooze. Those, like me, say their prayers, and say, "Good-night, Lord." A few, like Travis, say, "Here I am, Lord, send me." When I would awaken from my exhaustion, Travis would be toiling with long mathematical equations involved in turning flowing water into electricity. He was a man obsessed.

After our return to America, my zeal diminished, but that was not the case for Travis. He had a burning in his bones about the Philippines, which surpassed mine by leaps and bounds. Many men resist the moving of the Holy Spirit, while a few say, "Lord, what wilt thou have me to do?"

To make a long story shorter, it turned out that the mathematics involved in the generation of power from that mountain stream were not necessary. Through the blessings of God, and endless hours of legwork on Travis' part, connections were made between the power company in western Kentucky, where Travis was a vice president, and the power companies in the Philippines. Agreements were reached, whereby used materials could be sent from America, and power lines would be extended in the Philippines. The first of these extensions was to a little poverty-stricken village, called Matanao.

Since that time over sixty Filipino villages have received electrical power, and through these cooperative efforts thousands of people's lives have been improved. The Lord opened door after door, and blessed His servant to serve in phenomenal ways. There were many hurdles. Yet, Travis kept praying, kept knocking, kept seeking, kept asking, kept going, kept working, and kept on keeping on. Travis became a keynote speaker at national meetings of American electrical power companies. He shared his story of how the Lord had answered his prayers. He told of the opportunities to help the impoverished people of the Philippines. Electric companies from all over America came on board. CEO's, officers, presidents and vice presidents of power companies were writing personal checks, as well as pledging company support to the efforts. At one point during these events, I asked Travis what the people at our church could do to help him financially. His answer was that he had a rather unusual problem, in that he had more money than he knew how to spend. Praise God who opens the doors of opportunity, and the windows of heaven!

Through countless hours of immeasurable zeal, Travis continued to stay on track for years. The Lord continued to bless, and the mission continued to be accomplished. Huge shipments of materials were being sent. Villages all over the island were being lit up. Yet, in addition to electrical power, Travis desired to help the poor people find means to support their families. Along these lines, a factory was opened in the Philippines for the purpose of rewinding used electric transformers sent from America. A sewing factory was started in another village (*I was naked, and ye clothed me.*). A furniture factory was established. The bunk beds at a Primitive Baptist orphanage, called *Beauty for Ashes*, were made at this factory (*I was a stranger, and ye took me in.*). An ice plant was built in a remote fishing village. The men could catch plenty of fish, but the fish would spoil before getting to the market. Now cold fresh fish can be sold (*I was hungry, and ye gave me meat.*). In another village, loans were made for fishing boat motors. The fishermen can now go out to deep waters, where the 'big ones' are (*I was hungry, and ye gave me meat.*). In other villages, goat and rabbit raising operations were established (*I was hungry, and ye gave me meat.*). These operations, not only provide food and employment, but there are also agreements that a portion of the offspring animals will be given to others, so that new operations may be started. In all, fifty such '*Livelihood Projects*' have been established.

During one of Travis' many trips, a woman approached him with a difficult question: "Are you willing to get electricity to a village that is predominantly Muslim?" The Muslim situation on the island was, and is, volatile. The United States State Department routinely advises Americans not to go to this island. Christians are sometimes lined up and killed, execution style. Perhaps this woman was testing Travis, to see just how far his Christianity would go. Perhaps God was testing Travis, to see just how far his Christianity would go. It was probably much to the woman's surprise (and most likely to the surprise of many who read this), that Travis told her that he would go.

The arrangements were made for Travis to be at a certain place at an appointed time. He was picked up by men in a large vehicle, and told to get into the back seat. The driver made many loops and circles. Travis assumed that this was to insure that no one was following them. Eventually, they arrived at a secluded building. One of the men went in. After a time, the man returned, and told Travis he could go in now. At that point, Travis was escorted to a room where a man was seated; a man that Travis would later learn was the second most powerful Muslim on this island of political and religious unrest. When Travis entered the room, the man went into an extended rant of how the Muslim people had been mistreated and persecuted. Travis said the long moments were tense. I am sure he felt fearful, as he stood before this very powerful and very angry man (Or at least I am sure that I would have felt fear.). Travis said the man finally ended his tirade, and with a voice that seemed to be full of hatred, the man spoke the words: "Now what can I do for you?"

To this question, Travis immediately responded with the God-given words: "Sir, with all due respect, that is the question I have traveled 9000 miles to ask you. What can I do for you?" When Travis answered the furious man with these words, the whole atmosphere changed. The man calmed down, and plans were laid out to get electricity to the town. In January 2010, the 'Livelihood Phase' of this project was completed. Electric pumps are now being used to draw good water from deep wells. In addition, a new water distribution system extends this fresh water supply to other villages in the surrounding area (***I was thirsty, and ye gave me drink***.).

Before I leave this story of electrifying the Muslim town, let me share with you one more event. When the power would be officially turned on for the first time in a village, it was customary to have big celebrations. As might be expected according to human nature, it was not surprising that there were lots of politicians taking credit, lots of back slapping accolades, and lots of speeches at these big ceremonies. At some point during these festivities, Travis was always called on to speak. So the first few times that he was asked to speak, he shared with the people of the villages the words that had inspired him from the 25th chapter of Matthew. He told them how the Lord had answered his prayers concerning these words, and had given him the opportunities to get electricity to the people of the Philippines. He would conclude his message with the thought that it was 'by the help of Jesus Christ, and in the name of Jesus Christ, and to the praise of Jesus Christ' that he did these things.

Well, a Filipino electrical engineer, named Gil, who had become Travis' right-hand man in the whole project, would always be the one who introduced Travis as the featured speaker. So after a while, Gil began to undercut Travis, in that he would use Travis' Matthew 25 story of serving Jesus by serving others, as his way to introduce Travis. Thus, Travis had to come up with something else for his message.

Now when it came time to turn the lights on in the Muslim village, the celebrations were the same as always. The dignitaries were all on hand. Those in charge delivered their speeches. The important people took their turns. The time finally came for Gil to introduce Travis. So Gil took the platform, and began to tell the crowd about Travis. He explained the teachings found in the 25th chapter of Matthew. He concluded with the proclamation that these lights had come 'by the help of Jesus Christ, and in the name of Jesus Christ, and to the praise of Jesus Christ'. Travis confessed that the longer Gil talked about Jesus to these Muslims, the more he feared what might come from the words. Yet when the speech concluded, there was applause instead of executions. Thank God. And thank God for a man like Travis Housley, who in the name of

Jesus Christ gets electricity and clean water to thirsty and impoverished people. *"Inasmuch as ye have done it unto one of the least of these my brethren, ye have done it unto me."* —Jesus.

A while back, I made a return trip to the Philippines, without Travis. As I encountered people in that far-away land, I would introduce myself by saying that I was Jeff Winfrey, and that I was the pastor of the Primitive Baptist Church in Dawson Springs, Kentucky. At that point, the broken English response would go like this, "Ahh, I know *Kentucky.* That is where Travis Housley is from." Most hear the word, *Kentucky,* and think of racehorses, or bluegrass, or maybe 'hillbillies'. Filipinos hear the word, *Kentucky,* and think of Travis Housley. Indeed, this man from the *Commonwealth of Kentucky* is well known, and well respected, in the hearts of the *Common People of the Philippines.*

Is it his preaching of the truth that set him apart? It might be, in that he has a real grasp on truth, and can preach it well. Yet, I did not get the sense that it was the truth that he had preached to the Filipino people that they remembered. I think that it was more the love that he had shown for the Filipino people that set him apart.

Which group does Christianity right? Is it Primitive Baptists, who almost worship truth, and think too little about helping others? Or is it our friends in other churches, who help right and left, but have no idea what is in the Bible? I am afraid that neither of us does it exactly right. The truth about real Christianity is that it goes beyond words of truth, to ways of truth, and finally walking truth.

May no one ever have reason to question whether Primitive Baptists believe in helping others. Let our actions be the proof that we believe in serving Jesus by serving others.

15
Are Spiritual Gifts Still in the Church?

Friends carried bedridden loved ones to the streets, hoping Peter would pass by, for if Peter's shadow overshadowed, *they were healed every one* (Act 5:15-16). Diseases and evil spirits fled from those who touched something that Paul had touched (Act 19:11-12). These New Testament Apostles even raised the dead! Spiritual gifts in the early church produced amazing wonders, but are these gifts still in the church today? I question men who claim to be gifted with New Testament powers, yet no news of their miracles ever gets out. If these kinds of miracles were happening anywhere, surely television would be sending the news everywhere. I am not saying that our God does not still heal the sick. Yet I doubt the motives of men who want money for miracles. I fear that most of today's so-called 'spiritual gifts' are more sham and show, than real New Testament Christianity. So instead of arguing about whether men can still raise the dead, I want to focus on the less spectacular, but very important, seven spiritual gifts that follow.

> *Romans 12:6 Having then gifts differing according to the grace that is given to us, whether* **prophecy**, *let us prophesy according to the proportion of faith;*
> *Romans 12:7 Or* **ministry**, *let us wait on our ministering: or* **he that teacheth**, *on teaching;*
> *Romans 12:8 Or* **he that exhorteth**, *on exhortation:* **he that giveth**, *let him do it with simplicity;* **he that ruleth**, *with diligence;* **he that sheweth mercy**, *with cheerfulness.*

According to His grace, God still gives these seven spiritual gifts: **prophecy**, **ministry**, **teaching**, **exhortation**, **giving**, **ruling** and **showing mercy**. In 1 Corinthians 12, Paul likens the different gifts in the church to different body parts. The eye is not an ear. A foot serves differently to a hand. Some body parts seem more important, but all are needed. A church has members with varying gifts, but all are needed. Each gift focuses on the needs of others, and not on self. The use of the gifts helps others, and edifies the church itself. May each of us find which gifts God has given us, and find ways to use our gifts to honor our Lord and Savior.

We begin with the *gift of prophecy*. *Vine's Dictionary* states that "prophecy is not necessarily, nor even primarily, foretelling. It is the declaration of that which cannot be known by natural means." So the God-given gift of prophecy might be a pastor declaring the naturally unknown gospel to the church, or a mother declaring God's truths to her child, or a teacher declaring creation to a classroom, or a surgeon declaring the Great Physician to a patient prior to surgery. There are countless ways to declare: "that which cannot be known by natural means."

Yet, it is important to remember that God's gifts should be used in God's way. In 1 Corinthians 14, we find God's way to prophesy *when the whole church be come together into one place* (1 Cor 14:23). As far as prophesying during the church worship service, God's way is to *let your women keep silence in the churches* (1 Cor 14:34). Thus, some say that women cannot have the gift of prophecy. Yet the Bible tells of women who used the gift with God's approval, just not in the worship service.

At Pentecost, Peter proclaimed God's fulfillment of the prophecy: *I will pour out my Spirit on all flesh: and your sons and **your daughters shall prophesy**...* (Acts 2:17). Since it was God who poured His Spirit on the daughters, it was surely right that they would prophesy. Paul abode with Philip, who *had four **daughters**, virgins, **which did prophesy*** (Acts 21:9). If it was wrong for these women to prophesy, Paul missed a chance to correct the error. The Bible says of Aquila and Priscilla: **they** *took him* (Apollos) *unto them, and expounded unto him the way of God more perfectly* (Acts 18:26). "**They**" (Aquila **and Priscilla**) took Apollos aside (after the worship service), and declared to him 'that which cannot be known by natural means'. If it is done in the right place, the right time and the right way, it is okay (even Bible approved) for a sister to help a preacher better understand God's truth.

The woman at the well returned to her city and declared Jesus. *And many of the Samaritans of that city believed on him for the saying of the woman* (Jno 4:39). Jesus reprimanded this woman about other things, but not for telling others about Jesus. The angel told the women to declare the risen Savior to the men. *Go quickly, and tell his disciples that he is risen from the dead* (Mt 28:7). Jesus did the same. *Be not afraid: go tell my brethren...* (Mt 28:10). If Jesus sent the women to tell it, it was right for them to go.

If God gives a woman the gift of prophecy, it is right to use the gift, but only in the way that God designed. Women should not prophesy when *the whole church be come together into one place*. Yet outside the worship service, men and women, young and old, anyone with the gift of prophecy, should look for opportunities to declare 'that which cannot be known by natural means'. Let the church not place stumbling blocks that hinder those with gifts. Yet, may the church be on guard to worship God, only in God's way.

We move to the *gift of ministry*. This gift is not equal to being a 'minister of the gospel'. The word, *ministry*, is translated from the Greek, *diakonia*. The word means one who waits tables, or an attendant who serves others. So this is not the gift to preach, but the gift to serve.

The early church saw the need for men with the gift to serve. *There arose a murmuring of the Grecians against the Hebrews, because their widows were neglected in the daily ministration* (Gr. *diakonia*). *Then the twelve called the multitude of the disciples unto them, and said, It is not reason that we should leave the word of God and serve* (Gr. *diakonia*) *tables*. To solve the problem, the church appointed seven men to serve the widows and to tend to their needs. These 'deacons' (from the Gr. *diakoneo*) freed the apostles to give themselves *continually to prayer, and to the ministry* (Gr. *diakonia*) *of the word* (Acts 6:1-4). The deacons and preachers both had ministries. One ministered to natural needs, while the other ministered to spiritual needs. Each apostle and deacon served others by using his gift of ministry. Each gift was from God. Each was important. Yet the gifts differed according to the grace that was given.

Deacons and pastors are not the only ones with the gift of ministry. *Certain women... **ministered** (Gr. diakoneo) unto him (Jesus) of their substance* (Lk 8:2-3). This is not to say that women should hold the office of deacon, but they certainly can be ministers to others. Paul said of Stephanas' family: *They have addicted themselves to the **ministry** (Gr. diakonia) of the saints* (1 Cor 16:15). Paul further said we should submit ourselves to this family's ways. Paul desired that all get 'hooked on serving others'. We should all serve Jesus by serving others.

Yet the gift of ministry goes against our very natures. The apostles found it difficult to be servants. *And there was also a strife among them, which of them should be accounted the greatest. And he (Jesus) said unto them...he that is greatest among you, let him be as the younger; and he that is chief, as he that doth **serve** (Gr. diakoneo). For whether is greater, he that sitteth at meat, or he that **serveth** (Gr. diakoneo)? Is not he that sitteth at meat? But I am among you as he that **serveth** (Gr. diakoneo; Lk 22:24-27).* Surely if King Jesus was willing to become a servant, then the members of His church should follow His example, deny their selfish nature, and put to use the gift of ministering to others. The church is most glorious, when the members are addicted to serving the saints.

We go to the ***gift of teaching***. Jesus taught by preaching, *as one having authority* (Mt 7:29). Jesus likewise taught by example. He rose from supper, poured water into a basin, and washed His disciples' feet. Then He spoke these words. *Ye call me **Master** (Gr. didaskalos, or teacher) and Lord: and ye say well; for so I am. If I then, your Lord and **Master** (teacher), have washed your feet; ye also ought to wash one another's feet. For I have given you an **example**, that ye should do as I have done* (Jno 13:13-15). Jesus' entire life, all that He said, and all that He did, is a lesson to His disciples from the greatest of teachers.

God gives a specific gift called '*pastors and teachers*' to some men. The pastor-teacher is to be apt to teach. He is to teach by the example of his above-reproach lifestyle. He is to teach by preaching the word he has diligently studied, so that he may be ready always to give answer. Yet, the gift of teaching is by no means limited to the pastors. Parents must be teachers at home. Children are God's gift, but the gift comes with great responsibility. The teaching of our children is of utmost importance. *Lay up these my words in your heart and in your soul...And ye shall teach them your children, speaking of them when thou sittest in thine house, and when thou walkest by the way, when thou liest down, and when thou risest up* (Deut 11:18-19). Even grandparents share in this responsibility. *Teach them to thy sons, and thy son's sons* (Deut 4:9). As a child, Timothy was taught by his mother and his grandmother. Grandparents have much wisdom. May God bless our grandparents with the zeal to take hold of our God-given opportunities to teach our grandchildren about our God.

Some might say that they are not good with words.[1] Even if we could not say a single word, we can still teach the ways of Christ by a Christian lifestyle. If a picture is worth a thousand words, then a Christian act of love and kindness might be worth a thousand sermons. A Christian can teach the ways of Christ by the way he performs on the job, the way he treats his neighbor, the way he cares for his family, the way he serves his Lord, the way he reacts to situations, etc. Let each member of every church use the gift of teaching to God's glory.

We move to the ***gift of exhortation,*** *he that exhorteth, on exhortation.* *Exhorteth* is from the Greek *parakaleo*, which means to call another to one's side. *Exhortation* is from the Greek *paraklesis*, which means comfort. So the idea is that we call somebody to our side in order to comfort. The gift of exhortation is God's gift to be an encourager. Our Father is *the God of all comfort* (Gr. *paraklesis*), *who comforteth* (Gr. *parakaleo*) *us in all our tribulation, that we may be able to comfort* (Gr. *parakaleo*) *them which are in any trouble* (2 Cor 1:3-4). The same Greek words that describe God, also describe the gift that God gives to us. Thus, when we use this gift, we are conforming ourselves to be like Him. God often calls us to His side and comforts us. God's children are to do the same for each other. Oh, what a need there is for encouragers!

---

[1] Neither was Moses, but look at what God accomplished through him.

Barnabas personified the gift of exhortation. The apostles literally named this man, 'Barnabas', *which is, being interpreted, The son of consolation* (Gr. *paraklesis*) (Acts 4:36).[2] From the first of their relationship, this *son of consolation* took Paul to his side. Once converted, Paul was a man with nowhere to go. The Jews now hated him, and the church still feared him. Yet, Barnabas took Paul to his side and defended him. On Barnabas' testimony, the church received Paul. (Thank you, Barnabas, for being Paul's friend! What a friend Paul became to the church, and to us all!)

Barnabas remained Paul's encourager, even at the expense of self. In Acts 13:2-3, the church sent '*Barnabas and Paul*' to preach, but it quickly became apparent that Barnabas played second fiddle behind Paul. While Paul's fame increased, Barnabas' fame decreased. The group would soon be known as '*Paul and his company*' (Acts 13:13). Barnabas was still there, but it seems that he had ceased to be noticed. Paul had become the '*chief speaker*' (Acts 14:12). Paul's sermons are left on record, but none from Barnabas. Yet, in spite of all this, Barnabas remained true to his name. He was the *son of consolation*, even the encourager of others. He was content to lift up another, even at his own expense. So is anyone who practices the gift of exhortation.

Barnabas stuck with Paul until he finally had to choose between Paul and a man who needed consolation more than Paul. In Acts 15 Paul gave up on John Mark. Mark previously had deserted Paul and Barnabas. Thus Paul had no time for him. Yet the *son of consolation*, with the gift of exhortation, saw a man who needed encouragement. So Barnabas left Paul and took John Mark to be by his side. When others considered Mark to be of no use, Barnabas was his friend. Moreover, Barnabas' exhortation must have been successful, for near the end of Paul's life, he wrote a letter to Timothy and declared that Mark was profitable for the ministry (2 Tim 4:11). The loyal friendship of Barnabas, and his practice of gentle exhortation unto a weaker brother, evidently made a great difference in the life of John Mark.

---

[2] This is the same Greek *paraklesis* that is translated *exhortation* in the gift.

As our Father is the God of all comfort, let us give comfort to others. Let us follow the example of *the son of consolation*. If we desire to be exhorters, we must be willing to deny self and focus on the needs of others. Let each of us put into use the God-given gift of exhorting, in order to comfort others in the church, and to give glory to God.

We come to the ***gift of giving***. *He that giveth let him do it with simplicity.* *Giveth* is simple to understand, but *simplicity* needs some explanation. *Simplicity* is from the Greek *haplotes*, which means generosity. Yet it also means singleness (without hypocrisy or self-seeking). So the gift of giving is generous sharing with a pure and single motive, which is not selfish or self-centered.

Surely God is a generous, unselfish giver. *He **gave** his only begotten son* (Jno 3:16). *The good shepherd **giveth** his life for the sheep* (Jno 10:11). *I **give** unto them eternal life* (Jno 10:28). God ***giveth** us the victory* (1 Cor 15:57). God ***giveth** us richly all things* (1 Tim 6:17). God is the giver of good and perfect gifts. Yet even though God has given to us so abundantly, and even though God has given to some *the gift of giving*, it still seems that we oftentimes tend to be selfish and stingy toward others.

The Bible often uses the word 'first' in teachings about giving. Abel gave the ***firstlings** of his flock and the fat thereof* (Gen 4:4). Abel gave the **first** and the **best**. God told His people to *offer the **first** of thy ripe fruits* (Ex 22:29). Solomon said: *Honour the Lord with thy substance, and with the **firstfruits** of all thine increase* (Pro 3:9). Paul said to the church: *Upon the **first** day of the week let every one of you lay up by him in store, as God hath prospered him, that there be no gatherings when I come* (1 Cor 16:2). Human nature first thinks of self. God says first give to God. God deserves more than our leftovers.

Now the New Testament does not specifically teach tithing, but it teaches much about giving. *Every man according as he purposeth in his heart, so let him give; not grudgingly, or of necessity: for God loveth a cheerful giver* (2 Cor 9:7). If the church is not under the law to tithe, then what principles now apply? When our concern is more about self, than about God and others, we either give too little, or we give grudgingly. Remember the principle of 'first' giving. When we first think of self, we give too little. If we first think of God giving His Son for us, we cheerfully give more.

If the law cried for the tithe, then let our consciences figure what grace cries for. To give with *simplicity* is to give unselfishly. God unselfishly gave His Son. God freely gives all things to us, not by necessity, nor in a grudging manner, but cheerfully. Let us ever follow His example. The Bible commands all to give, but the person with the gift of giving is different from others. He knows the blessing in giving and looks for opportunities. Blessed are the givers. Giving members result in a giving church. A giving church gives glory to Christ. Christ has given all. Let us be generous and unselfish givers, and thus give Him glory.

We move to the **gift of ruling**. The word, *ruleth,* is from the Greek *proistemi,* which has two meanings. It means to preside. Preachers and deacons are to rule (*preside over*) their houses well (1 Tim 3:5). The word also means to practice or maintain. Paul said *that they which have believed in God might be careful to maintain* (Gr. *proistemi*) *good works* (Titus 3:8).

Combining these two usages gives a more complete meaning to the gift of ruling. This gift is not the authority to be the 'boss' of the church. It is to 'preside in the practice of maintaining good works'. A pastor must practice the gift of ruling, but not as the word *rule* is often used. He is a 'ruler', but he is not to make the rules. He is not a dictator, but a servant. He rules by example. As the model, he is to 'lead in the practice of good works'.

The prophet said: *A little child shall lead them* (Is 11:6). How can a little child lead adults? The disciples desired greatness and power. They yearned to be 'rulers', but not in the sense of *proistemi.* Jesus said to them: *Except ye be converted, and become as little children, ye shall not enter into the kingdom of heaven* (Mt 18:3). What did the child have that the disciples lacked? The child had humility. Jesus declared the child to be the true 'ruler', in that he was in a position to 'lead (even the apostles) in the practice of good works'. These big-headed men needed to follow the lead of an unnamed child, and become more humble. How often might this be the case in churches today?

Much can be learned from the young people in the Bible. Surely the young men, David and Daniel, led by their practice of good works. So can the children in the church today. It is truly an inspiration for the adults in the church to observe a faithful young person.

Yet the gift of ruling is by no means limited to the children. At the near stoning of the adulterous woman, Jesus declared: *He that is without sin among you, let him first cast a stone at her* (Jno 8:7). Beginning at the eldest, they turned and walked away. Here the oldest (and probably the most respected) man in the crowd led the whole group in the practice of good works. Sometimes leading in the practice of good works requires an old man to swallow his pride and repent. The truly effective old leaders in the church are the humble old leaders. From the young child to the old sister, many have the ability to lead others in the practice of good works. Some 'rule' by visiting the sick. Others 'rule' by helping the poor. Some 'rule' by maintaining the church building. Each person, by his example, can 'lead in the practice of good works'. As one 'rules' (uses the gift to lead in the practice of good works), let others be humble followers.

We finally come to the **gift of showing mercy**: *he that sheweth mercy with cheerfulness. Vine's Dictionary* defines *mercy* as, not just a feeling of sympathy, but also an action that is brought on by the feeling. To show mercy is to first feel compassion toward one in distress, and then to follow up the feeling with action to relieve the distress. The word, *cheerfulness*, is from the Greek *hilarotes* (derived from *hilaros*). To see the extent of cheer connected with showing mercy, think of our word, *hilarious.* Showing mercy is not to be drudgery, but a time to get *hilarious.* The use of this gift is associated with extreme pleasure.

The ultimate act of mercy of all time was when Jesus voluntarily went to the cross. In His compassion for us, He sacrificed Himself. We learn much from His example. We may have feelings of compassion, but true mercy requires self-sacrifice. Alleviating the distress of others generally demands money, resources and time. The Good Samaritan felt compassion, but went far beyond just having pity. Unlike the more religious types who walked on by, the Samaritan stopped to help. His showing of mercy required: bandages, oil, wine, transportation to an inn, time at the inn, money for the inn, and a return trip to the inn to pay any further debts that had been incurred during recuperation.

Our selfish human nature leads us to turn away from the distressed, but Jesus never turned away. He always showed mercy. He said to His children, *Go, and do thou likewise* (Lk 10:37). Jesus sought out the lost, the troubled, the discouraged, the poor in spirit, the afflicted, the distressed, the hurting. His life and His death were wrapped around showing mercy. What better way can God's children show their love for God, than to be like Him? Yet it seems that today's world is not much different than the days of the half-dead man and the Samaritan. How many times a day, do those who claim that they want to be like their Savior pass by on the other side? How often do the recipients of God's mercy make the effort to stop and show mercy? Of those who stop, how many get hilarious at the opportunity? Oh what mercy God has shown toward us!

How can we be so unmerciful? Let us, who have received mercy, show mercy: not grudgingly, nor of necessity, but cheerfully. The cheerful showing of mercy brings glory to God from the person who received mercy, in that he sends up prayers of praise for his relief. The cheerful showing of mercy brings glory to God from the one who showed mercy, in that he shines forth God's glory in his cheerful obedience. Surely, the chief purpose of man is to glorify God. So if showing mercy achieves this purpose in a twofold way, let every member of every church look for opportunities to show mercy. And may just a few of us get hilarious about the idea.

In conclusion, our most gracious God has given many wonderful gifts to His children throughout the ages. The unspeakable gift of His Only Begotten Son is beyond human comprehension. The gift of eternal life far exceeds man's dreams. The gift of His church affords us such refuge. Yet beyond the gift of the church itself, God gives spiritual gifts to each member of His church. In order for the church as a whole to be glorious, each individual member must use his, or her, gifts to the edifying of the body, and to the praise of its head, Jesus Christ. If each person in the church earnestly strives to use the God-given gifts that he, or she, has received, then the church collectively will accomplish her mission. She will truly be a light to the world, a city on a hill, and a glory to God.

16
How Can We Understand the Bible's 'Salvation'?

The tract title reads, *"HAVE YOU BEEN SAVED?"* The evangelist asks, "Have you been saved?" Modern Christianity equates *save* to *born again*. If *save* is limited to *born again*, I am confused by Paul's words to Timothy. *Take heed unto thyself, and unto the doctrine; continue in them: for in doing this thou shalt both save thyself, and them that hear thee* (1 Tim 4:16). If this *save* is *born again*, we must assume that Timothy was still not born again. If Paul's right-hand-man preacher still needed to continue in his ministry, so that he might finally **born himself** again, then I wonder if any of us have a chance to get to heaven.

The first key to understanding the Bible's *'salvation'* is to realize that the Bible talks about different salvations. Consider the *save* in the angel's statement: *Thou shalt call his name Jesus: for he shall save his people from their sins* (Mt 1:21). Contrast that to the *save* in Peter's near-drowning cry: *and beginning to sink, he cried, saying, Lord, save me* (Mt 14:30). The angel's *save* has to do with going to heaven, while Peter's *save* has to do with not going to heaven, just yet. James said *the prayer of faith shall save the sick* (Jas 5:15). Again this prayer is not to be saved *to heaven*, but to be saved *from heaven*. These examples may seem frivolous, in that any reasonable person can understand these differences. Yet the same reasonable person might struggle with why the Bible says that **God...hath saved** us (2 Tim 1:8-9), and then it says that you need to **save yourselves** *from this untoward generation* (Acts 2:40). Here the reasonable person might ask, "Which is it? Has God already saved us? Or do we need to save ourselves?"

It is not easy to understand the Bible's *saves*. The Bible says that we are saved by Jesus, saved by God, and saved by the Holy Ghost.

It also says that we are saved by ourselves, saved by the preacher, and saved by our husbands or wives. Which is it? Does God save man? Or do men save men?

The confusion multiplies when we go past the question of who saves the sinner, and also consider what saves the sinner. The Bible says that we are saved by grace, saved by faith, saved by grace through faith, saved by faith (but not without works), saved by hope, saved by the gospel, saved by preaching, saved by hearing, saved by calling on the Lord, saved by confession, saved by baptism, saved by conversion, saved by enduring to the end, etc. If all this is necessary to get to heaven, who then can be saved?

So how do we reconcile all these *saves*? The solution is to rightly divide the word of truth. *Study to shew thyself approved unto God, a workman that needeth not to be ashamed, **rightly dividing the word of truth*** (2 Tim 2:15). To rightly divide is not to discard unwanted sections, as the woman who tore out pages that talked about election. God warns against adding to, or detracting from, His word. To rightly divide is to dissect and expound the parts, so that they fit the whole.

In olden days, preachers *read in the book in the law of God distinctly, and gave the sense, and caused them to understand the reading* (Neh 8:8). Surely a preacher of the gospel is to rightly divide the word of truth in such a way, as to give the sense, and to cause God's people to understand the Bible's 'salvation'.

The Bible's 'salvation' can be sensibly divided into five parts: the **planning part**, the **judgment part**, the **life-giving part**, the **life-living part**, and the **heaven part**. Let us begin with the *planning part* of salvation. This is the mind of God part. Surely the all-wise God always had a plan and knew how to work it out. *Known unto God are all his works from the beginning of the world* (Acts 15:18). Concerning His plan, God said, *I have spoken it, I will also bring it to pass; I have purposed it, I will also do it* (Is 46:11).

The *planning part* provides the basis for all the other parts. In God's mind Jesus was *the Lamb slain from the foundation of the world* (Rev 13:8). In the *planning part* God elected whom He would save. *According as he hath chosen us in him before the foundation of the world...* (Eph 1:4). In the *planning part* God predetermined the final destiny of those He would save. *Having predestinated us unto the adoption of children...* (Eph 1:5). In the *planning part* God gave His elect to Jesus *that he should give eternal life to as many as thou hast given him* (Jno 17:2). All that God chose in the *planning part* must finally end up glorified in heaven. *Moreover whom he did predestinate, them he also called: and whom he called, them he also justified: and whom he justified, them he also glorified* (Rom 8:30). All the *'whoms'* that God put in the *planning part* will become glorified *'thems'* in the *heaven part.*

In today's Christianity, the *planning part* is the ignored and rejected part. Most people pretend it is not in the Bible. Some try to explain it away, by saying that God looked into the future and based His choice on some merit that He foresaw in the one that He chose. That might be okay, except the Bible specifically says that election was not based on foreseen works. *The children being not yet born, neither having done any good or evil, that the purpose of God according to election might stand, **not of works**, but of him that calleth...* (Rom 9:11). Moreover, the Bible clearly states that God's ordained plan of salvation is **unto good works**, not because of good works. *We are his workmanship, created in Christ Jesus unto good works, which God hath before ordained that we should walk in them* (Eph 2:10). Along the same line, Jesus said that He chose us, so we would bring forth fruit, not because we had. *Ye have not chosen me, but I have chosen you, and ordained you, that ye should go and bring forth fruit* (Jno 15:16).

Some say that God foresaw which men would choose God. So God simply chose the ones that He knew would choose Him. The problem with this twisted thinking is that the Bible says that God is the 'chooser', and that God's choice is what causes the sinner to approach unto God. *Blessed is the man whom thou choosest, and causest to approach unto thee, that he may dwell in thy courts* (Ps 65:4). Furthermore, election and predestination are said to be *to the praise of the glory of his grace* (Eph 1:6). If God's choice was based on God foreseeing who would choose God, then man is the real 'chooser', and God is a hypocrite for claiming that election praises His grace. Man's belief is not the basis and cause of his election. Man's belief is the result of election. *As many as were ordained to eternal life believed* (Act 13:48). Election is *not of him that willeth, nor of him that runneth, but of God that sheweth mercy* (Rom 9:16). Election is unconditional. The *planning part* is entirely of God.

The second part of salvation is the *judgment part*. This part occurred on the cross and in the courtroom of heaven. This part saves God's children from the penalty of sin and from the wrath of God's judgment. The *judgment part* is all of Christ. Jesus redeemed us. *By his own blood he entered in once into the holy place, having obtained eternal redemption for us* (Heb 9:12). Jesus cleansed us from our sins. *I, even I, am he that blotteth out thy transgressions for mine own sake, and will not remember thy sins* (Is 43:25). Jesus suffered God's wrath in our place. *But he was wounded for our transgressions, he was bruised for our iniquities: the chastisement of our peace was upon him; and with his stripes we are healed* (Is 53:5). Jesus made God to be at peace with us. *God ...hath reconciled us to himself by Jesus Christ* (2 Cor 5:18). Jesus made us righteous. *For he hath made him to be sin for us, who knew no sin; that we might be made the righteousness of God in him* (2 Cor 5:21). Jesus perfected us. *For by one offering he hath perfected for ever them that are sanctified* (Heb 10:14). Jesus satisfied God. *He shall see of the travail of his soul, and shall be satisfied* (Is 53:11). Jesus is our justification. *Being now justified by his blood, we shall be saved from wrath through him* (Rom 5:9). Jesus is our salvation. *Thou shalt call his name JESUS: for he shall save his people from their sins* (Mt 1:21).

Every person Jesus died for must get to heaven. Each is paid for, cleansed, reconciled, made righteous, perfected, justified and saved. God is satisfied that Jesus justified. So what can keep anyone Jesus died for out of heaven? The point is that each one Jesus died for has been saved on the cross, and will be saved to heaven. The Bible exalts 'The Successful Savior'. Most people like the idea of a successful Savior, but modern confused theology does not allow Jesus to succeed. Its first error is to **overstate the scope** of the *judgment part* of salvation, by saying that Jesus died for all people. This error fabricates a Savior, who tries to save all, but must settle for only saving some. This first error inevitably leads to a second error, which is to **undervalue the power** of Jesus in the *judgment part* of salvation, by admitting a weak Savior, who is unable to save all that He tried to save.

Bible truth mandates that every person Jesus died for will be saved. So if Jesus died for all, then all must get to heaven. Yet all will not get to heaven, because Jesus did not die for all people. Jesus died for His people, for God's elect people, for those the Father had given to Him. The *judgment part* is all of God, and Jesus finished it all, for all that were in God's *planning part* of salvation.

The third part of the Bible's plan of salvation is the *life-giving part*. The *life-giving part* is an act of God on the sinner's soul at some time between natural conception and death. This is the born again part. *The wind bloweth where it listeth...so is every one that is born of the Spirit* (Jno 3:8). The Holy Spirit (independently, self-sufficiently and without aid) accomplishes the *life-giving part* of salvation for each and every child of God that God chose in the *planning part*, and for the exact same each and every child of God that Jesus died for in the *judgment part*. God's salvation of His children to heaven is a perfectly fit together, perfectly successful process for finally securing each and every one of God's children to heaven.

The *life-giving part* saves from spiritual deadness to spiritual life. *You hath he quickened, who were dead in trespasses and sins* (Eph 2:1). Today's common belief is that the sinner must cooperate in this part of salvation, but the Bible teaches that the *life-giving part* is entirely an act of God. Speaking of natural man, Jesus said: *Ye will not come to me, that ye might have life* (Jno 5:40). Jesus further said: *No man can come to me, except the Father which hath sent me draw him* (Jno 6:44). Natural man does not come to God, unless God first comes to him.

The *life-giving part* of salvation is described as a birth. Can a man cause his own birth? Did you have to ask to be born? Could you have refused to be born? What did you do before you were you? As there is no natural will or action prior to natural birth, there is no spiritual will or action prior to spiritual birth.

The *life-giving part* of salvation is also described as raising the spiritually dead to spiritual life. A dead man cannot help resurrect himself from the dead. God alone must give life to the dead. How dead is dead? As there is no natural will or action in the naturally dead, there is no spiritual will or action in the spiritually dead. The analogies of a birth and a resurrection clearly show that the *life-giving part* is all of God.

The Bible teaches Holy Spirit unassisted regeneration. In the *life-giving part* of salvation man does not choose God. God chooses man. Man does not first come to God. God first comes to man. Sinful man is impotent to recover himself from the fallen state he is in by nature. He cannot by his own free will and ability come to God. The *life-giving part* is totally by the purpose, power and grace of God. God does not save, '*if*' the sinner will do his part. God does not do His part, '*but*' the sinner then has to do his part. The *life-giving part* is entirely God's part. The *life-giving part* is by God's sovereign grace—period.

The fourth part of salvation is the *life-living part*. This is the part where the born again child of God lives the spiritual life that he has been given. It is the '*Livin' Whatcha Been Given*' part. It begins at spiritual birth, and should lead to spiritual maturity. More of the Bible's *saves* are in the *life-living part* of salvation than in any other part. Yet modern Christians seem to have no idea that this part of salvation even exists. Most people misunderstand God's plan of salvation, because they try to fit all the *saves* of the *life-living part* into the other parts. The *saves* of the *life-living part* have nothing to do with getting to heaven. They have to do with how we live our spiritual lives, while still in this world. The *life-living part* saves from the practice of sin, and saves to a 'closeness' with God, even while we are still living in this world. If we come to understand the particulars of the *life-living part* of salvation, we will be equipped to sort out and rightly divide all the Bible's *saves*.

All the other parts of salvation are entirely of God, but the *life-living part* is a joint work between the Holy Spirit and the born again child. **After God gives spiritual life**, you are to *work out your own salvation with fear and trembling*. Yet you are able to work it out, only because *it is God which worketh in you both to will and to do of his good pleasure* (Phi 2:12-13). In the *life-living part*, we work out what God works in. God does not just born us again and leave us on our own. After giving us spiritual life, God influences us to live the life that He has put in. With the giving of spiritual life comes direct teaching from God. *They shall be all taught of God* (Jno 6:45). With the giving of spiritual life comes leading from the Spirit. *God hath sent forth the Spirit of his Son into your hearts, crying, Abba, Father* (Gal 4:6). Without the giving of spiritual life, *Ye will not come; No man can come*. With the giving of spiritual life, God gives the desire and ability to come to Christ. Spiritually enlivened ears can hear Jesus' invitation: *Come unto me, all ye that labour and are heavy laden, and I will give you rest* (Mt 11:28). Once God has given us spiritual life, it is time for us to come to Jesus. It is time to start *'Livin' Whatcha Been Given'*.

Since the *life-living part* is the only part where man helps in the saving, it must be the part where you can *save yourselves from this untoward generation* (Acts 2:40). This must be the part where the preacher can both save himself and his hearers. *Take heed unto thyself, and unto the doctrine; continue in them: for in doing this thou shalt both save thyself, and them that hear thee* (1 Tim 4:16). These *saves* have nothing to do with anybody getting to heaven. Jesus does that part. *Thou shalt call his name Jesus: for he shall save his people from their sins* (Mt 1:21). The Holy Spirit does that part. *The wind bloweth where it listeth…so is every one that is born of the Spirit* (Jno 3:8). These *saves* come through *'Livin' Whatcha Been Given'*.

If God's people turn toward God and live life His way, they can be saved from much despair that comes from turning to *this untoward generation*. If God's preachers will take heed unto themselves and God's doctrines, they can save both themselves and their hearers. First of all, they can save themselves from drowning in the waves of despair that come into their lives. Secondly, they can save themselves to be able to live an abundant life (even in this life). This abundant life happens when they look to Jesus and walk on the water, somewhere above the waves.

The *life-living part* is the part where man is saved by something in addition to grace. Paul said that *it pleased God by the foolishness of preaching to save them that believe* (1 Cor 1:21). Man's preaching does not save anybody to heaven. God saves to heaven in the parts of salvation that are entirely of Him. The preaching of the gospel of grace lets us know that God does the 'heaven-saving parts'. To know that God does the 'heaven-saving parts' saves us from doubts and fears about the next world, even while we are still living in this world. Preaching that saves a believer belongs in the *life-living part* of salvation.

Paul said that *we are saved by hope* (Rom 8:24). Paul did not mean that we save ourselves to heaven by hoping real hard. God's parts of salvation save us to heaven. We are saved by hope, when we come to know that God's parts of salvation get us to heaven. The certain hope that God saves us to heaven by grace, and grace alone, saves us from doubts and fears, while we are still living this life. Saved by hope is a *life-living part* of salvation.

Jesus *said to the woman, thy faith hath saved thee; go in peace* (Lk 7:50). The woman came to Jesus weeping over her sins. Jesus told her that her sins were forgiven. Her faith was not the means to forgiveness. Forgiveness comes in the *judgment part* of salvation that occurs on the cross. Jesus did not tell her that her faith had saved her, so that she could now go with eternal life. Jesus told her that her faith had saved her, so that she could **go in peace**. Faith does not save to eternal life. God's grace does that in the parts of salvation that are entirely of God. Yet, when we by faith come to know that our sins were forgiven in the *judgment part,* then we are saved by our faith in what Jesus accomplished, so that we can experience a sense of peace concerning the certainty of our eternal salvation. To experience this peace that comes by faith in Jesus is to be saved by faith in the *life-living part* of salvation.

Where does faith fit into all the parts of salvation? Faith in the gospel is not the basis for the *planning part* of salvation. The Bible does not say, "as many as would believe were ordained to eternal life." It says, "*as many as were ordained to eternal life believed*" (Acts 13:48). So the *planning part* was not based on who would believe, or whether we would believe. Neither is faith in the gospel the basis for the *judgment part* of salvation. Jesus has finished the *judgment part* of salvation, whether we believe it or not. God knows that Jesus finished the *judgment part*, whether we know it or not. So the *judgment part* was not based on who would believe, or whether we would believe. Neither is faith in the gospel the basis for the *life-giving part* of salvation. The Holy Spirit independently does the *life-giving part*, without means or assistance. *The wind bloweth where it listeth... and so is every one that is born of the Spirit* (Jno 3:8). God does not need our faith to let Him give us eternal life. As a matter of scriptural fact, we have no faith until God gives us eternal life, in that faith is not the cause, but the result of the *life-giving part*. Faith is a fruit of the Spirit (Gal 5:22). So the *life-giving part* is not based on who would believe, or whether we would believe.

Yet the *life-living part* is based on believing in the gospel of grace. A life that is lived by faith in God, as to the *planning part* of salvation, and as to the *judgment part* of salvation, and as to *life-giving part* of salvation, is a life that is saved from the fear of hell. It is a life that is saved to know with certain assurance that it will one day live forever in heaven. To believe that God planned to save you (personally and specifically) before the world began, and to believe that Jesus successfully saved you (personally and specifically) on the cross, and to believe that the Holy Spirit was pleased to seek you out (personally and specifically) in order to give you eternal life, will even now bring you to live a life filled with joy, peace, hope and rest. Faith in the gospel of grace will even now motivate you to begin *'Livin' Whatcha Been Given'*. If you are *'Livin' Whatcha Been Given'*, then you are living a life worth living. If you are living the spiritual life, which you have been given, then you are saved from the despair of living a life of vanity and vexation of spirit.

There is a power in believing the message of grace, which leads believers to change how they live. The gospel motivates God's children to live their lives by faith, not just believing in Jesus as their Savior, but also believing in Jesus in their times of troubles. Faith is not for getting things. Faith is for facing things. Faith is not for getting life. Faith is for living life. Faith is not just to believe in Jesus. Faith is to believe Jesus, as to how to live life. Living by faith not only saves you from the futility of this world, but also saves you to fellowship with Jesus while still in this world. The *life-living part* of salvation is the here and now part.

The fifth part of the Bible's salvation is the *heaven part*. The *heaven part* saves from the presence of sin, and saves to an eternal presence with God. There are two parts to the *heaven part* of salvation. The first part concerns our spirits when we die. At the instant of death, our spirits go to be with Jesus. Paul said *absent from the body…present with the Lord* (2 Cor 5:8). Jesus said to the thief: *To day shalt thou be with me in paradise* (Lk 23:43). That thief's spirit has been in paradise with Jesus in the *heaven part* of salvation for the last few centuries.

The second part of the *heaven part* of salvation concerns our bodies at the final resurrection. Jesus is coming back. He will resurrect the dead bodies. He will change the bodies of those who are still alive at His coming. Mortal bodies will be changed to immortal bodies. Bodies of corruption will be made incorruptible. Jesus *shall change our vile body, that it may be fashioned like unto his glorious body* (Phi 3:21). *When he shall appear, we shall be like him* (1 Jno 3:2).

All that God designed in the *planning part* will be fulfilled in the *heaven part*. All that Jesus saved in the *judgment part* will see their final salvation in the *heaven part*. All that began their spiritual lives in the *life-giving part* will live their eternal lives in the *heaven part*. These four parts of eternal salvation are entirely of God. They have to be of God. We were not there in the *planning part* or the *judgment part*. We were still dead in the *life-giving part*. We have no idea how to get to the *heaven part*. Our eternal salvation is sure, because it is entirely of God, and in no way hinges on us.

Yet the *life-living part* does hinge on us following the leadership of the Holy Spirit. Let us work out our own salvation. Let us save ourselves from this untoward generation. Let us live our lives by faith. Let us be saved by faith, and go in peace. Let us come unto Jesus and find rest. *Let us therefore fear, lest, a promise being left us of entering into his rest, any of you should seem to come short of it* (Heb 4:1).

17
How Can We Know if We are Saved?

A re we condemned to face death, wishing and wanting, yet wondering? Is there no certainty about eternity? How can we know if we are saved? What do we need to know, so we can know?

We basically need to know two things, in order to know if we are going to heaven when we die. We first need to know that God's plan of salvation is entirely of God, and nothing of us. We then need to know, how to know, if we are a part of God's plan.

As long as we believe that we have a part in our own eternal salvation, we can never be sure that we are saved. Whatever part that we perceive to be ours is the weak link in our proposed plan of salvation. God is never a weak link. God accomplishes His purposes all the time, every time. Yet we are not so perfect. So the very idea that we have a part, would forever keep us from knowing for sure that our salvation is sure.

If we think our eternal salvation hinges on our good works, we can never know for sure if we are saved. How much good is good enough? Our best works still cry: *When I would do good, evil is present with me* (Rom 7:21). If we think our eternal salvation hinges on our believing, we still can never know for sure if we are saved. How much faith is faith enough? Our best faith still cries: *Lord, I believe; help thou mine unbelief* (Mr 9:24). So to believe that salvation is based in any way on self, is to admit that there is no way to know for sure that we are saved.

On the other hand, if we understand the truth about salvation, even that God successfully saves His people entirely by Himself, then the weak link (me) is eliminated. If we are not at all involved in saving ourselves, and if God is totally involved in saving us, then the chance of our being saved increases infinitely, even to the point of certainty. The Bible does truly teach that God successfully saves

His people, entirely by Himself. So the first step in becoming sure that we are saved is to become sure that our salvation is all of God.

The Bible's plan of salvation is all of God's grace, and in no way depends on the sinner. Perhaps most who sing *Amazing Grace* are not so sure about how amazing grace really is. By definition grace cannot be earned or merited. Grace ceases to be grace, if cooperation is required. The whole idea of grace becomes a contradiction, if man has to do something, so that God can give the man an 'unearned and undeserved gift'. The very idea that man has to do something makes grace, not be grace. The amazing truth about amazing grace is that it stands alone. The amazing thing about amazing grace is that nothing else is needed.

Perhaps the most amazing thing about God Himself is that God eternally saves sinful man, exclusively by His amazing grace. Nobody has to cooperate with God, so as to help God save anybody. We do not help save ourselves. We do not help God save others. The angel said: *Thou shalt call his name Jesus: for he shall save his people from their sins* (Mt 1:21). Jesus did completely, and precisely, what the angel said He would do. Jesus (and Jesus alone) saved His people from their sins. He did not call for help. Indeed, there was none to help. He does not now call for help. Indeed, there is no help needed. Yet the vast majorities, who claim to believe in Jesus, believe in a Jesus who needs help in order to save. They fail to recognize the sovereign ruling Jesus who accomplishes His salvation according to His will. They fail to acknowledge that salvation is by God's sovereign grace and His grace alone. They miss the point that grace is really grace.

Evidently, most people find that real grace is hard to swallow. Most, who claim to believe in grace, prove they do not by adding their '*but*'. They believe in grace, '*but*'… They preach grace for fifty minutes, and then get to what the sinner has to do, so as to help their little god do what he cannot do by himself. Their salvation by grace gets all tied up in what the sinner has to let God do. Their salvation is not *to the praise of the glory of his grace*, but to the merit of the response of the sinner. They cry, "Oh yes, we believe in grace, but surely there must be a fig leaf or two somewhere in this plan, which we have to stitch together to complete the salvation." They cry, "Oh yes, we believe in grace, but we believe in a lesser kind of grace than pure grace will allow. We believe in grace, but we only believe in the kind of grace that has to be agreed to. We know that God saves by grace, but even the sovereign God of grace cannot save us, unless we help grace to be grace, by agreeing to grace." I say, "My, oh my!"

The Bible makes the case for amazing grace, and grace alone, that successfully saves all God's people. The Bible's amazing grace is controlled by God, and not man. Amazing grace began with God's unconditional election of a vast host of people from every nation and family under heaven, not based on foreseen works or cooperation in the ones chosen. Amazing grace shined brightest, when God sent His Son to a cruel cross (and when the Son willfully went). Amazing grace was accomplished in Jesus' particular redemption, not offered to everybody, but certain for the multitudes, which amazing grace had chosen. Amazing grace prevails through unassisted Holy Spirit regeneration, not based upon the consent of man, but wholly, and solely, based in amazing grace. By God's amazing grace, each one that God chose, got died for; and each one that got died for, gets born again; and each one that gets born again goes to heaven. Amazing grace will finally put in heaven, all that it initially put in the plan. Amazing grace is the plan of salvation that is: perfect in its design, perfect in the way it fits together, and perfect in the success of its completion.

So let us imagine that we have just come to know the gospel of grace. We have come to understand that God entirely saves His children by amazing grace. We breathe a sigh of relief, in that we now know that we really never had a part in our own eternal salvation. Thus we rejoice, because we no longer have to worry about whether God is satisfied with our part. We now know that God was satisfied with Jesus' part, and we further understand that when God got satisfied, we got justified. We now know that God even does the born again part. So that takes a load off our minds, not only about our own salvation, but also about the rest of the world that we thought we had to help God save.

Perhaps, for the first time in our lives, we experience the peace that passes understanding in truly knowing: SALVATION IS OF THE LORD. Yet, as we are meditating upon salvation by grace, and grace alone, haunting thoughts begin to flood our minds. There are still very personal questions that scream for answers. Has grace saved me? Am I one of the ones that God saves by grace? Am I going to heaven when I die?

The way to know if we are going to heaven is to know if we have been born again. Remember that amazing grace is the plan of salvation, where each one that God chose, got died for; and each one that got died for, gets born again; and each one that gets born again goes to heaven. So if we can know that we are in the born again part of the plan, we can be sure that we must also be in all the other parts of the plan. And if we are sure that we are in the entirety of God's plan of salvation, we can know for sure that we will end up in heaven.

So how can we know if we are born again? Generally speaking, there are two ways we can know. We can either know it by remembering that it happened. Or we can know it by proving that it must have happened. If we assume that Paul was born again on the road to Damascus, then Paul could remember his instant of 'born again'. Paul's case is easy, but all are not so easy. Paul often told his experience, but John the Baptist had no experience to share. Yet that does not mean that John had not been born again. The Bible says that John leaped for joy, while still in his mother's womb (Lk 1:44). Now all babies 'leap' in the womb, but God's word says that John leaped because of joy. The Bible further says that joy is a fruit of the Spirit (Gal 5:22). So if joy is a result of having the Spirit, then John must have had the Spirit in him, while still in the womb. If John had the Spirit in him, he was already born again. Since John was born again before he was born, he would have had no memory of his 'born again'. Yet both the Bible, and the life that John lived, testify that he must have been born again.

Some have a great story about their 'born again' moment, while some have no memory of the moment at all. Yet it is possible to be sure, even without having a moment. We do not remember the moment of our natural birth, but if we are now living a natural life, we can be sure that we must have already been born. It is very possible that we do not remember the moment of our spiritual birth either, but if we are now living a spiritual life, we can be sure that we must have already been born again. So we have our answer, either way. If we remember a 'born again' moment, then we are sure that we are saved. If we cannot remember a 'born again' moment, but are now doing things that pertain to living a spiritual life, then we too are sure that we are saved.

Thus some find their answer by straightforward thinking. All they have to do is remember what happened. Others need to use backward thinking to find their answer. Yet in the end, one can be as sure as the other. So let those of us, who cannot remember a born again moment, learn how to think backwards.

Paul said: *The natural man receiveth not the things of the Spirit of God: for they are foolishness unto him: neither can he know them, because they are spiritually discerned* (1 Cor 2:14). So if we understand that the unborn again natural man will not receive spiritual things, because such things are foolishness to him, then by backward thinking, we can rationalize that if we have received spiritual things, and if these things are not foolishness to us, then we must be different to this natural man that Paul spoke of. Paul went on to say that the natural man cannot know spiritual things, because only a spiritual man can understand such things. So if we do know the things that Paul said a natural unborn again man cannot know, then we must be beyond just being a natural man. Thus, by recognizing what a natural man will not and cannot do, and by realizing what we have been willing and able to do, we can deduct that we must be already born again. This is a backward way of thinking in order to prove that we must be born again, but it does provide logical proof that we are.

Let us go further in our backward way of proving things. Jesus said: *Ye will not come to me, that ye might have life* (Jno 5:40). Jesus also said: *No man can come to me, except the Father which hath sent me draw him* (Jno 6:44). At this point, you may argue that you came to Jesus years ago. Please do not misunderstand what I am saying. I am not saying that you did not come. If you say you came, I believe you.

Yet, if you think you came to Jesus in order to be born again, you are thinking backwards, and this time your backwards thinking is an error in your thinking. According to Jesus, the only way you could have come to Jesus was by the Father first drawing you. Thus, if you understand that your coming to Jesus was because of the Father having drawn you (through the means of 'born again'), then you understand the right kind of backward thinking, which provides you undeniable proof that you must have already been born again before you ever came. The right kind of backward thinking says: If no man will, or can, come to Jesus until he is first born again, then the fact that you came to Jesus is your proof that you must be born again.

Paul said: *You hath he quickened, who were dead in trespasses and sins* (Eph 2:1). To quicken is to make alive. To quicken the dead is to raise the dead. God raises those who are spiritually dead in trespasses and sins, so that they become spiritually alive. Jesus said: *The hour is coming, and now is, when the dead shall hear the voice of the Son of God: and they that hear shall live* (Jno 5:25). This is not the final resurrection. Jesus said that this raising of the dead was '*now*' happening, and would continue. This is the same as the ongoing process of 'born again'. Jesus did not liken this 'born again' to healing the sick or giving strength to the weak. Jesus likened 'born again' to raising the dead. How dead is dead? Dead folks do not see, do not hear, do not believe and do not come. So how is it with you? Can you see and hear the good news of the gospel? If you can, you are not still spiritually dead. Do you believe Jesus is the Son of God and your Savior? You must have spiritual life before you can believe such a thing. So if you believe, you are not still dead. Have you come to Jesus? Dead folks will not come. The spiritually dead cannot come. So if you have come, you are not still dead. In a backward way of thinking, if you are not still dead, you must be now alive. If you are now alive, it must be because Jesus has already spoken His life into you. If Jesus has spoken His life into you, you are born again. If you are born again, you will live forever in heaven. By backward thinking, if you are sure that you are not still spiritually dead, then you must be spiritually alive, and if you are spiritually alive, you will live forever.

The Bible says that the Spirit moves into the heart at 'born again'. So does the Spirit just slip in, or can we know He is in there? John said we can know. *Hereby know we that we dwell in him, and he in us, because he hath given us of his Spirit* (1 Jno 4:13). Here John went beyond stating that God dwells in us after 'born again'. He said that the Spirit in some way lets us know that God is dwelling in us. In yet another verse, John said the same thing. *Hereby we know that he abideth in us, by the Spirit which he hath given us* (1 Jno 3:24). So how does the Spirit tell us? Paul said that we know that the Spirit is in us, if our hearts cry to God, as children to a father. *Because ye are sons, God hath sent forth the Spirit of his Son into your hearts, crying, Abba, Father* (Gal 4:6). Paul said that we can know that we have the Spirit, if the Spirit is leading us. *As many as are led by the Spirit of God, they are the sons of God* (Rom 8:14). Paul said that the Spirit even testifies to us that we are His. *The Spirit itself beareth witness with our spirit, that we are the children of God* (Rom 8:16). So if you cry to God, or are led to goodness, or feel a testimony, then the Spirit is in you. You are indeed born again.

We can know that the Spirit is dwelling in us, if we exhibit the fruit of the Spirit in our lives. *The fruit of the Spirit is love, joy, peace, longsuffering, gentleness, goodness, faith, meekness, temperance* (Gal 5:22-23). Paul said that these character traits are the fruit of the Spirit, or things that grow from the Spirit. The first fruit listed is love. So since love comes from the Spirit, we can reason that anyone who has the character trait of love must already have the Spirit. Thus anyone who has love is already born again and is going to heaven.

As Paul said that love is a fruit of the Spirit, John said: *For love is of God; and every one that loveth is born of God* (1 Jno 4:7). To say that *love is of God* is to say that love comes from God. If love comes from God, then anyone who now loves must already have God in him. Moreover, anyone who has God in him is already born again. So anyone who now loves is already born again. Thus, if we have the love, we have the proof that we are born again. Along the same line, John further declared that we can know we have spiritual, even eternal life, if we love our brothers. *We know that we have passed from death unto life, because we love the brethren* (1 Jno 3:14). It is apparent that John considered love to be our proof that we are born again, even our proof that we already have spiritual eternal life.

The Bible often speaks of our faith as the proof that we have spiritual life. The Bible's premise is that we can know that we are born again, if we believe in Christ. John said: *Whosoever believeth that Jesus is the Christ is born of God* (1 Jno 5:1). Do not look at this statement as if it says, "Whoever believes gets born again." That will not fit with the rest of God's word. Belief cannot be the means to 'born again', in that faith is a fruit of the Spirit, which results from 'born again'. The teachings of the Bible declare that except a man be born again, he cannot see, hear, know, understand, or believe. So whoever believes does not become born again by his belief. Whoever believes must already be born again. The fact that we believe is our proof that we already have eternal life.

Jesus said: *He that heareth my word, and believeth on him that sent me, hath everlasting life* (Jno 5:24). Jesus did not say whoever hears and believes gets everlasting life. He said whoever believes **has** everlasting life. Paul declared: *No man can say that Jesus is the Lord, but by the Holy Ghost* (1 Cor 12:3). If confession is *by the Holy Ghost*, then confession cannot be how we get the Holy Ghost. So we do not confess that Jesus is the Lord in order to receive the Holy Spirit and be born again. Our confession is instead our proof that we already have the Holy Ghost, and that we are already born again. Thus, anybody who now confesses that Jesus is the Lord must have already been born again. John said: *Whosoever shall confess that Jesus is the Son of God, God dwelleth in him* (1 Jno 4:15). Again notice that we do not confess in order that God will move in. Whoever *shall confess* (future tense), *God dwelleth in him* (present tense). The thought is that the confessing part happens after the God-dwelling-in part.

There are some things that God directly teaches His children. *They shall be all taught of God* (Jno 6:45). We cannot know that Jesus is the Son of God, unless the Father reveals it to us. *Simon Peter answered and said, Thou art the Christ, the Son of the living God. And Jesus answered and said unto him, Blessed art thou, Simon Barjona: for flesh and blood hath not revealed it unto thee, but my Father which is in heaven* (Mt 16:16-17). Furthermore, we cannot know the Father, unless Jesus reveals Him to us. *Neither knoweth any man the Father, save the Son, and he to whomsoever the Son will reveal him* (Mt 11:27). One man cannot truly teach another man to know God, but God teaches His children to know Him. *They shall not teach every man his neighbour, and every man his brother, saying, Know the Lord: for all shall know me, from the least to the greatest* (Heb 8:11). So do you know Jesus is the Son of God? Do you feel that you know your heavenly Father to whom you pray? If you know your God, it is because God has taught you of Himself. If you know your God, it is because He dwells in you. If God is in you, you are born again.

We can know we have eternal life, if we do right. *Every one that doeth righteousness is born of him* (1 Jno 2:29). Again we do not do right in order to be born again. Everyone that does right is already born of God. God does not make us to be new creatures because of good works. God makes us to be new creatures, so we will do good works. *For we are his workmanship, created in Christ Jesus unto good works, which God hath before ordained that we should walk in them* (Eph 2:10).

There is a sense of truth in the statement, "Good guys go to heaven." Now the fallacy in the statement is that *there is none that doeth good, no, not one* (Rom 3:12). So I admit that there is truly no such thing as a 'good guy'. Another fallacy in the statement is that going to heaven is not based on being a 'good guy'. *Who hath saved us, and called us with an holy calling, not according to our works...* (2 Tim 1:9). The third misconception in the statement is that if there are any so-called 'good guys', it is God who has put His goodness in them. *Ye have not chosen me, but I have chosen you, and ordained you, that ye should go and bring forth fruit* (Jno 15:16).

Yet after all these disclaimers, let me share with you a conversation that I had with my wife after preaching a friend's funeral. I questioningly said to her, "Maybe I should have explained how we get to heaven. Everybody knew he was a 'good guy'. Yet, he drank a few beers. He sometimes played cards. He wasn't much on church. I wonder if people might have been wondering about whether he is in heaven. Maybe I should have told them about God's plan of salvation, which is all by grace, and not by us. Yet, maybe they were not in a state of mind to hear such details at a funeral." I sarcastically ended my words by saying, "Maybe they just figure he got there on the 'good guy' plan."

My dear wife answered, "That's how we know if anybody gets there." Her words were profound truth. She did not say that his being a 'good guy' is how he got there. She said his being a 'good guy' is **how we know** he got there. Nobody does good works, good enough to get to heaven by good works. Yet, we can know the ones who are going to heaven by the good works they do. My friend was a 'good guy'. I expect to see him soon.

God totally does the getting us to heaven part, but how can we know if we are going? Do you believe? Faith is a fruit of the Spirit, and whoever believes is born of God. Do you love? Love is of God, and everyone that loves is born of God. Have you come to Christ? Without being born again, you will not come, and no man can come. So if you have come, then you are born again. Do you have the Holy Spirit in you? You can know He is in you, if He is leading you to right, and convicting you of wrong. Do you do the 'good guy' thing? The Bible says that everyone that does righteousness is born of God.

Perhaps we can never be absolutely sure about our eternal destiny. In a real sense we do fail in all these things. Our belief falters. Our love falls short. We often catch ourselves going from Christ, instead of coming to Him. We certainly fail in the 'good guy' part. We may sometimes even wonder if the Holy Spirit is really in us. Yet perhaps the last evidence that we need to mention is that if it bothers us to fail, then we must have the Holy Spirit in us. It is the Spirit within who convicts our consciences. So the very idea that we are concerned about whether we are going to heaven is evidence that we will end up there. If our desire for heaven is real, then our getting there is real, too. I hope to see you there!!

18
Is Christianity the Means to Eternal Salvation?

The Bible claims exclusivity in Christ for eternal salvation. *Thomas saith unto him, Lord, we know not whither thou goest; and how can we know the way? Jesus saith unto him,* **I am the way***, the truth, and the life: no man cometh unto the Father, but by me* (Jno 14:5-6). Jesus said that Jesus is the way, even the only way to the Father. *Neither is there salvation in any other: for* **there is none other name** *under heaven given among men, whereby we must be saved* (Acts 4:12). Jesus is the way, even the only way to salvation.

If Jesus is the exclusive way to heaven, then that eliminates everybody else. One man, one name, one way: Jesus Christ. No other man, no other name, no other way: only Jesus Christ. Nobody ever went to heaven through the way of a totem pole or a sacred cow. Nobody will be in heaven through the name, Mohammed. Nobody goes to heaven through the name, Buddha. Everybody who ends up in heaven will be there through nobody else, but Jesus Christ. Jesus is the only way to get to heaven.

If Jesus is the exclusive way to heaven, then that eliminates, not only everybody else, but also everything else. If Jesus is the lone way to heaven, that even eliminates Christianity as the way to heaven. The Bible declares exclusivity in Christ for eternal salvation, but not in Christianity.

This crucial distinction has been lost in most of today's thinking. Jesus said to Thomas: *I am the way.* Jesus did not say anything about Christianity being the way. There is an important distinction between Jesus being the way, and 'being a Christian' being the way. The only way to go to heaven is to go through Jesus Christ, but people can go to heaven without going through Christianity. Christ can get people to heaven who were never Christians. There are

Muslims in heaven, but they did not get there by Mohammed. They got there by Christ.

There is a big difference in Jesus being the way, and 'knowing Jesus is the way' being the way. Thomas asked, *"How can we know the way?"* If Thomas had known the way, he would not have asked the question. He had been with Jesus for three years, and though Jesus had taught it, Thomas still did not know that Jesus is the way. Yet he sensed a need to know the way. Maybe Thomas was concerned about how Thomas could get himself to heaven. If there was a way to get to heaven, Thomas needed to get on that way. Yet how could he get himself there, if he did not even know the way? Jesus answered, *"I am the way."* Jesus did not say, "Thomas, you knowing that I am the way is the way." Thomas did not have to know that Jesus is the way, in order for Jesus to be the way. Thomas did not have to know the way to get to heaven, in order for Thomas to get to heaven. If Thomas had died prior to knowing that Jesus is the way, he would have still gone to heaven.

This same Thomas had been willing to die with Jesus in this world. He had previously spoken the words: *Let us also go, that we may die with him* (Jno 11:16). Surely a man who is willing to die with Jesus in this world is certainly going to live with Jesus in heaven. Thomas was already heaven-bound before he asked the question. Thomas was already going to heaven before he knew the way. Jesus can take those to heaven who do not know that Jesus is the way.

In a sense this idea of 'Thomas having to know the way, in order for Jesus to be the way' is what many preach today. Modern preachers go farther than stating that Jesus is the way to heaven. They go on to say that we have to know that Jesus is the way, before we can get to heaven. Many people are already in heaven who never knew that Jesus was the way. Now Jesus is the way that they got there, because Jesus is the only way that anybody gets there. Yet they never knew that very important point, until they got there.

Before the time of Christ, or after the time of Christ (BC or AD), Jesus is the only way to get to heaven. Whether an infant, or a life-long Christian, Jesus is the only way. Whether the intellectual Bible scholar, or the mentally challenged who lacks understanding, Jesus is the only way. They all get to heaven one way. There is one way for the Baptist, and that same way can get a Hindu to heaven. I am not saying that it is unimportant whether we are a Baptist or a Hindu. Let me walk this tightrope carefully. Christianity does matter, but being a Christian is not what gets us to heaven. Jesus gets us to heaven.

Jesus is the way to salvation, the only way, and the complete way. Jesus came to save His people. Jesus successfully saved all He came to save. My knowing these truths does not make them so. Nor does my not knowing these truths make them not so. Truth is truth, whether I know it or not, whether I believe it or not. My knowing that Jesus is the way is not my way to heaven. My knowing that Jesus is the way is my way to peace. Whether Thomas and I know the way, or do not know the way, is irrelevant, as to whether Thomas and I end up in heaven. Yet, whether Thomas and I know that Jesus is the way, or do not know that Jesus is the way, is very relevant, as to whether Thomas and I have peace of mind about getting to heaven. If Thomas and I know that Jesus is not only the exclusive way (in that there is no other way), but also know that Jesus is the complete way (in that there is nothing needed in addition to Jesus), then Thomas and I can have peace that passes understanding about our eternal standing with God.

Jesus is the way to heaven. Knowing that Jesus is the way to heaven is the way to peace. The more we eliminate everything except Jesus in our thinking about how we get to heaven, the more peace we will have. Anything we add to Jesus being the complete and only way, takes away from the peace we experience. Yet if we just leave it where Jesus left it, if we just assume that Jesus was right when He said, *I am the way*, if we just conclude that Jesus does it all, then we can have real peace about our eternal salvation.

So if Jesus is the exclusive way that eliminates all other ways, even the complete way that eliminates all additional ways, where does Christianity fit into the picture? Is Christ the exclusive way, or is hearing the Christian message the way? Is Christ the total way, or must the way also include the necessity of coming to know that Christ is the way?

The words, *I am the way*, get everybody to heaven that Jesus wants in heaven. Yet some are not content with Jesus' words. They add their own word. They say, *'believing* Jesus is the way', is the way. Adding just one word causes the real problem of how to save unbelieving babies. If you add an extra word, you need an extra plan, in order to save all the people that the added word eliminated. If the way to heaven is to know that Jesus is the way, then babies do need another plan. Yet if Jesus is the way, whether we know it or not, then babies can get to heaven the same way old sinners do. Neither the baby, nor the old sinner, has to know in order to go. Jesus finished the work of salvation for both of them, whether they know it or not. There is one plan. There is one way. Jesus is the way.

The Bible says people get to heaven out of every nation and family under heaven. The extinct nations of the Incas and Mayans lived and died, never hearing the name of Jesus, never hearing the gospel. How did any from those families get to heaven? Some say, "God is not unfair. Since these never had a chance to accept the gospel, God got them to heaven in some other way." I say that God had a way for them. It was not Christianity. Christianity never got to them, but that is okay. Christianity was never God's way to get His people to heaven anyhow. Jesus is God's way to get people to heaven. Jesus can get His people to heaven, no matter what extinct nation they might have come from. Jesus can get His people to heaven, no matter what remote family they might now be in.

There is no doubt that some people have a much better chance to believe in Jesus than others. If you grew up in a Christian home and went to a church where the only one you heard about was Jesus, then you had a much better chance of believing in Jesus, than children all over this world, and all through history, who grew up learning about somebody other than Jesus. These vast hosts of children had no chance to believe in the Jesus that they never heard of. So some say that since the gospel never got to them, they are again under a different plan. They get to heaven some other way.

If that be the case, it would never be good to take the gospel to anybody. The gospel would be a curse, and not a blessing. It would be bad news, and not good news. If some preacher takes the gospel to those who are already going to heaven anyway (through the 'never-had-a-chance way'), then he critically cuts their chances of getting to heaven. Suppose he goes and tells them the story of Jesus. Suppose half believe the story, but half reject it. That preacher just condemned the rejecting half to hell. If they were all going to heaven before he got there, look what a mess he made by bringing them the gospel. To have a supposed way of salvation where it would be harmful to preach the gospel is not only unreasonable, but also unscriptural.

The point is not that we should not take the gospel to all the world. The point is that Jesus is the sole way to heaven, without the means of the gospel. If we add anything to 'Jesus is the way' (including the gospel), we just complicate God's simple and perfect plan. It is much less confusing, and so God honoring, just to leave it all with '*I am the way*', and then praise Jesus for being the way.

It is important to take the gospel to all the world, so that many will praise Jesus. We should strive to spread Christianity, but at the same time we should realize that Christianity is not a new salvation, which Jesus introduced when He came into the world.

For centuries prior to Christianity, Jesus had already saved multitudes without the means of Christianity. Since the introduction of Christianity, Jesus still saves His people without the means of Christianity. Christianity is not a necessity for salvation. Christianity is a revelation about salvation. God has always saved His people through Christ, and Christ alone. Christianity reveals to God's people that God always saves His people through Christ, and Christ alone. Jesus is the way. Knowing His name and His story is a bonus. The revelation that occurs in Christianity inspires God's people to follow Christ and become Christians. Yet Jesus can save His people, even if they never heard the gospel, and never became Christians.

Though Christianity is not necessary for eternal salvation, it is still important to worship the right God. Jesus is God, and Jesus should be worshipped. Jesus is the way. Jesus should be worshipped. Yet what about those who do not know that Jesus is the way? Native Americans worshipped a totem pole sincerely, but it is not okay to worship a totem pole. Muslims worship their god sincerely, but sincere worship of a false god is still wrong. All men should worship the true God. Yet there are children of the true God, who do not worship Him, because they do not know who He is. Christianity's job is to go into all the world with the gospel of grace, and to proclaim the name of Jesus Christ. This message does not give life. Jesus can do that without the means of Christianity. Salvation is by Christ. Revelation is by Christianity. Christ is the way to eternal life. Christianity is the way to enlightenment about Christ being the way to eternal life. Jesus is the way to heaven. The message that Jesus is the way to heaven is the way to peace.

You do not have to look far in this world to find 'good folks' who are not worshipping Jesus. Though they worship somebody other than Jesus, they still appear to be deep down good people. Jesus said we could tell good people by their fruits. I know people who are not Christian by name, but they are more Christ-like, than many who claim Jesus' name.

The Bible says about carnal man: *There is none good, no, not one* (Rom 3:12). This is a universal statement for all mankind in their natural condition. The Bible explains what is required in order to make people to be 'good folks'. When Jesus speaks spiritual life into a carnal man, the man is different than before. The born again man is a new creature, with a new nature, even a nature of goodness. He now thinks in a new way, even a good way. Jesus made him into one of the 'good folks', and this changed man begins to do good things. By their fruit you can know them. This goodness is a fruit of the Spirit, and it shows itself by the way the born again child of God lives his life.

I often see 'good folk' fruit in people who are not that 'churchy'. I even see 'good folk' fruit in people who are not Christian, and wrongly serve a false god. My Mom has a doctor who is non-Christian in his beliefs, but not in his kindness and compassion. I really believe he is a 'good folk' (made to be that way by the Jesus, he is yet to serve). On the same line, I recently preached a man's funeral who had been my friend since childhood. Some were concerned, as to whether he had ever 'accepted' Christ. Another friend had convinced him to recite the 'right words' on his deathbed. Yet even prior to the man's confession, I had not been so worried about his eternal status. I knew some special things about him. Though he was just a common working man, I knew that he had made regular large donations to help poor children. He did not do this to be seen of men. Only a few ever knew that he did it. He did it, because deep down he had a good heart. He was pretty crusty on the outside, but full of love on the inside.

These kinds of Christ-like actions are stronger evidence than a deathbed confession. Faith is no doubt a fruit of the Spirit, but love is the first one on the list (Gal 5:22-23). An outworking of love for others is evidence of a prior in-working of the Spirit of God. I could tell that the Spirit was on the inside by the fruit on the outside. I feel sure that my friend was one of the 'good folk'. I saw the fruit. The same Spirit that produced the fruit gave the eternal life. I believe my friend is with God in heaven.

In Acts 8, Philip preached Jesus to the Ethiopian eunuch. The eunuch confessed belief in Jesus and was baptized. Was Philip's preaching what put the man through? Was Philip the way, or is Jesus the way? When Philip found the eunuch, he was reading God's word, after having been to Jerusalem to worship. Those are two 'good-fruit' signs, indicating that the Spirit's fruit of goodness was leading the man to do 'good folk' things. The Spirit was in the eunuch, before Philip ever got to him. The man had already been born again, without any help from a preacher.

Yet the born again eunuch did not understand what he was reading, or who to worship. Here is where the preacher comes in. Philip told the eunuch about Jesus. At that point the eunuch did other 'good folk' things, like confessing his belief in Jesus, and being baptized. Yet these things were not the way to heaven. Neither was the preacher the way. Jesus is the way, whether Philip had gotten there or not.

In Acts 9, Jesus cornered the Christ-hating, Christian-killing Saul of Tarsus. With His life-giving voice, Jesus spoke to Saul, and he was born again. At that point, Saul was a changed man who submitted his whole life to Jesus. *Lord, what wilt thou have me to do* (Act 9:6)? That sounds like a 'good folk' to me. In Acts 8, the eunuch was already worshipping before the preacher got to him. In Acts 9, Saul was already born again, and going to heaven, without help from a preacher. That is the pattern. That is how it works every time. Jesus is the way to salvation. Jesus does not need a preacher to help Him be the way. Jesus is the way.

In Acts 10, Cornelius was a devout man, who feared God, who gave much alms, and who prayed always. All these things were true about the man before the preacher ever got to him. That sounds like a 'good folk' to me. I would have trouble preaching that man into hell. After a while, Peter preached the gospel of Jesus to Cornelius. At that point, Cornelius believed and was baptized. Yet, what if Peter had refused to go preach to that Gentile? Or what if Cornelius had died before Peter got there? Would Cornelius be now burning in hell if the preacher had never gotten to him? No! Heaven does not depend on a preacher. Cornelius was already born again, and exhibiting a Christ-like nature, before Peter got to him. Cornelius was going to heaven without Peter's help. Peter was not the way to eternal life. The preacher is not the way to heaven. The gospel is not the way to heaven. Belief is not the way to heaven. Confession is not the way to heaven. Jesus is the way to heaven. Jesus, and Jesus alone, is the way to heaven.

There is an exclusiveness in Jesus for eternal life, but not in the route of Christianity. There are people in heaven who did not believe in Jesus, while they were in this world. Belief is not a necessity in order to get to heaven. *For what if some did not believe? shall their unbelief make the faith of God without effect* (Rom 3:3)? What if somebody does not believe? Maybe they never had a chance, because nobody ever got Jesus' name to them, so that they might believe. Maybe whoever told them the story was so far off in his beliefs that his version was more wrong than right. Maybe they had seen enough Christian hypocrisy to turn them off to the whole thing. Maybe they believed in their soul, but refused to publicly profess. I do not know what goes on in somebody else's mind. Yet I do know the answer to the question: *Shall their unbelief make the faith of God without effect?* The Bible answers: *God forbid.*

Man's unbelief cannot make God ineffective in His faithfulness to His plan of salvation. *If we believe not, yet he abideth faithful: he cannot deny himself* (2 Tim 2:13). God will never deny the death of His Son, and what that death accomplished, even if nobody ever believes it. Our unbelief cannot undo what has already been done. Christ died for every one of His children, a vast host that no man can number, even a number far beyond anything Christianity has ever reached. Christ paid for the sins of every one of them. That has been done. It is finished. God knows that Christ died for and saved His people, whether we know it or not. Jesus was the way. Jesus is the way. Salvation is accomplished. Now belief is very important in that it gives contentment to the believer, but belief is not what gets the believer to heaven. Jesus does that. Christ is the way for the Native American, the Old Testament Jew, the man on the uncharted island, the infant who never believed, and the devout believer. Jesus is the way for all His children. Jesus needs nobody's help in order for Him to be the way. Jesus is the way.

Jesus is the way to heaven, because Jesus' voice is the way to being born again. *The hour is coming, and now is, when the dead shall hear the voice of the Son of God: and they that hear shall live* (Jno 5:25). The dead shall hear Jesus' voice and live. There is no doubt that this raising from the dead was something that was going to happen in the future: *The hour is coming.* Yet it was also already happening, even as Jesus made this statement: *The hour...now is.* So this cannot be the final resurrection, when dead bodies will be raised.

These are spiritual resurrections, where Jesus speaks to those who are dead to the spiritual realm of existence and gives them spiritual life. This is where Jesus gives life to those who are dead in trespasses and in sins. *And you hath he quickened, who were dead in trespasses and sins* (Eph 2:1). The preacher's voice is not the way. Jesus' voice is the way. Only Jesus can speak spiritual life into the spiritually dead. The Bible describes unborn again humanity as being dead to spiritual things. Until Jesus speaks spiritual life into them, they cannot hear the preacher's cry. They have no spiritual ears. *Why do ye not understand my speech? even because ye cannot hear my word* (Jno 8:43). They cannot see the light. They have no spiritual eyes. *Except a man be born again, he cannot see the kingdom of God* (Jno 3:3). The voice of Jesus first gives life. Then the voice of the preacher can be heard. Then the gospel can give enlightenment. The only ones who can respond to the preacher are the ones who have life. The gospel does not give life. The gospel gives light. The true gospel preacher does not preach himself as the way. The true gospel message is that Jesus is the way, that Jesus is the sole way, and that Jesus is the whole way.

All of God's children must be born again. Yet not a one of them knows how to do it. We did not born ourselves naturally. We cannot born ourselves spiritually. We do not help God do it. God does it for us. God does His part, and His part is to do everything necessary to get us to heaven. As a preacher, my part is to preach to you that God does His part, and that God will one day get you to heaven. As a hearer, your part is to believe that God does His part, and that God will one day get you to heaven. Your hearing and believing is not what gives you the life. By the time you get to the point of hearing and believing, Jesus has already given you the life. Our hearing and believing is not the way to heaven. Jesus is the way to heaven. Our hearing and believing is our way to peace. The preacher's job is to guide our feet into the way of peace (Lk 1:79).

It is all very simple. Jesus is the way. Jesus can find those that we cannot find. He saves those that we can never know. He can even save those who never knew Him. 'Knowing Jesus' is not the way to heaven. Jesus is the way. Christianity is not the way to heaven. Many are in heaven who never followed the way of Christianity in this world. The truth that Christ saves without the means of Christianity is a much broader way of salvation than all the man-made ways. Jesus gets to people that Christianity never gets to. 'Jesus plus Christianity' for salvation is far more restrictive, than the simple words, '*I am the way*'. Jesus is the sole way, and the whole way. The exclusivity is in Christ, not in Christianity.

19
What is the Covenant of Grace?

In the long ago, God created all things in six glorious days. After completing His masterpiece, *God saw every thing that he had made, and, behold, it was very good* (Gen 1:31). Yet the man, Adam, whom God had created after His own image, soon sinned against his Holy Creator, and by that *one man sin entered into the world, and death by sin; and so death passed upon all men* (Rom 5:12). In the day that Adam committed his sin, he was cast from God's presence, and in his separation from God, Adam experienced a death. Moreover, the death that Adam experienced by sinning against God was extended to all that were in his loins, so that all mankind received the death sentence that was placed upon Adam. When that one man sinned, all men died. Since man has no cure for death, his case would have been forever hopeless, unless God by grace would intervene.

To the praise of the glory of his grace, before God ever started creating, even prior to the beginning of anything, God had a plan to save the man He would create. Long before the man ever sinned and needed saving, God had already worked out all the details, as to how He would save the man. This eternal plan of salvation that was forever in the mind of God has come to be called God's Covenant of Grace.

In one sense, the Covenant of Grace is a rather simple idea. Yet when considered in its fullness, it is quite profound. Simply stated, the Covenant of Grace is a solemn agreement (even a contract or pact) entered into by God with God before the world began, for the purpose of saving God's children from their sins. Profoundly stated, the idea of a Covenant of Grace is the grid and groundwork of all the Bible. Although the particular term *'Covenant of Grace'* is not found in the scriptures, the very purpose of the scriptures is to make known to man God's plan of salvation, which originated in the Covenant of Grace. Moreover, most of the Bible's teachings are in some way connected to the revelation of the details of this covenant.

Let us begin with some basics. Generally speaking, a covenant is a contractual agreement, entered into by two or more parties. Yet the Covenant of Grace is somewhat different, in that God is the only party involved in the agreement. Since this covenant was made before creation, and since no one but God existed in eternity past, the Covenant of Grace is a covenant, where God entered into an agreement with God. Yet if we consider that God is three persons, it is real to say that God the Father, God the Son and God the Holy Spirit entered into an agreement with each other.

A key point here is that man was not actively involved in any way in this contract. The Covenant of Grace was already a fully functional harmonious pact between Father, Son and Spirit, well before man ever existed. The covenant concerned man, but was not entered into by man. The covenant was God's agreement with Himself to save man. Man had no part in the original agreement, and man would have no part in the execution of the terms of the agreement. In no way would man be asked to actively bring about any aspect of the agreement. The established ends of the covenant are not brought to pass by the will of man, the words of man, the works of man, or anything else of man. The only way man is ever involved in this Covenant of Grace is to be the passive recipient of the grace that was established in it. Moreover, the covenant is a Covenant of '**Grace**', and by definition, any benefits that man might receive according to the terms of this agreement must be received totally and completely by the agreed upon and established means of grace. According to the terms of this agreement God would save his people by a most amazing means, even by the means of amazing grace.

The Covenant of Grace makes up the very foundation and framework for understanding the Bible. As we approach God's word, it is so important to know that the ideas portrayed in the Covenant of Grace are the keys that unlock the mysteries of the entire scriptures. Only through the premise of covenant theology can the complexity of Bible truths be seen and understood. Most of the Bible in some way alludes to the Covenant of Grace. From Genesis to Revelation the terms and conditions of the agreement continue to be revealed in more and more detail. The shadowy representations of the Old Testament become the sharp reality of the New Testament.

For instance, the woman's bruised seed, which God knew about immediately after the fall, became the Christ of the cross. Likewise, the 'seed' that God spoke of in His covenant with Abraham became the Jesus who saved His people from their sins. The Passover lamb pictured the Lamb of God, whom God would eventually send. So in scriptures and history, God's plan of salvation, which originated in the Covenant of Grace, came into view. The vague prophecy of early teachings is the vivid history of today. From the fall in the garden to the final resurrection, the terms of the covenant unfold. From before creation to the end of time, the events established in the covenant are brought to pass. From the redemption of the cross to the regeneration of every child of God who was named in the covenant, the Covenant of Grace becomes reality in all its glorious detail. In the Covenant of Grace was the basic outline, from which comes all the details of God's whole Bible. In the Covenant of Grace was the basic outline, from which comes all the details of God's salvation by His grace. Such Bible concepts as election, predestination, redemption, reconciliation, justification, regeneration, calling, glorification, and many more have their basis in the Covenant of Grace. In the Covenant of Grace lies everything that will one day be declared to be to the praise of the glory of God's grace.

In an attempt to understand more about God and His word, let us delve into this idea of Covenant of Grace. With our limited simple minds, let us even attempt to go back in time and visualize God in eternity past. God must have always known all about all He would ever do. *Known unto God are all his works from the beginning of the world* (Acts 15:18). Surely, God always knew the time when He would create (even when there was no such thing as time). Surely, God always knew the place where He would create (even where there was no such thing as place). God always knew that He would lastly create man in the image of God. Though God did not cause the man to sin, God always knew that the man would sin, and that the man would cease to be in the image of God. God knew that if men were ever again to be in God's image, that God would have to do it for them. Men's works could never bring about their return. It would have to be by God's grace.

Knowing these things, God had already taken upon Himself to do something quite amazing. Before God ever created man, and before man ever sinned, God had already entered into a covenant agreement with Himself, as to how He would save fallen men. The salvation would be by God's grace. Father, Son, and Spirit would each have a part, and each one agreed to His part. Thus, God entered into a holy covenant, by which God would save His people from their sins.

In this covenant agreement of grace, God established His purpose to save a vast host of people from every nation and family under heaven. God's plan of salvation began with the Father's election of a foreknown, ever-loved and much-loved, particular people to be His people. In the Covenant of Grace, God the Father predestinated that these particular chosen people would be saved by His grace, and would eventually, and eternally, be conformed to the likeness and image of His Beloved Son Jesus Christ. So, even before there were people to choose, the Father chose particular people. His choice was not based on anything that the people would do. He did not gaze into the future and choose according to foreseen goodness, for there was none good, no not one. God the Father did not elect His people according to His omniscience. God's election was based only in God's grace.

From the most extensive explanation in the Bible about God's election, we find these words: *So then it is not of him that willeth, nor of him that runneth, but of God that sheweth mercy* (Rom 9:16). Election was not according to man's will or man's actions. God's election is based only on God's mercy and grace. Everything that God established in His Covenant of Grace will eternally be to the praise of the glory of His grace. Man had no active part in the covenant.

When all the details of the covenant are finally fulfilled, God will share His glory with no man.

In this covenant agreement of grace, God the Father gave each of His chosen people to God the Son. In covenant agreement, God the Son accepted each of the beloved ones that the Father gave to Him. In receiving those that the Father gave, the Son also accepted the responsibility of giving eternal salvation to each of the God-chosen, God-given children. Jesus often referred to this covenant transaction between Father and Son with similar words to: *all that the Father giveth me.* Without an understanding of the concept of the Covenant of Grace, the idea expressed in these words remains hidden. Yet these words have clear meaning, if we first understand that the Father elected His people in the Covenant of Grace, and then gave His elected people to His Son, so that His Son Jesus Christ would save each of them.

Let us look at verses where Jesus said the Father had given Him the people for whom He would die, even given Him the people to whom He would give eternal life. *As thou hast given him power over all flesh, that he should give eternal life to **as many as thou hast given him*** (Jno 17:2). Few Christians question that Jesus had God-given power over all flesh, but few ever go on to notice that Jesus had God-given power, in order to save God-given people. Jesus used His power to give eternal life to the ones the Father had previously given to Him. It was all part of the covenant agreement between Father and Son before the world was.

Jesus repeated the same truth: *Thine they were, and **thou gavest them me...*** (Jno 17:6). These had first belonged to the Father, and at some point the Father had given them to His Son. This transaction between Father and Son is very agreeable to what is explained by the idea of a Covenant of Grace.

Jesus further said: *I pray for them: I pray not for the world, but for **them which thou hast given me**; for they are thine* (Jno 17:9). Again, we see that the Father had given His elect people to Jesus, but it is comforting to also notice the present tense statement, *for they are thine*. Here Jesus acknowledged that even though the Father had given His people to Jesus, they still belonged to the Father, too.

Since Jesus is God, God had really only given His people to Himself, and thus He never really lost His claim to them.

In the same prayer Jesus finally said: *Father, I will that they also, whom thou hast given me, be with me where I am; that they may behold my glory...* (Jno 17:24). Jesus' will about the God-given ones was in total agreement with the Father's will. *And this is the Father's will which hath sent me, that of all which he hath given me I should lose nothing, but should raise it up again at the last day* (Jno 6:39). They both had willed, and agreed to, the same things in the Covenant of Grace before the world began. When the world ends, all that the Father chose, and gave to Jesus, will be with Jesus. Jesus will lose nothing of all He had been given. He will raise every one of them up at the last day.

Then the victory statement: *Behold I and the children which God hath given me* (Heb 2:13). Think of the significance of these words from our 'Successful Savior'. *Behold!* Look Father! I have them all. You gave them to me. I paid for them. I cleansed them. I redeemed them. They are mine. I give them back to you, who chose them so long ago. How glorious and reassuring it is to know that each one, whom the Father gave to Jesus in covenant agreement before the world began, will eventually, and eternally, be with Jesus when the world ends!

In this covenant agreement of grace, Jesus knew full well what would be required of Him in accepting the people that the Father gave to Him. He totally understood His covenant commitment. He always knew what it would take to save His people from their sins. In agreeing to save His people, Jesus amazingly agreed that He would die for them. In order to die for them, the Creator agreed to be made of a woman, and to become one of them. The Son of God agreed to live a sinless life for an appointed time, and then to shed His blood in laying down His life in death upon a cruel cross. In this act, He would be surety for God's chosen people. In His suffering and death, He would take the place of each one that the Father had given to Him. He would pay the ransom demanded by the justice of God for all the sins of all His people.

The Savior of sinners had surely anticipated the time of His death, even from before time. Yet at the appointed time when He squarely faced the cross, Jesus stated His will in His prayer. When He prayed that all the God-given elect be with Him in glory, He knew exactly what it would take to make that prayer reality. He had always known. Jesus left that prayer and walked to the cross. He fulfilled His own will. He saved His people from their sins, even God's elect people, whom He had agreed to save so long ago. When Jesus laid His life down on the cross, the Son of God fulfilled the united will of Father, Son and Spirit that had been forever established in the Covenant of Grace.

Finally, in this covenant agreement of grace, God the Holy Spirit agreed to give spiritual life to each one that the Father had chosen, even the same ones for whom the Son had agreed to die. The Holy Spirit would do this according to His sovereign will and purpose. At the time that He deemed to be the right time, He would find each of the elected persons. At a precise point in each of their natural lives, He would breathe into each one of them a glorious spiritual and eternal life. It would be as a new birth, a spiritual birth from above, and the irresistible grace of God would be its cause. The result of the new life would be a new and heavenly nature. The spiritually born again new creature would have spiritual character traits that can only come from God. God, the Holy Spirit, even agreed to dwell within the heart of each of these regenerated creatures, teaching and guiding them in spiritual things.

So it can be seen that there is no disagreement within the Godhead regarding the entered into agreement. The Son died for the exact ones that the Father chose. Likewise, the Holy Spirit finds the same exact ones that the Father chose. The Son saved the identical ones on the cross that the Holy Spirit saves in the new birth. Every individual that the Trinity determined to save in the Covenant of Grace will finally be saved in heaven. *Moreover whom he did predestinate, them he also called: and whom he called, them he also justified: and whom he justified, them he also glorified* (Rom 8:30). In this one simple verse, we see the Father's election and predetermination unto salvation. We see the Spirit's effectual call to salvation. We see the Son's justification unto salvation. We see an absolutely aligned cooperation of the Trinity. We see the perfect success in the working out of God's Covenant of Grace plan of salvation. Every predestinated *'whom'* ends up a glorified *'them'*. What a God! What a plan!

Before there were sinners to save, Father, Son and Spirit agreed in covenant to a foolproof plan of salvation, whereby each person of the Trinity united to do His part to save each individual in the plan. God even united in agreement with Himself to fulfill every aspect of the Covenant of Grace. The idea of a Trinity without unity is absurdity. Before time began, Father, Son and Spirit agreed in unity to save all who were named in the Covenant of Grace. When time is no more, Father, Son and Spirit will be united in agreement that each of the three has fulfilled what He agreed to. All who became God's people in eternity past will experience God's glory in eternity future. Everything that was established in God's Covenant of Grace will forever be to the praise of the glory of God's amazing grace.

To know the basics of this covenant is to have the keys to the scriptures. God's Covenant of Grace is both the groundwork and the fulfillment of God's word. It is both the centerpiece and the encompassing of all God-given revelation. Searching for Bible truth without the foundational grid of the Covenant of Grace is like looking for the proverbial needle in a field of haystacks. It is like groping for light in the midst of utter darkness, where you look as hard as you can, but you still cannot see. Yet with a little insight into the Covenant of Grace, the darkness becomes light, and the blindness becomes sight. Only through the unveiled secrets, which are uncovered by a glimpse of God's Covenant of Grace, can the profound, be made to appear rather simple. Only in the unfolding of the Covenant of Grace, can the Bible be understood.

To know covenant theology wipes out all need for dispensational thinking. The same Covenant of Grace that saved Adam will save the yet to be born again, last child of God. God does not need seven plans for seven dispensations of time. God has one plan for all time. In covenant salvation, one plan fits all. One God saves all. One way is the way. God does not need multiple plans. God never saved a single Israelite through goat blood. *For it is not possible that the blood of bulls and of goats should take away sins* (Heb 10:4). Yet Old Testament saints are in heaven. Jesus said that Abraham, Isaac and Jacob were living with God. Moses and Elijah came down from heaven to the mount. These children of God got to heaven the same way Paul and Peter got to heaven. The only way anybody gets to heaven is through the plan of salvation described by the Covenant of Grace.

Some argue that Old Testament saints had to get to heaven some other way, because they had already gotten there before Jesus ever died. God knew men would make such an objection. So God made it clear how He was right in letting those sinners in. *Whom God hath set forth to be a propitiation through faith in his blood, to declare his righteousness for the remission of sins that are past, through the forbearance of God* (Rom 3:25). God did not claim that He was right to let them in because of animal blood. God did not claim that He was right to let them in some other way, since they lived in another dispensation of time. God went straight to the Covenant of Grace to defend His righteousness. The words, *whom God hath set forth to be a propitiation*, are words of covenant theology. The *whom* is Jesus, and in the Covenant of Grace before time, God had already set forth Jesus to be the satisfying atonement for the sins of all His people. Moreover, *through faith in his blood* (that is through God's faith in His Son's covenant promise, even God's confidence in His Son's eternal promise that He would keep His covenant commitment to come and shed His blood to pay for the sins of God's people), God does *declare his righteousness for the remission of sins that are past*. In other words, God said that He was right to go ahead and let them in, even tolerating the sins of the past while His patient *forbearance* waited for the promised blood to be shed.

The Covenant of Grace is the only plan that ever has been, or ever will be, needed. If we propose a plan of salvation that adds something to what God agreed to do in the Covenant of Grace, we end up having to add a plan to God's plan, in order to save those that our man-made addition knocked out. If we add belief to what God agreed to in His Covenant, we have to add a plan for babies and the mentally deficient. If we add the gospel, we have to add a plan for Old Testament saints and Mayans. The only plan of salvation that can save all God's people, through all time, in all places, is the plan that God agreed to in the Covenant of Grace.

The plan is profound, but basically simple. Before time, the Father chose a vast host of people from every nation and family under heaven. In covenant agreement, the Father gave His chosen people to His Son, so His Son would save each of His God-chosen, and God-given, people from their sins, by His death on the cross. In covenant agreement, the Holy Spirit seeks out and finds every one of the God-chosen, God-given, and Jesus-died-for children of God. In covenant theology, all that were ever in the Covenant of Grace will forever live with the God of grace. What a covenant! What a plan! What a simple gospel! The salvation by grace, and only by grace, which was agreed to in the Covenant of Grace, will forever be to the praise of the glory of God's grace. May we who are in God's Covenant of Grace, and who are destined to be in God's eternity by grace, even now live our lives to the praise of the glory of His grace.

20
What is the Significance of Baptism?

The ritual of baptism began under God's authority, when John *was a man sent from God ...to baptize with water* (Jno 1:6, 33). So ministers continue to baptize, and believers are still baptized, because it is of God. Yet baptism is much more than just obedience to God's command. Baptism is a God-given ritual, which portrays more meaning and significance than words have ever expressed.

Baptism is perhaps the simplest, but at the same time, the most profound of all New Testament teachings. In one sense, baptism is so simple that the small child can see its greatest meaning. Yet in its deepest sense, baptism is so profound that the greatest scholars cannot fully appreciate all its significance. Who, but God, could merge such simple complexity? Only God could consolidate so many things that Christianity represents into one sacrament. In symbolic, show-and-tell fashion, baptism paints pictures of many Bible truths. When properly understood a baptism is a sermon without words, proclaiming the gospel message without preaching.

The simplest, and most important, of the wordless sermons represented by baptism is *'Death, Burial and Resurrection'*. The crucifixion and resurrection of Jesus is the greatest of Bible truths. The fact of Jesus' death, burial and resurrection is the very centerpiece and foundation of Christianity, without which there is no Christianity. When the one baptized is placed under the water, and is raised from the water, the child's mind grasps the message of death, burial and resurrection. As Jesus literally experienced death, burial and resurrection, even so His followers continue to paint, and repaint, that scene in the watery grave of baptism. For centuries, the words of preachers have loudly proclaimed Jesus' death, burial and resurrection, while the baptisms of believers have silently preached the same.

As the common sense of a child connects baptism to death, burial and resurrection, so do the words of Jesus. *But I have a baptism to be baptized with; and how am I straitened till it be accomplished!* (Lk 12:50). At the time of these words, Jesus had already been baptized by John in the Jordan River. Yet Jesus spoke of a baptism that was still to come.

The clue as to what Jesus meant by a baptism that was yet to come lies in the words, *and how am I straitened till it be accomplished!* To be *straitened* is to be preoccupied about a troubling situation. Surely what preoccupied Jesus here was the same thing that troubled Him when He prayed in the garden: *Father if it be possible, let this cup pass from me* (Mt 26:39). Jesus was willing to die, but there is little doubt that He was troubled at the thought of it. The baptism that Jesus was *to be baptized with*, and about which He was *straitened till it be accomplished*, was His literal death, burial and resurrection. Thus, Jesus figuratively used the word, *baptism*, to express His literal death, burial and resurrection.

Paul's words further equate baptism to death, burial and resurrection. *Know ye not, that so many of us as were baptized into Jesus Christ were baptized into his death? Therefore we are buried with him by baptism into death: that like as Christ was raised up from the dead by the glory of the Father, even so we also should walk in newness of life* (Rom 6:3-4). Paul said, *know ye not*, as if this was common knowledge, even something that a child would know. Then he spoke of our baptisms, and Jesus' death, burial and resurrection, as if they are the same thing. Paul took it as common knowledge that we who are baptized, are *baptized into his death*, are *buried with him by baptism*, and *like as Christ was raised up from the dead* with new life, even so we are raised to a new life. So first and foremost, we see from the scriptures that baptism represents Jesus' death, burial and resurrection.

Yet from this same text, we see a second significance of baptism in the words, *even so we also should walk in newness of life*. Lest there be confusion, let us clarify that baptism is not the cause of this new life. The new life is the direct work of the Holy Spirit, without any means or assistance. He moves where He pleases, and so it is with everyone that is born of the Spirit. As we cannot assist in our natural births, neither can we assist in our spiritual births. Prior to being born again, the carnal man is spiritually dead, and incapable of action in the spiritual realm. The Spirit must first give the new birth (and its associated new spiritual life) before the new creature can do new and spiritual things, like believing the gospel and coming to Jesus.

So after having been given spiritual life, the new creature can hear the gospel with new ears. Now he might cry out, "Men and brethren, what shall I do?" Some preacher might say, "Repent and be baptized." So the preacher baptizes this one, who already had the new life. Here is where he is raised from baptism to *walk in newness of life*. From now on, he is to have a new walk, even a new way of living. So as baptism pictures death, burial and resurrection, it also pictures one who is raised from the dead to live a new kind of life, even a life that would honor the God, who gave him the life.

A very similar significance of baptism is found in yet another verse: *For as many of you as have been baptized into Christ have put on Christ* (Gal 3:27). Here baptism pictures putting on the very character of Christ. To put on Christ is to be enrobed in Christ, to be shrouded with His presence. To be baptized is to be wrapped in the aura of Christ. What a thought! What a mission for life! To *walk in newness of life*, or to *put on* Christ, is to let our light shine in a dark world to the glory of our Father which is in heaven.

Our next significance of baptism is what we might call an engulfing of the Holy Spirit. Just prior to His ascension, Jesus reminded His disciples of John's literal water baptism, but then promised them that they would soon be baptized with the Holy Ghost. *For John truly baptized with water; but ye shall be baptized with the Holy Ghost not many days hence* (Acts 1:5). Jesus fulfilled this promise on the Day of Pentecost. He prayed the Father to send the Holy Ghost, and the Holy Ghost literally came down as cloven tongues of fire, filling the place and engulfing them with His very presence. The Holy Ghost covered them, surrounded them, filled the house, and filled them. What a scene!

It is significant to notice that these people were not baptized **by** the Holy Ghost, but **with** the Holy Ghost. Jesus had said, as John baptized **with** water, you shall be baptized **with** the Holy Ghost. Jesus had not depicted the Holy Ghost as the 'baptizer', but as the water of baptism. The God of heaven did the baptizing. The people were plunged into, surrounded by, encompassed with, and engulfed in the wonderful presence of the Holy Ghost. As the water of baptism covers, surrounds, and engulfs, even so the Holy Ghost did the same.

Now I do not expect another Pentecost, but I do believe that baptism with the Holy Ghost still applies to us in our day. Listen to Peter's closing words on that glorious day: *Repent, and be baptized every one of you in the name of Jesus Christ for the remission of sins, and ye shall receive the gift of the Holy Ghost. For the promise is unto you, and to your children, and to all that are afar off, even as many as the Lord our God shall call* (Acts 2:38-39). Peter first said, *repent and be baptized,* **then** *ye shall receive the gift of the Holy Ghost.* This *gift of the Holy Ghost*, which was to come after their baptisms, cannot be the new birth. The Bible says that they were already pricked in their hearts. Besides, they had just responded to the preached word in such a way, as to prove that they were already born again. So *the gift of the Holy Ghost* must be something other than, and beyond, the new birth. Moreover, *the gift of the Holy Ghost* must be something beyond the miracle of that day, in that they already had the cloven tongues of fire around them. So *the gift of the Holy Ghost*, which they were yet to receive, could not have been that which they already had.

So if *the gift of the Holy Ghost* is not the new birth, nor the appearance of cloven tongues of fire, what might it be? Peter referred to this gift as something in the future, something *ye **shall** receive*, even *the **promise*** of something yet to come. They had already received Jesus' promise that they would be baptized with the Holy Ghost that day, but Peter here called a yet to be received gift of the Holy Ghost, *the promise*. Peter further said that *the promise* was far reaching, in that it was not just to those who were there that day, but also to their children, and to those who were afar off, even to *as many as the Lord our God shall call.* So since *the promise* made at

Pentecost extends to God-called children, and since God is still effectually calling His children, it seems that *the promise* would in some way still be available today.

The promise is indeed available today. The promise is to us, even now. The promise is with us all the time. As the one who is baptized is surrounded and engulfed with water, even so the one who is called is surrounded and engulfed with the Holy Ghost. Thus the engulfing waters of baptism paint a beautiful picture of *the promise* of the surrounding presence, even the engulfing power, and the ever-encompassing providence of the Holy Spirit, who is with us today, and will never leave us or forsake us.

As we come to the next significance of baptism, Paul tells us that we can be baptized and wash away our sins. *And now why tarriest thou? arise, and be baptized, and wash away thy sins, calling on the name of the Lord* (Acts 22:16). These words must be true. They are in God's word, and *thy word is truth* (Jno 17:17). Yet, how can these words be in agreement with the basic doctrine that only Jesus' blood can wash away our sins?

First notice the sense of urgency in the words, *why tarriest thou?* It is as if the baptizing needs to take place right now. Many people in the Bible sensed this immediate seriousness. The eunuch heard the gospel, and nothing could hinder him from being baptized. Jesus sent Saul of Tarsus to the preacher, who immediately baptized him. Peter preached to Cornelius, and the same day baptized him, and many who were gathered with him. Paul preached the gospel to the jailer and his family, and the same night baptized them. Surely we see a pattern of immediate baptism without tarrying.

So why did the New Testament hearers sense such an urgency for immediate baptism? The alarming message of New Testament preaching was that men had crucified the Son of God. Peter told his listeners that they *by wicked hands have crucified* God's Son. Philip preached Christ as the sheep who was slaughtered in the stead of the eunuch. Cornelius heard how Jesus was *hanged on a tree.* Paul *determined not to know anything among them, save* [except] *Christ, and Him crucified.* When these Spirit-filled men preached the crucifixion of the Savior of sinners, something powerful happened in the Spirit-filled (yet sin-filled) hearts of the hearers. The heart-pricked, Christ-killing multitude cried out, *Men and brethren, what shall we do?* With trembling voice, the soul-convicted, Christian killer, Saul, mouthed the words, *Lord, what wilt thou have me to do?* In deep despair, the jailer who had shackled the preachers exclaimed, *Sirs, what must I do to be saved?*

These were not Bible scholars with inquiries to fill the gaps in their commentaries. These were not theologians questioning one another over the finer points of doctrine. These were pitiful pleadings of guilt-stricken sinners battling dark sins. These were mournful cries from consciences, thought to be condemned to hell. These were soul-wrenching confessions from the deep recesses of the very being. It was urgent. It was serious. It was pressing. It was real.

It was not the time to sort out the different *saves* taught in the Bible. It was not even the time to distinguish between grace and works. It was especially not the time to correct the wording of the question that had just been asked. As important as sound doctrine might be, these times were not the times to talk to the head. These moments were heart moments. These questions were soul questions. These troubles were not related to theology, but to conscience. The things of the head could be addressed at a later date, but right at the moment, something urgent was going on in the heart. Misunderstood doctrine was not the problem. Self-understood depravity was the problem. It was time for baptism to wash away those vile sins from the conscience of a vile sinner. Paul's words to these troubled souls were: *And now why tarriest thou? arise, and be baptized, and wash away thy sins, calling on the name of the Lord.*

Now there is no doubt that Paul consistently preached the blood of Christ as the eternal cure for sin. Paul preached the washing away of sins by the blood, the payment of debt by the blood, the forgiveness from God by the blood, the reconciliation to God by the blood, the perfection of sinners by the blood, the justification of the ungodly by the blood, the salvation of sinners by the blood, etc. Paul understood that the only way for a sinner to stand without condemnation at the judgment seat of God was by having been washed in the blood of Jesus. Paul was not confused about his doctrines, nor was he negligent to preach the truth. Paul could logically spell out the details of salvation by the blood of Jesus, as well as any man alive. Just look at the Book of Romans or the Book of Ephesians. Paul knew that it was important to understand that God's eternal salvation is by grace and blood, but he also knew that understanding the details of the plan was not the immediate solution to the problem of a guilt-stricken conscience.

Thus even though the blood of Christ is the only thing necessary, when it comes to God's eternal judgment of the sinner in the courtroom of heaven, it seems that something else might be necessary when it comes to the sinner's immediate judgment of himself in the courtroom of his own conscience. The ultimate thing, which will eventually reconcile the sinner within his own conscience, is to understand the doctrines of salvation by grace. Yet this is not the immediate answer to the urgent questions that come from the pricked heart. The night was too short to explain to the jailer all the doctrines in the Book of Romans. Maybe that time would come later, but for that night, the jailer's question needed a short answer.

The part of the story concerning the washing by blood for eternal judgment could come later, but the washing of the conscience by baptism was the most needed thing for the moment. Sometimes a man does not need to tarry. Some times are urgent times. There are times when guilty sinners need immediate answers, even solutions for right now. There are times when the conscience needs more attention than the cortex. There are times when the right words for the guilty sinner are: *Why tarriest thou? Arise, and be baptized, and wash away thy sins.*

So Paul offered baptism as an urgent cure for the guilty conscience. Likewise, Peter told those at Pentecost, who were pricked in their hearts over crucifying Jesus, to repent and be baptized. Thus, both men considered baptism to be the right response for guilt-stricken sinners. Yet in another place, Peter described baptism not as the solution for a **guilty** conscience, but the answer of a **good** conscience. *The like figure whereunto even baptism doth also now save us (not the putting away of the filth of the flesh, but* **the answer of a good conscience toward God**,*) by the resurrection of Jesus Christ* (1 Pet 3:21).

Before we tackle the guilty and the good conscience, let us consider Peter's statement in some detail. First of all, Peter called baptism a *figure*. This is what we have been saying all along. Baptism figuratively represents other things. Baptism is not the literal, but the figurative portrayal of the literal. Baptism is not the literal death, burial and resurrection of Jesus, but a figurative picture of His death, burial and resurrection. Baptism is not literally rising from the dead to a new life, but it figuratively represents rising up from the dead to walk in newness of life. Baptism is not the literal putting on of Christ, but the figurative putting on of Christ. In baptism the person is not literally engulfed with the Holy Ghost, but baptism represents the idea of an all-encompassing presence of the Holy Ghost.

Secondly, Peter said that *baptism doth also now save us.* The words, **now save**, certainly imply that Peter was not talking about eternal salvation. Yet, Peter even further made sure that we would not jump to the wrong conclusion about how baptism saves us, in that he immediately declared that baptism was *not the putting away of the filth of the flesh.* In this disclaimer, Peter clarified that he was not talking about the eternal salvation pertaining to the cleansing by the blood, which forever puts away the filth of the flesh in God's eyes. Thus, Peter fully agreed with Paul that baptism was not God's means to wash away sins eternally.

Yet it seems that Peter may have disagreed with Paul, when he finally stated that baptism is *the* **answer of a good conscience** *toward God.* Remember Paul's sense of urgency, when he told those who were under the burden of a **guilty conscience** to rise and be baptized. According to Paul the appropriate response (**answer**) of the **guilty conscience** is baptism. Yet Peter said that baptism is *the* **answer** *of a* **good conscience** *toward God.* Furthermore, it seems that Peter even contradicted himself with this statement, in that here he recommended baptism as the answer of a good conscience, whereas at Pentecost he had recommended baptism as the response to those with the guilty consciences.

So how can the one act of baptism be both the answer of a guilty conscience and the answer of a good conscience? The solution to this apparent contradiction lies in understanding that different people have different states of mind at different times. One person may be full of fears, as he thinks of himself, and feels to be a condemned sinner. Another person may be full of faith, as he thinks of his Savior, and feels to be a saved sinner. Where we previously learned of Paul's (and Peter's) words, spoken to guilt-stricken sinners, who had troubled hearts, here we have Peter's words, spoken to reconciled believers, who have peace in knowing that Jesus has successfully saved them.

Peter's words at Pentecost were to the sinner who had come to know that he had crucified God's Son. Peter's words here are to the sinner who has come to know that his sins are forgiven, because of the crucifixion of God's Son. Peter's words here are to the sinner who knows that salvation is not based on the corrupt works of the sinner, but on the perfect work of Jesus in saving sinners. Peter's words here are to the sinner, who according to his own conscience knows that he is guilty, but according to the gospel, he also knows that God judges him to be righteous, through the imputed righteousness of Christ.

The purpose of the gospel is to tell the sinner that Christ has washed away his sins, even to the point where God no longer sees any of his sins, and thus God has declared him to be innocent. When the sinner comes to realize and believe that God no longer judges him to be guilty, his guilty conscience is cleared. Instead of continuing to see himself to be condemned by his own guilty conscience, he now sees himself to be justified by his own cleared conscience, because he has come to see what Jesus accomplished in his behalf. Thus the guilty conscience that once feared God's eternal condemnation is now the good conscience that anticipates God's eternal justification, even a justification not based on the sinner's own works, but on the work of Christ. Baptism is the *answer of a good conscience*, that is the response of the cleared conscience of the sinner, who knows that he stands sinless before a Holy God, because of the salvation that is by Jesus. Any sinner whose conscience has been cleared by knowing that Jesus' death, burial and resurrection has accomplished his salvation is to respond from that good conscience by being baptized.

So Peter calls for the same response from the guilty and the good conscience. Peter says that baptism is the right response for the convicted sinner, who comes to know his sinfulness, and whose guilty conscience judges him, according to his own works. On the other hand, Peter says that baptism is also the right response for the relieved sinner, who comes to know the gospel of salvation by grace, and whose good conscience judges him, according to Jesus' finished work.

So sometimes the guilt-stricken, haunted-by-sin conscience cries: *Men and brethren, what shall we do?* The right answer for that conscience is: *Repent, and be baptized.* Yet sometimes the guilt-relieved, soothed-by-the-gospel conscience cries: *What doth hinder me to be baptized?* The right answer for that conscience is: *If thou believest with all thine heart, thou mayest.* Thus the response is the same for the guilty conscience, or the good conscience. The answer is the same for the sinner who has only come so far as to see his depravity, and for the sinner who has further come to see his deliverance. In either case, it is right for the sinner to confess his sins, to profess his Savior, to be baptized, and thereby, to enter into the church.

That brings us to our final significance of baptism. As we come out of the waters of our baptisms, we have come into the church. *Then they that gladly received his word **were baptized**: and the same day there **were added** unto them about three thousand souls* (Acts 2:41).

So we now recall that baptism is the non-word sermon that preaches Jesus' *death, burial and resurrection.* Baptism also pictures one who is raised to *walk in newness of life.* To be baptized is to figuratively *put on Christ.* Baptism represents *the promise* of the engulfing presence of the Holy Ghost around God-called children. Baptism is the answer for the convicted sinner, who feels the urgency to *wash away thy sins.* Baptism is the *answer of a good conscience* for the relieved sinner, who knows that Christ has already washed away his sins. Last but not least, baptism is the way to enter the church, and join with others who profess Jesus.

And now why tarriest thou? Arise, and be baptized!

21
What is Christian Joy?

The joy of the LORD is your strength (Neh 8:10). The joy of the Lord supports us in our journey. It is our crutch to lean on. Yet, we need to be sure as to what *the joy of the Lord* is before we lean too heavily on the wrong crutch.

The joy of the Lord is much different to the so-called joy of this world. *Folly is joy to him that is destitute of wisdom* (Pro 15:21). The unwise man imagines that he finds joy in the foolish things of the world. He senses a fleeting escape from his troubles in the frolicking of a night on the town. His supposed joy may endure for a night, but a hangover comes in the morning. Unlike the world's folly, the joy of the Lord is real and lasting joy. With the joy of the Lord, *weeping may endure for a night, but joy cometh in the morning* (Ps 30:5).

Perhaps every child of God is looking for an elusive 'something'. It is a mystical 'something' that often seems just out of our reach. We are not sure exactly what this 'something' even is, but we have this emptiness somewhere deep inside us that yearns to be filled. It is almost like a hole in our soul. We crave this obscure soul-satisfying 'something' that would make us feel contented.

The world's wisdom searches for this 'something', but it has no idea what it is looking for, or where to find it. The wise man Solomon looked for it in many places. He looked for it in his much gold. We sometimes think, "Oh, if I were just a rich man..." Solomon had enough money to buy anything his heart desired, but he did not find what he was looking for in what he could buy. Solomon had seven hundred wives and three hundred concubines, but he did not find what he was looking for in women. Solomon sought it in the works of his hands, but it was not there. He searched through wine and entertainment, but his answer was not there. Solomon tried it all. Solomon had it all.

The world would say that such a man would surely be content. Yet Solomon concluded that everything under the sun (all that is in this world) was *vanity* (nothingness or emptiness) *and vexation of spirit* (not contentment of spirit). Surely, we would think that the wisdom of Solomon could have found whatever it is that men are looking for. Yet, Solomon found that *in much wisdom is much grief; and he that increaseth knowledge increaseth sorrow* (Ecc 1:18). It seems that more wisdom only gives more realization of the emptiness of this world, even the nothingness of everything. We will never find what we are looking for in the things of this world.

Like Solomon, America looks for this elusive 'something' in what the world has to offer. In our so-called earthly wisdom, we chase after riches, lust after women, go for the gusto, and expand our horizons. Yet as far as finding what our souls truly seek, we are probably the most troubled nation ever. Spirits are vexed. Hearts are haunted. Souls are lonely. Booze is guzzled. Pills are popped. Minds are blown. Suicide runs rampant. Just listen to the popular songs of our times. The lyrics tell of the same emptiness that Solomon described. The songwriters do not tell us where to find what it is that we are seeking, but they do understand that we do not have it, and they sense that we all need it.

Solomon should have paid more attention to the words of his father, David. While Solomon was chasing his rainbows, David had left the words: *The LORD is my shepherd; I shall not want* (Ps 23:1). Instead of having a life filled with nothingness, David lived life wanting nothing. If the Lord was his shepherd, he wanted nothing more. Instead of vexation of spirit, David had contentment of spirit. He was filled with the very present presence of his Lord, and his soul rejoiced. The joy of the Lord was his strength.

America also needs to pay more attention to the words of David. We are a people obsessed with covetousness, with things, even with 'wants'. David had one thing, and no 'wants'. We have everything, and want more.

What did David have that eliminated all his desires for anything else? David knew the reality of the words: *The LORD is my shepherd.*

It is great to know that Jesus is the *good shepherd* (Jno 10:11). It is good to know that Jesus is the *great shepherd* (Heb 13:20). Yet David knew Jesus as: **my shepherd**. He belonged to Jesus, and Jesus belonged to him. David needed nothing beyond that. He wanted nothing more. He had the one thing that counted for everything. He had the one thing that made nothing else matter. His shepherd filled his life with *green pastures* and *still waters*. His shepherd restored his soul from the vexation of spirit that troubles the world. David did not fear his *walk through the valley of the shadow of death*. His shepherd would be there with him. David's cup ran over with joy. He knew that his shepherd's *goodness and mercy* would sustain him all the days of his life, and he had the certain hope that he would *dwell in the house of the LORD for ever*.

What more could a little lamb want beyond these things? The understanding that comes from this Psalm turns the world's nothingness into heaven's fullness. This Psalm restores the empty soul to one that overflows with joy. As I think about the Psalm, I am filled with joy, and the joy of the Lord is my strength.

Like David, Paul knew what it was to have no 'wants'. *Not that I speak in respect of want: for I have learned, in whatsoever state I am, therewith to be content. I know both how to be abased, and I know how to abound* (Phi 4:11-12). Paul did not speak about earthly 'wants'. He was not concerned with earthly 'wants'. He was in a prison and literally had nothing. Yet he could honestly say that he had no earthly 'wants'. He was content, whether he had lots or little. He was content with wherever he was and with whatever happened. His motto was: *I can do all things through Christ which strengtheneth me* (Phi 4:13). The joy of the Lord was Paul's strength.

Our lives should not be consumed with our earthly 'wants'. We can be content with whatever, if we have the one thing that really matters, even the promise that our Jesus will never leave us, or forsake us. *Be content with such things as ye have: for he hath said, I will never leave thee, nor forsake thee* (Heb 13:5). If we have the promise that God is with us, we need nothing more. If we know that *the LORD is my shepherd*, then our cups run over. If we truly have the joy of the Lord's presence in our lives, we want nothing else.

There is joy in knowing that the Lord is with us. When Jesus came into this world, the angel brought *good tidings of great joy* (Lk 2:10). In the Lord's presence, there was joy. When the seventy returned to Jesus, they came into His presence *with joy* (Lk 10:17). In the Lord's presence, there was joy. When Jesus came back from the grave, their sorrow turned to *great joy* (Mt 28:8). In Jesus' presence, there was joy. Indeed, those were joyful days, when God came into the world as a babe, and left the world as a resurrected King and Savior. In His presence, there was joy.

Since there is joy in the presence of the Lord, it seems that there might have been sadness after Jesus ascended back into heaven. Yet, there was still joy. *And it came to pass, while he blessed them, he was parted from them, and carried up into heaven. And they worshipped him, and returned to Jerusalem* ***with great joy*** (Lk 24:51-52). The Lord was gone, but they still had great joy. They had heard the angels say: *This same Jesus, which is taken up from you into heaven, shall so come in like manner as ye have seen him go into heaven* (Acts 1:11). They no longer enjoyed Jesus' physical presence, but they knew He was coming back. They no longer had His physical presence, but they still felt His spiritual presence, and the joy of the resurrected Lord became the strength of the Apostles.

So with great joy the Apostles returned to Jerusalem, as changed men, strong men, even fearless men. The cowards, who had stood afar off at Jesus' crucifixion, now boldly took their stands in the temple, publicly preaching the resurrected Jesus to all. The same Peter, who had three times said *I know him not*, took his stand at the judgment seat of Annas and Caiaphas. They asked Peter for the name of the man who had caused the lame man to leap. *By what power, or* ***by what name****, have ye done this?* (Act 4:7). They wanted a name. These were the same men who had crucified Jesus, the same men Peter had cowered to a few days ago. Now of all things, these men asked Peter to say the name of the man that Peter had previously claimed not to know. What a test of faith!

Surely, Peter remembered that Jesus had told him that he would someday be crucified for following Jesus. Surely, Peter considered that this might be the very day. Yet Peter boldly proclaimed: *Be it known unto you all, and to all the people of Israel, that by the name of Jesus Christ of Nazareth, whom ye crucified, whom God raised from the dead, even by him doth this man stand here before you whole* (Acts 4:10). Wow! Peter called Him by name.

Peter was a changed man, a different man. What if they killed him? So what! He had seen the reality of resurrection. His fears were gone. They all were changed. Those who had been consumed with fear became courageous. Those who had been so prone to strife came together. Jesus was gone, but they were filled with the Holy Ghost. Jesus was physically no longer with them, but His Spirit filled their souls. They were full of joy, and the joy of the Lord was their strength.

Long after Jesus had ascended, the Apostle John began a letter with the words: *That which was from the beginning, which we have heard, which we have seen with our eyes, which we have looked upon, and our hands have handled, of the Word of life* (1 Jno 1:1). John had heard the voice of God, had seen the face of God, had even touched God. He had known and loved the *Word of life*, even the Word that was God. After his reminiscing, John stated the purpose of his reflection. *That which we have seen and heard declare we unto you, that ye also may have fellowship with us: and truly our fellowship is with the Father, and with his Son Jesus Christ* (1 Jno 1:3). John claimed to still have a fellowship with the Father, and with His Son Jesus Christ. He wanted us to have this same fellowship with God.

John was not here referring to what he once had with Jesus, when he had seen Him eye to eye. He did not want to go back to a time when he was a younger man, so he might again find fellowship with Jesus. Jesus was long gone, but John still felt to be in the presence of Jesus, and Jesus was still in the presence of John. John wanted us to have this same kind of fellowship with the Father, and with the Son, so that we could be full of joy. Listen to the next words of John: *And these things write we unto you, that your joy may be full* (1 Jno 1:4).

John wrote to us so that our joy may be full, so that we may find what we are looking for in this world. John told us how we can have fullness, instead of emptiness. He told us how we can have contentment of spirit, instead of vexation of spirit. The one thing that can make a child of God happy in this world is fellowship with Jesus Christ. If we have the fellowship of Jesus, we have the way to be okay, even when everything is not okay. We need the fellowship of Jesus, so that our *joy may be full*, so that the joy of the Lord will be our strength.

Jesus said it like this: *The kingdom of heaven is like unto treasure hid in a field; which when a man hath found, he hideth, and **for joy thereof** goeth and selleth all that he hath, and buyeth that field* (Mt 13:44). In order to understand what Jesus was talking about, we must know what He meant by the *kingdom of heaven*. It is not surprising that this man from heaven would often talk about the kingdom of heaven. He even began His ministry with the subject. *From that time Jesus began to preach, and to say, Repent: for the kingdom of heaven is at hand* (Mt 4:17). Yet, what most people would find surprising is that Jesus' teachings about the kingdom of heaven had little to do with where we go when we die. Jesus said that *the kingdom of heaven is at hand*. If something is at hand, it is within reach. It can be taken hold of. It is 'right here' and 'right now'.

To show how Jesus used the words, consider the following passage: *Then cometh he to his disciples, and saith unto them, Sleep on now, and take your rest: behold, **the hour is at hand**, and the Son of man is betrayed into the hands of sinners. Rise, let us be going: behold, **he is at hand** that doth betray me* (Mt 26:45-46). "*The hour is at hand.*" As to time, it is happening 'right now'. "*He is at hand.*" As to place, it is happening 'right here'. The point is not that there is no such thing as an eternal heaven. Jesus sometimes spoke of that, too. The eternal heaven is real, but it is in another place and time. It is not 'right here' and 'right now'. We cannot now take hold of it. It is not *at hand*. Whatever Jesus was talking about is here and now.

If we assume that Jesus limits the idea of the *kingdom of heaven* to where we go when we die, we will never understand His message. When I was a teenager, I decided that I would read through the New Testament. Yet I only read a few chapters. At Matthew 13, when I read Jesus' teachings about selling all that you have and buying the kingdom of heaven, I became confused, and even frustrated. If heaven was by the sovereign grace that I had heard preached and learned to love, then why did I need to buy it? In my confusion, I shut my Bible and quit reading. I must have read over the *at hand* part. I had missed the 'right here' and 'right now' aspect of heaven, which followers of Jesus can experience in their hearts, and even in their lives, while still in this troubled world. I failed to understand that Jesus was talking about something that is available in this world, even something that is closely akin to the heaven that awaits us in the next world. I had not related the *kingdom of heaven* to experiencing the spiritual presence of Jesus in this present world. I had no idea that Paul talked about the same thing, but called it the *earnest of our inheritance* (Eph 1:14). I did not know about John's fellowship with Jesus in this world, so that our *joy may be full*, even that we may feel to be almost in heaven now. I had failed to realize that if I know that *the LORD is my shepherd*, then I do not want those things that Jesus said to sell anyway. Oh, the joy of the kingdom of heaven that is at hand far exceeds all we could otherwise have!

About the same subject, Jesus further said: *The kingdom of God cometh not with observation: Neither shall they say, Lo here! or, lo there! for, behold, the kingdom of God is within you* (Lk:20-21). We cannot see the 'at hand kingdom of heaven' with natural eyes. Neither can we hold it in natural hands. We experience it on the inside, even in our hearts and souls. It is real, but it exists in the spiritual realm. Paul said: *The kingdom of God is not meat and drink; but righteousness, and peace, and joy in the Holy Ghost* (Rom 14:17). It is not so much something that we do on the outside, like eating or drinking. It is something that we feel on the inside, like peace and joy. It is spiritual fellowship with the Father and Son, so that our *joy may be full*.

Surely, God's children, who are now in the eternal heaven with God, even now experience joy in the presence of Jesus. Surely, there is joy in singing the new song. *They sung a new song, saying thou art worthy...for thou wast slain and hast redeemed us to God by thy blood out of every kindred, and tongue, and people, and nation* (Rev 5:9). Yet, there is also joy for us down here, when we feel the presence of the Lord. Paul said: *The Lord is at hand* (Phi 4:5). We can now take hold of the

Lord. He is at hand. We can enjoy His presence 'right here' and 'right now'. The kingdom of heaven is at hand.

Jesus said that we are to sell all that we have in order to have this joy. John desired that we have this same joy. When we are in the spiritual presence of the Lord, our joy is full. When we are in the presence of the Lord, we have that elusive 'something', for which our souls crave. When we are in the presence of the Lord, we have that one thing that will give contentment. When we are in the presence of the Lord, we have the thing that will get us through, even give us strength. *The joy of the LORD is your strength.*

The same Holy Spirit that dwells in us inspired John to write the words about this personal relationship with Christ that we can take hold of even now. Oh, that we might have what John had! Oh, that we might experience the close, personal, spiritual fellowship with the Father and with His Son Jesus Christ! Oh, that our *joy may be full!*

Peter spoke of joy that we can experience, even while in the midst of the fires of the trials of this world. *Though now for a season, if need be, ye are in heaviness through manifold temptations: That the trial of your faith, being much more precious than of gold that perisheth, though it be tried with fire, might be found unto praise and honour and glory at the appearing of Jesus Christ: Whom having not seen, ye love; in whom, though now ye see him not, yet believing, ye rejoice with **joy unspeakable** and full of glory* (1 Pet 1:6-8). Consider the wonder in these words. A season of heaviness is upon me. Many and varied troubles engulf me. I am in a trial of fire, as gold in the refiner's furnace. As my faith is truly being tested and purified, *the appearing of Jesus Christ* is brought before my eyes of faith. In the turmoil of the scene, though I have never literally seen my Jesus, I know that I love Him (maybe more than I have ever known it before). Though I do not now see Him with my natural eyes, I believe in Him with all my heart. The wonder of it all is that as I see Him, I begin to rejoice even in the midst of my fiery trial. By God's grace, I am able to *rejoice with joy unspeakable and full of glory.*

I have felt this unexplainable joy. At the loss of my granddaughter, I felt this joy unspeakable in the saddest moment of my life. No doubt, I had mixed feelings. There was real sorrow, but there was also real joy. I am not promising you that it will all feel good, but there is good in the midst of the bad. There is peace that passes understanding. When Jesus appears, we rejoice in the Lord, even in the midst of our troubles. When we have fellowship with Jesus Christ, even when we are in His presence, there is joy.

The Bible does not teach that we should joy in the troubles themselves. While imprisoned in Rome, Paul wrote one of his last letters to the church at Philippi. Joy is the central theme of that prison epistle. Among other things, Paul told them: *Rejoice in the Lord alway: and again I say rejoice* (Phi 4:4). Paul did not tell us to rejoice in the troubles, but he told us that we can still *rejoice in the Lord*, even in the midst of the troubles.

Paul did not rejoice about being in prison, but Paul knew how to *rejoice in the Lord*, even in the midst of a prison. He had previously proved such, even while at Philippi. After being whipped and shackled in stocks in the inner prison, *at midnight Paul and Silas prayed and sang praises unto God* (Acts 16:25). Yes indeed, Paul practiced what he preached. He knew how to find joy in the Lord, even when there was none to be found otherwise.

Let us look at the following verse, in order to find two secrets as to how to experience joy in the worst of times. *Looking unto Jesus the author and finisher of our faith; who for the joy that was set before him endured the cross, despising the shame, and is set down at the right hand of the throne of God* (Heb 12:2). First of all, we take the verse to mean that we can use the faith that Jesus has given us to look directly to Jesus, in order to find direct help in our time of need. Secondly, we take the verse to say that we are to look to Jesus as our example of how to face our troubles. When Jesus faced His most difficult trial, even His crucifixion, He looked to the other side. He looked *for the joy that was set before him.* Looking toward heaven did not make the cross go away. He still had to endure it, and He still despised the shame of it. Yet, as He endured what was upon Him, He looked at what waited for Him.

We need to first use the faith that Jesus has given us, and look to Him, while in the midst of what we must endure. We also need to use that faith to see the other side, where our Jesus is *set down at the right hand of the throne of God*. Oh, the joy that is being experienced up there even at this moment! As we endure our daily crosses, may we look to Jesus, who looked *for the joy that was set before Him*. May we with patience wait for the joy, which waits for us. Like Jesus, we must sometimes endure the troubles. Yet in our troubles, may we use our faith to *rejoice in the Lord alway, and again I say rejoice*. May the joy that we find in the Lord be our strength.

Someday soon, we will leave this world of troubles. When that moment comes, may God bless us to see Jesus, even as Stephen saw Him. May we even *see the heavens opened and the Son of man standing on the right hand of God* (Acts 7:56). As the thief had his day so long ago, it will be our day. We will finally be with Jesus in paradise, where we will forever *rejoice with joy unspeakable and full of glory*. We will truly be where we *shall not want*. We will have said 'good-bye' to this world of vanity and to all its vexation of spirit. Even beyond contentment, we will be fully satisfied. *I shall be satisfied, when I awake, with thy likeness* (Ps 17:15).

As Jesus was heading home, He endured His cross knowing that joy was just ahead. He knew that *weeping may endure for a night, but joy cometh in the morning*. He looked for that joy that was set before Him, knowing that the joy would be forever and ever.

Yes, there will be joy in heaven, when we are blessed to be in the presence of the Lord forever. And there is joy in this world when we are blessed to be in the presence of the Lord right now. *These things write we unto you, that your joy may be full. The joy of the LORD is your strength*.

22
What is Christian Peace?

From his deathbed, Jacob spoke this prophecy to his son, Judah. *The sceptre shall not depart from Judah, nor a lawgiver from between his feet, until Shiloh come; and unto him shall the gathering of the people be* (Gen 49:10). The word, *Shiloh*, means *tranquil*. One named *Tranquil* was to come. He is called the *Prince of Peace* and the *King of Peace*. When He came, the heavenly hosts proclaimed, '*On earth peace*'. As Simeon held the *way of peace* in his arms, he said that he could now *depart in peace*. This Jesus was his *Peacemaker*.

Though the Bible never specifically divides peace into five levels, we can find much Bible truth by considering five levels of peace connected to this one called, *Shiloh*. What we will call *Level One Peace* is experienced in God's natural creation. Since the one called *Tranquil* is the Creator, it is not surprising that a sense of tranquility can result from His Creation. We feel this kind of peace while looking out at sunset on the ocean, or while looking up at the stars on a summer night, or while looking down at a newborn in our arms. This peace lies somewhere between contentment and amazement. The creature can sense it, as he ponders the Creator. It occurs when the mortal mind imagines the Eternal.

I recollect having this peace at the quiet dawning of a new day of a wilderness morning. Once upon a time, my teenage son and I were backpackers. We would spend days in the back country with only what our packs could hold. After miles of trekking, we would make camp, filter water, re-hydrate the powder we called supper, recollect the day beside a small fire, and retire to separate tents. (I snored too much for us to share a tent.)

Typical of a teenager, the '*boy*' slept in, but the '*old man*' awoke before the first hint of light. In the solitude of the darkness I would crawl out of my little tent and watch the woods come to life. I still remember the moments: the dawning of a day in the woods; the dim glow of near-dead embers from last night's fire; the silhouette of trees on the soft light in the east; the hint of the stir of the first breeze; the song of praise from an early bird; the steady breathing of a sleeping firstborn son (though by then a man, still my little boy); the smile of God on an old man by a little tent; the dawning of a day in the woods.

In these quiet moments of solitude, the wonder of creation captures us. As we pause to ponder the Creator's masterpiece, our minds are led to prayer and worship. *Shiloh* grants us this *peace like a river*, which H. G. Spafford spoke of in his song, "It Is Well with My Soul". Yet there are levels of peace that far exceed *peace like a river*. Spafford spoke of a greater peace with the words:

> *When sorrows like sea billows roll;*
> *Whatever my lot, Thou hast taught me to say,*
> *It is well, it is well with my soul.*

This man had just lost four daughters to the depths of the Atlantic Ocean. Leaning on the rail of his ship of disaster, the sorrows pounded his heart, like the never-ending waves on the side of the ship. Yet, in spite of his circumstances, and no matter his lot in life, Spafford spoke of a wellness in his soul.

This is what we will call *Level Two Peace*. Anybody can have 'gentle-flowing-river' peace, but Spafford claimed peace on a 'sea-billow-sorrow' day. The world cannot know peace in these moments. *And the way of peace have they not known* (Rom 3:17). Yet, God's children are able to know *the peace of God, which passeth all understanding* (Phi 4:7). This peace truly goes past what we can understand. Even the one who is experiencing this peace cannot understand how it is happening. Yet this peace really happens, when the Spirit of God touches the troubled spirit of His child.

The key to gaining a little understanding about the peace *which passeth all understanding* is to put the words in their context. Paul first said: *Rejoice in the Lord alway: and again I say, Rejoice* (Phi 4:4). Notice the words, **in the Lord**. We cannot rejoice in the loss of four daughters. Yet a child of God can rejoice *in the Lord*, even after such a loss. *In the Lord*, a man has hope of seeing those daughters again. *In the Lord*, a man finds grace to help in time of need. *In the Lord*, a man finds one that cared enough to give His life, so that those four daughters might live forever in heaven. Even at times *when sorrows like sea billows roll* a man can *rejoice in the Lord alway: and again I say, Rejoice.*

Paul further said: *The Lord is at hand. Be careful for nothing* (Phi 4:4-5). If *the Lord is at hand*, we can feel His presence. We can even put our hands in His hand. If we face trials holding the hand of the God of eternity, we can *be careful for nothing.* That is, we need not be full of cares about anything. We can cast our cares on Him. Our world may fall apart, but our God is still on His throne. His promises remain sure. He stands by our side. He holds our hands. *Whatever my lot, Thou hast taught me to say – The Lord is at hand.* And if *the Lord is at hand*, then *it is well with my soul.*

It surpasses all reasoning to think that Spafford could say, "Whatever my lot, it is okay." It blows our natural minds to think of saying such words at such a time. Yet, if we have learned to *rejoice in the Lord alway*, and if we truly know that *the Lord is at hand*, then we are to the point where *the peace of God, which passeth all understanding, shall keep your hearts and minds through Christ Jesus.*

When *the peace of God, which passeth all understanding* is keeping our *hearts and minds through Christ Jesus*, we have 'troubled heart' peace. Jesus began His last sermon with the words: *Let not your heart be troubled* (Jno 14:1). In the middle He said: *Peace I leave with you, my peace I give unto you: not as the world giveth, give I unto you. Let not your heart be troubled, neither let it be afraid* (Jno 14:27). Jesus ended His sermon with these words: *These things have I spoken unto you, that in me ye might have peace. In the world ye shall have tribulation: but be of good cheer, I have overcome the world* (Jno 16:33).

Jesus did not promise us the world's prosperity. Nor did He tell us that great faith would deliver us from the world's troubles. Jesus said *in the world ye shall have tribulation.* In this world sorrows like sea billows will continue to roll. Yet Jesus said we can *be of good cheer*, because He has *overcome the world.* Though the world is troubled, *let not your heart be troubled. Peace I leave with you, my peace I give unto you.* Not in the world, but in Jesus we find peace. Even in the midst of the world's troubles, when we have the peace that Jesus gives us, we have *the peace of God, which passeth all understanding.* Even though the world does its best to trouble our hearts, *the peace of God, which passeth all understanding shall keep your hearts and minds through Christ Jesus.*

So *Level One Peace* hinges on external circumstances. It only happens when we stop to smell the roses, while life's river is flowing gently. Yet *Level Two Peace* can occur even *when sorrows like sea billows roll.* It is *'whatever my lot'* peace. It makes no sense how we can feel peace in spite of overwhelming situations, but the Bible and our experiences teach us that this peace of mind does happen. Thus, *'whatever my lot'* peace far exceeds *'peace like a river'* peace. Yet the next level of peace surpasses anything yet mentioned. So far, we have looked at peace of mind in the mind of a man about earthly circumstances. What we will call *Level Three Peace* considers peace of mind in the mind of God about eternal circumstances. If the peace of mind in man about earthly things passes our understanding, how much more could be said of the peace of mind in the infinite mind of God about heavenly things? What we call *Level Three Peace* is the peace of mind that God feels toward sinners.

God has a deep hatred of sin. His justice demands vengeance against sinners. *The Lord was as an enemy* (Lam 2:5). Can anything appease such an angered God? Who could bring this Holy God to be at peace with sinful men? *When we were enemies, we were reconciled to God by the death of his Son* (Rom 5:10). Jesus' death reconciled the enmity. *God...hath reconciled us to himself by Jesus Christ* (2 Cor 5:18).

Since Jesus is God, God has reconciled us to God by God. God reconciled us to Himself, all by Himself. We did not help. God gets all the glory! We had no means to make peace with an angry God, but Jesus took away all the sins of all for whom He died, and thereby made peace between Holy God and His children.

This Jesus-accomplished peace changed God's disposition toward sinners. This Jesus-made peace spared God's children from the burning hell reserved for His enemies. This peace affords us entry into the eternal peace of heaven itself. Thanks to Jesus, the God who *was as an enemy* is now at peace with His children.

We think again of the Savior called *Shiloh*. When He came into this world, the angels sang, *'Peace on earth'*. Before He left this world, He had made eternal peace in heaven, between the Holy God of heaven and some of the vilest sinners of earth. Surely, there must be a significant difference between peace on earth and peace in heaven. Surely, *Level Three Peace* far surpasses the first two levels. Surely, eternal peace in heaven goes much beyond a quiet morning in the woods! Please do not misunderstand. I still like a quiet morning in the woods. I even cherish those moments. Yet eternal peace in heaven has to be infinitely greater than any momentary *peace like a river*. Furthermore, *the peace of God, which passeth all understanding* is as nothing, when contrasted to the eternal peace of God in heaven. The temporal peace of God that gets us through the world's troubles pales in comparison to the eternal peace of God that gets us through heaven's gates. If the wonder of the peace of providence passes our understanding, how much more does the wonder of eternal peace go beyond our imagination!

There is an infinite difference between *Level Two Peace* and *Level Three Peace*. There is a quantum leap from the peace of mind that man experiences regarding earthly circumstances to the peace of mind that God experiences regarding eternal circumstances. This attitude of peace, which occurs in the mind of God, as He considers a sinner that had been His enemy, far exceeds the peace that occurs in the mind of man, as he finds reassurance in God's providence. As far as the heavens are higher than the earth, so is the peace of heaven higher than any peace experienced by those who reside on this earth. As far as His ways are higher than our ways, so is the peace in the infinite mind of God higher than anything pertaining to the finite minds of men.

Praise *Shiloh* for this eternal peace! Surely the greatest moment of all moments was when *Tranquil* made peace between the God of heaven and hell-bound sinners. The greatest event of all events was when *Shiloh* made atonement for wretchedness in the mind of

Holiness. The most glorious thing of all things was when God reconciled us to Himself by Jesus Christ. How can it be that the all-righteous God can accept something like me? *Shiloh* is the answer. *Tranquil!* Wow! The perfectly righteous God will forever dwell with a sinner like me, thanks to a man named *Shiloh!* Jesus was my 'Way of Peace', even my 'Peacemaker'. Peace! Reconciliation! I am justified! God is satisfied! Christ is glorified! *Shiloh! Tranquil!* What a name for my Savior!

Thus far, we have considered *Level Two Peace* that exists in the mind of the man, who knows the God of providence. We have also considered *Level Three Peace* that exists in the mind of God, who knows that *God...hath reconciled us to himself by Jesus Christ.* What we will call *Level Four Peace* somewhat combines these two. Like the second level of peace, this fourth level is a peace that exists in the minds of men. Yet, like the third level of peace, this fourth level concerns what is in the mind of God.

This fourth level of peace occurs in the mind of a man, when the man comes to know what is in the mind of God. This peace of mind in man happens, when a man comes to know what God already knows about the eternal peace that Jesus made between God and man. When we come to know that God already knows that Jesus has made God to be at peace toward us, then we can in our minds feel to be at peace toward God. To put it simply, *Level Four Peace* is the peace that exists in the mind of the man, who knows that the mind of God is at peace with him.

We return to the words: *God...hath reconciled us to Himself by Jesus Christ.* Since God did the reconciling, we can be sure that God knows He has done it. Surely from before time, God knew that this reconciliation was going to occur. As it occurred, God watched all the details unfold, just as He had planned. God even now knows what the Bible clearly proclaims, even that Jesus has made peace between God and sinners. In the mind of God, there is no doubt, as to what Jesus accomplished on the cross. God knows for certain that the result of this peace is that all His children will be with Him forever in heaven.

Now, God knows what God knows, whether we know it or not. Moreover, our not knowing what we do not know, cannot make God not know what He already knows. The point is that God knows that He has *reconciled us to Himself by Jesus Christ*, whether we know it or not. Some think that man has to believe that Jesus did what He did, in order for it to become real. God said in His Bible that He has *reconciled us to Himself by Jesus Christ*. That statement is fact, and God knows it is true, whether we know it or not, whether we believe it or not. If we do not know that God has *reconciled us to Himself by Jesus Christ*, our lack of knowledge cannot make God not know what He already knows. Yet if we do know what God already knows about having *reconciled us to Himself by Jesus Christ*, then we can have peace in our minds, like God has in His.

Do we know this truth that God knows so well? Are we sure that God has *reconciled us to Himself by Jesus Christ*? God's mind is at peace concerning what Jesus accomplished, but do we have peace of mind concerning what Jesus accomplished? Do we have peace of mind concerning the idea that God is at peace with us? Do we know for sure that Jesus has already made God to be at peace toward us?

Many of God's heaven-bound children have eternal life, but still wonder if they have it. There is a difference in having eternal life, and having the assurance of knowing that we have eternal life. Many of God's children go through life wondering if they are saved. There is a difference in being eternally saved, and having the peace in knowing that we are eternally saved. It is possible to have already been born again, and to exist in the state of having eternal salvation, yet still to exist in the state of mind of not knowing that we have the eternal salvation. *Level Four Peace* is the peace of mind that exists in the mind of the man, who knows (and is sure) that God knows (and is sure) about the eternal peace that Jesus made.

Surely we come to have this peace, when we come to know what God already knows. We have peace of mind about our eternal destiny, when we come to know that God already knows that He has *reconciled us to Himself by Jesus Christ*. If we do not know this thing, we have doubts and fears in our minds. Yet, if we come to know this thing that God already knows, and if we come to know that God is sure of this thing, then we can have a contented peace of mind concerning our eternal acceptance with the Holy God.

The very purpose of the true gospel minister is *to guide our feet into the way of peace* (Lk 1:79). True peace comes in knowing that our salvation is of the Lord. God's plan of salvation, which is by grace, and grace alone, needs no *ifs, ands* or *buts* added to it. God's grace stands alone to save God's people. God is totally satisfied with Jesus' finished work on the cross. By Jesus, and Jesus alone, God is at peace with us.

If we know these things about our salvation, then we know what God already knows. If our minds know what God already knows, we have the peace of mind of knowing that God's mind is at peace toward us. If we know, without doubt or disclaimer, that Jesus has reconciled us to God, then we can have a peace of mind that few of God's heaven-bound children now experience. This peace is what we call *Level Four Peace*.

As we near the end of our thoughts on peace, let us return to the words of H. G. Spafford. He described what we call *Level One Peace* with the words: *When peace like a river attendeth my way.* This is that soul-soothing, pause-and-ponder God kind of peace. Imagine what the Apostles felt when Jesus said to the raging storm, *Peace, be still* (Mr 4:39). There was *a great calm* in the presence of the one named *Tranquil.* There still is!

Spafford wrote of *Level Two Peace* with the words: *When sorrows like sea billows roll, whatever my lot, Thou hast taught me to say, It is well, it is well with my soul.* A declaration of soul wellness while gazing into the depths that held his daughters seems quite impossible. The world cannot understand such an irrational attitude. Even the child of God who experiences this providential peace of God does not understand how it can happen. This peace passes all understanding. Yet, men like Spafford (and Winfrey) can attest to the world that it is real. It is not explainable, but it is real peace that can overcome real despair.

Spafford expressed *Level Three Peace* in the words:

My sin, oh the bliss of this glorious thought!
My sin, not in part, but the whole,
Is nailed to His cross and I bear it no more.

Oh, the bliss of the wonder that God's Son died on a cross for me! In the words of Stuart Hine:

And when I think of God His Son not sparing,
Sent Him to die, I scarce can take it in;
That on the cross, my burden gladly bearing,
He bled and died to take away my sin.

To think that God sent His Eternal Son, His Perfect Son, His Beloved Son! It seems too good to be true. My mind cannot fathom such a God.

For some unexplainable reason God loved me enough to send His Precious Son to a cross to pay a debt that I owed. When I further think that Jesus willingly died for me, I am brought to tears. Tears of sorrow and tears of joy! What love! What a Friend of sinners! What a God!

Moreover, when God spared not His Son, but sent Him to die, God *reconciled us to Himself by Jesus Christ*. When Jesus gladly bore our burdens by nailing our sins to His cross, God *reconciled us to Himself by Jesus Christ*. Peace was made. God is satisfied. To God be all the glory! Eternity will be too short to praise our God for the gift of His Son. Eternity will be too short to praise our Savior for His unselfish, sufficient salvation of sinners. *Praise the Lord, praise the Lord, Oh, my soul.*

Perhaps Spafford alluded to *Level Four Peace* with the words:

Let this blessed assurance control.

A child of God can have eternal salvation, without having the assurance that he has the salvation. In God's mind, the salvation of His children is past tense, even a 'done deal'. Their debt is paid in full. Nothing further is required. It is finished. God is satisfied. Salvation is accomplished.

Since God has reconciled us to Himself by Himself, God's children have eternal salvation, and none can pluck one of them from the God who saved them. When a hell-bound sinner comes to understand God's foolproof plan of salvation, he senses the assurance that only salvation by grace can offer. When the sinner understands that he has already been reconciled to God by Jesus Christ, his guilt-stricken mind experiences indescribable relief. He has peace of mind concerning his eternal destiny. He has joy in his heart, and rest in his soul. He has *blessed assurance*. He has the peace and assurance about his eternity that only comes through understanding that salvation is of the Lord. This peace of mind concerning the next world is the greatest thing a man can have in this world. *Let this blessed assurance control.*

We finally come to what we will call *Level Five Peace*. Spafford certainly proclaimed this ultimate peace with the words:

> *And Lord haste the day when the faith shall be sight,*
> *The clouds be rolled back as a scroll;*
> *Tthe trump shall resound and the Lord shall descend;*
> *Even so, it is well with my soul.*

The voice of the archangel! The blast of the trumpet! The coming down of the Lord Omnipotent, Savior King! The glorious appearing of that Great God, and our Savior Jesus Christ! Resurrection morning! The dead live again! Wow!!

All has changed. No more death; no more tears. No more doubts; no more fears. No more battles with sinful flesh. No more looking through a glass darkly. Our faith is sight! The clouds are rolled back, all barriers removed, heaven's door opened, nothing between Jesus and me! No more envisioning the Savior's face. No more imagining what He looks like. Oh, to see Him, as He is! To finally be able to glorify Him with perfect untainted praise! To at last be totally satisfied! All will be well with my soul, with my mind, with my heart, and with my resurrected body. *Lord, haste the day. Even so, come Lord Jesus* (Rev 22:20).

The hope of eternal life! A time of timeless, endless, perfect peace is a few days away!

> *There is coming a day when no heartaches shall come,*
> *No more clouds in the sky, no more tears to dim the eye;*
> *All is **peace** forevermore on that happy golden shore.*
> *What a day, glorious day that will be!* (Jim Hill)

All is 'what'? All is peace. Everything peace. Everywhere peace. All-the-time peace. Peace without end. Forevermore peace. Ultimate peace! A life forever, and ever, where all is peace! What a day! What a glorious day! What an eternity! What a glorious eternity! All by a man named *Shiloh*! What a God!!

23
What is Christian Hope?

The wonder of joy, peace and hope! If we can sense joy when the world is sad, if we can find peace when the world is troubled, and if we can have hope when the world is hopeless, we are of all men most blessed. Feelings of joy, peace and hope will sustain our souls, even in the midst of the daily trials of life. Each of the three provides its own unique kind of comfort, but the three are so intertwined, that each depends on the others to bring full contentment to the soul.

In a prayer for the Christians at Rome, Paul tied together the three Bible concepts: joy, peace and hope. *Now the God of **hope** fill you with all **joy** and **peace** in believing, that ye may abound in **hope**, through the power of the Holy Ghost* (Rom 15:13). Paul did not pray for a little joy and peace, just to get them through. He asked *the God of hope* to *fill you with **all** joy and peace*. Paul noted that this soul-filling joy and peace comes *in believing*. He further explained that the joy and peace was so *that ye may abound in hope*. So 'abounding hope' was Paul's ultimate desire. As Paul ended his prayer, he acknowledged that all this was possible *through the power of the Holy Ghost*.

Let us start by focusing on the words: *in believing*. I suppose God can directly pour joy, peace and hope into our souls, but Paul did not pray for that in this prayer. He prayed that by the means of believing, we would be filled with joy and peace, so that our hope might abound. So if believing is the means to joy, peace and hope, many would say that we just need to believe ourselves into this blissful triad. Yet, such a belief about believing is not based on the Bible.

I do not argue that believing is a prerequisite to joy, peace and hope. I just say that God's gift of faith is a prerequisite to believing. Most of today's Christians seem to think that we can just dream up faith by our natural abilities. It is as if we can just do a little faith, and rise up to a spiritual realm, where we see and hold to heavenly things. Faith is not imagination. Faith is not fantasizing about spiritual things with a natural mind. God defines faith as *the substance of things hoped for, the evidence of things not seen* (Heb 11:1). God's miracle of faith gives real present substance to future hoped for things, so that what we hope for becomes as if it is already real. The wonder of faith proves to our souls the truth of spiritual things, to such an extent that we can even see invisible things in the spiritual realm. God's miraculous faith allows God's child to (even now) take hold of what he hopes for, to (even now) see what he looks for. Through the miracle of faith, we can begin to experience something akin to what is in heaven, even while we are still on earth.

So faith is not something that we just decide to have. Faith is not something that we just do on our own. Faith is a God-given miracle. The Bible is clear about the source of faith. Faith is the gift of God (Eph 2:8). Faith is a fruit (result) of the Spirit (Gal 5:22). Jesus is the author of our faith (Heb 12:2). It is given unto God's people to believe (Phi 1:29). The Bible teaches that it takes the great power of God for us to be able to believe, even the same exceeding great power that it took to raise Jesus from the grave (Eph 1:19-20). Believing is not something we choose to do on our own. In order for a person to believe, God must first directly implant the gift of faith into that person. Faith is a miracle!

So joy, peace and hope come through believing, and the ability to believe comes by the God-given miracle of faith. Yet beyond the ability to believe, we also need to know what to believe, in order to experience real joy, peace and hope. This is where preaching the gospel comes in. True joy, peace and hope come in hearing and believing the gospel of salvation by grace, and grace alone. Genuine joy, peace and hope come in believing that our eternal salvation is totally of the Lord. If we know that our eternal life is grounded in God's unchangeable plan of amazing grace, and if we know that nothing can stop that plan, then we have the assurance that affords us real joy, peace and hope.

So God's gift of faith *through the power of the Holy Ghost* lets God's children be able to believe, and the preaching of the gospel *through the power of the Holy Ghost* lets God's children know what to believe, so that *in believing* the gospel of salvation by grace alone, *the God of hope* will *fill you with all joy and peace, that ye may abound in hope*. To *abound in hope* is to be on Peter's mountaintop of '*joy unspeakable*'. To *abound in hope* is to be in Paul's paradise of the '*peace that passeth understanding*'. To *abound in hope* is to mount up on wings as eagles, and to walk above the troubled waves. Oh, the wonder of 'abounding hope'!

Now joy, peace and hope are each important. Yet hope is perhaps the greatest of the three, because of its essential view of the future. By definition, hope is present desire, based on future expectations. So we possess joy, peace and hope, all three for help through the trials of today. Yet hope is the one that always looks toward tomorrow. It is hard to imagine real joy or peace in this present world, without a hope-filled view of the future. Joy and peace come by knowing that the troubles we endure down here are nothing, compared to the glory that awaits us up there. So the more hope we have in the 'up there', the more joy and peace we have in the 'down here'. Christian hope is not based in the things of this world. Christian hope is based in heaven. Paul put the empty hopes of this world in perspective with these words: *If in this life only we have hope in Christ, we are of all men most miserable* (1 Cor 15:19).

The Bible does not generally connect hope with this world. The Bible ties hope to resurrection. As Paul faced death, he tied his hope to resurrection three different times. He declared to the mob of Jews: *...of the **hope** and **resurrection** of the dead I am called in question* (Acts 23:6). He confessed to Governor Felix to *have **hope** toward God...that there shall be a **resurrection** of the dead* (Acts 24:15). He preached to King Agrippa: *I stand and am judged for the **hope** of the promise made of God unto our fathers: Unto which promise our twelve tribes, instantly serving God day and night, **hope** to come. For which **hope**'s sake, king Agrippa, I am accused of the Jews. Why should it be thought a thing incredible with you, that God should **raise the dead**?* (Acts 26:6-8).

In Paul's letters, he tied his hope to the appearing of Jesus at the resurrection. *Looking for that blessed* **hope**, *and the glorious* **appearing** *of the great God and our Saviour Jesus Christ* (Titus 2:13). John tied his hope to Jesus' appearance at the resurrection. **When he shall appear**, *we shall be like him; for we shall see him as he is. And every man that hath this* **hope** *in him purifieth himself, even as he is pure* (1 Jno 3:2-3). Peter's hope hinged on the resurrected living Jesus, who has promised to come back for us: ...*a lively* **hope** *by the* **resurrection** *of Jesus Christ from the dead* (1 Pet 1:3). The hope of God's people is that Jesus is coming back to raise the dead, even that He is going to give us eternal life. The Christian hope is resurrection.

The *hope* of the Bible is not the same as the *hope* we often speak of in our everyday conversation. In today's language someone might say, "I hope I win the lottery." Yet everybody knows that such a thing is very doubtful. The Greek word, *elpis*, (which is translated as *hope*) does not refer to some long-shot, pie-in-the-sky, happily-ever-after, never-really-going-to-happen fairytale. *Elpis* speaks of a future event with assurance of its happening. At this point, resurrection is still just a hope that is somewhere out in the future. Yet resurrection is a certain hope. It is reality. It is just not here yet. The hope of eternal life is a hope that is going to happen.

Three times in his letter to Titus, Paul spoke of our hope of eternal life, and each time he proved in a different way the certainty of our hope. Paul first said: *In* **hope of eternal life**, *which God, that cannot lie, promised before the world began* (Titus 1:2). Even before creation, the God who cannot lie had already promised eternal life. In His Covenant of Grace, God had already established His unchangeable plan of salvation, even before He created Adam. So by two irreversible actions of God, we can be certain that eternal life is certain. Our sure hope of eternal life is based in both the irreversible purpose of God, and the irrefutable promise of God: *Wherein God, willing more abundantly to shew unto the heirs of promise the immutability of* **his counsel**, *confirmed it by* **an oath**: *That by* **two immutable things**, *in which it was impossible for God to lie, we might have a strong consolation, who have fled for refuge to lay hold upon the* **hope** *set before us* (Heb 6:17-18). God's immutable counsel is His irrevocable, irresistible determinate purpose to give eternal life to His children. God's immutable oath is His inflexible, inevitable binding promise to give eternal life to His children.

Eternal life is certain because God always does what He purposes and promises. *I am God, and there is none else; I am God, and there is none like me, Declaring the end from the beginning... My counsel shall stand, and I will do all my pleasure ...I have spoken it, I will also bring it to pass; I have purposed it, I will also do it* (Is 46:9-11). Because God is unchangeable, His people will never perish. *I am the LORD, I change not; therefore ye sons of Jacob are not consumed* (Mal 3:6). We have strong hope in God's unchangeable promise of eternal life. This hope is truly a refuge for our souls. Eternal life is certain. God promised it.

Paul next mentioned hope in the words: *Looking for that blessed **hope**, and the glorious appearing of the great God and our Saviour Jesus Christ; Who gave himself for us...* (Titus 2:13-14). Here hope is tied to Jesus' appearance at the resurrection, but further tied to the thought that Jesus ***gave himself for us***. The point here is that if Jesus came the first time to give His life for us, so that we would have eternal life, then He will surely come back the second time to give us the eternal life. Since Jesus endured the shame of the dying part, we can be certain that He will not miss the honor of the resurrecting part.

Along the same line of reasoning, since God went so far as to give His Son, it is sensible that He will also give the eternal life that His Son secured. *If God be for us, who can be against us? He that spared not his own Son, but delivered him up for us all, how shall he not with him freely give us all things* (Rom 8:31-32)? If God spared not His own Son, but delivered Him up for us, there can be no doubt that God is for us. If God was for us to the point of giving His Son for us, then nothing can ever turn God against us. The God, who went so far as to deliver up His Son in order that we might have eternal life, will certainly someday give us the eternal life.

So since the God who cannot lie has promised eternal life, it is improper to think that He will not give the eternal life. Yet, for the sake of finding certain assurance of our hope of eternal life, let us attempt to reason in what is unreasonable. If God could have

denied His very essence of being truth, and taken back His promise
of eternal life, He surely would have done it before Jesus' death on
the cross. Or if God could have changed His immutable plan of
salvation, He surely would have changed it before Jesus' death on
the cross. The point is that since God followed through with the
death on the cross part, nothing can stop Him from the eternal life
part. If God did not take back His promise, or change His plan, at
the moment when He faced the cross, then it is certain that He is
totally committed to saving His people from their sins.

So on the basis of reasoning (which is admittedly based in the
unreasonable realm of the impossible), I submit to you that if God
has gone so far as to deliver His Son to the cross, and if God has
gone so far as to go to the cross, then nothing can stop God from
giving eternal life to all the ones Jesus died for. As we consider the
commitment God has thus far proved toward His plan of salvation,
it is only reasonable, even absolutely certain, that eternal life is
absolutely certain. God has already paid for it.

Paul finally spoke of hope in the words: *Not by works of
righteousness which we have done, but according to his mercy he saved us,
by the washing of regeneration, and renewing of the Holy Ghost; Which he
shed on us abundantly through Jesus Christ our Saviour; That being
justified by his grace, we should be made heirs according to the **hope of
eternal life*** (Titus 3:5-7). Some admit that God promised eternal life,
and they further affirm that Christ paid for eternal life, but then
they ask the sinner to someway work his way into the eternal life.
This loophole in their proposed plan of salvation takes all the
certainty out of our hope of eternal life. If our eternal life depends
on us, then our certain hope of eternal life goes out the window. If
we have to do something good enough, or think something right
enough, in order to save ourselves to heaven, then our certain hope
of going to heaven inevitably becomes uncertain.

If our hope is in our works, how much good is good enough? If
our hope is in our faith, how much faith is faith enough? If the
apostles' faith was such that Jesus called it *little faith*, or even *no
faith*, how can we put any faith in our faith? If our hope is in our
hoping hard enough, we flail in a sea of doubt. If our eternal life

hinges in any way on us, our hope of eternal life becomes more uncertain, than certain.

According to Paul's words, our eternal salvation does not hinge on our works, but on the work of the Holy Ghost to regenerate us to that eternal life. We do not actively do anything to cause our new births. We are passive recipients, while the new birth is *shed on us abundantly through Jesus Christ*. We do not actively do anything to make ourselves heirs. We are passive recipients, as we are *made heirs according to the hope of eternal life*. There is no weak link in God's plan of salvation, because in God's plan of salvation, God does all the saving. From start to finish, our eternal life is totally of God. God promised it. God paid for it. God applies it. That is what makes it so certain! Indeed, our hope of eternal life is **a hope that is going to happen!**

So how can we have the certain hope of eternal life? To have certain hope of eternal life, we need to be certain about God's plan of salvation that gives eternal life, for certain. Our eternal life is anchored in God's plan of salvation by grace, and grace alone. Before time, the Father purposed to save His people, and His purposes always come to pass. In the Covenant of Grace, God promised to save His people, and He is the God who keeps His promises. God's infallible plan and failsafe promise guarantee the certainty of salvation for all God chose to save.

On the cross, Jesus redeemed His people from their sins and secured for them eternal life. The angel said, ...*He shall save His people from their sins* (Mt 1:21). Jesus did save His people. The successful finished work of Jesus guarantees the certainty of the salvation of every one for whom Jesus died. In time, the Holy Spirit breathes eternal life into each one of God's elected and redeemed people. Salvation is not by man's help. 'Born again' is totally by God's grace. The Spirit moves as He pleases, and so it is with everyone that is born of the Spirit. The life giving work of the Holy Spirit guarantees the certainty of the salvation of all God's children.

At the natural death of each of God's children, their spirit goes to paradise. At the last day, each of them will be in glory. There will be none lost, and none missing. From start to finish, salvation is of the Lord. God planned it before the world began. God paid for it on the cross. God applies it at the new birth. God assures it in the end. To God be all the glory!

God's children can have eternal life, without knowing anything about the certainty of God's plan of giving eternal life. Yet only God's children, who are certain about the certainty of God's plan to save them, can have a certain certainty about their hope of eternal life. Oh what joy and peace comes from the certain hope of eternal life!

There are many benefits in knowing the certainty of God's plan of salvation, and having the certain hope of eternal life. Knowing the truth about certain salvation frees you from doubts. *Ye shall know the truth, and the truth shall make you free* (Jno 8:32). Having the certain hope about certain salvation guards the mind: *...putting on the breastplate of faith and love; and for an helmet, the hope of salvation* (1 Ths 5:8). Knowing the certain hope of resurrection gives patience in troubles: *...if we hope for that we see not, then do we with patience wait for it* (Rom 8:25). Knowing the certain hope of resurrection leads to purity. *And every man that hath this hope in him purifieth himself, even as he is pure* (1 Jno 3:3). Knowing the certain hope of resurrection saves us. *For we are saved by hope* (Rom 8:24).

Let us look closer at the words: *For we are saved by hope.* This does not mean that we can hope our way into heaven. That is Wizard of Oz mentality. That sham of a wizard told Dorothy to close her eyes, click her heels together three times, hope real hard, and she could hope herself from Oz to Kansas. Only a child would really believe such a thing. *The Wizard of Oz* was a movie. Besides that, Dorothy was dreaming. Heel clicking and hoping have never gotten anybody to Kansas, and if we cannot hope ourselves to a nearby Kansas, how can we expect to hope ourselves to a faraway heaven? Now we all may hope to get to heaven, but our hoping to get to heaven is not what saves us to heaven. The Lord Jesus Christ saves us and gets us to heaven.

Yet that certain hope that Jesus is going to get us to heaven will save us right here. In the context of Paul's writing, '*we are saved by hope*', is sandwiched between groaning within ourselves as we wait for the resurrection, and being in such despair that we forget how to pray. When we come to this point, we need help. We need deliverance. We need to be saved from the misery that we feel. Having the certain hope of eternal life lifts us above the troubles of this life. Having the certain hope that we will soon be in heaven helps us get through a few more days of 'down here'. That is how we are saved by hope.

Oh the sadness of living life without hope! Job knew what it was to lose hope. In his troubles he cried: *My days...are spent without hope* (Job 7:6). Satan tries to rob us of our hope. Some mocked when Paul preached the hope of resurrection. Some said that there was no resurrection of the dead. Others said the resurrection was already past. With feeble arguments, the Sadducees challenged Jesus that such a thing could not be. Scoffers still say, "How can the dead be raised?" I cannot tell you how the dead are raised. I do not know how. Yet with certainty, I can tell you **that** the dead will be raised. I can also tell you with certainty that God certainly knows how to do it. Oh, the blessing of having a certain hope!

Paul prayed *that ye may know what is the hope of his calling* (Eph 1:18). If we know this hope, it will save us in times of despair. The hope of something better helps us through our troubles now. We read of a day when all troubles will be gone. *God shall wipe away all tears from their eyes; and there shall be no more death, neither sorrow, nor crying, neither shall there be any more pain: for the former things are passed away* (Rev 21:4). I regularly preach to imprisoned souls in nursing homes. Those lonely dying mortals know how it feels to be close to death. They know pain and sorrow. They know misery. Yet, they hope for something better. When I preach of resurrection, smiles replace the tears. When we sing together of heaven, joy comes alive. They yearn for their ultimate peace. Their hope is now real, but their hope will soon be sight.

Paul put things in perspective when he compared this world to the next: *For I reckon that the sufferings of this present time are not worthy to be compared with the glory which shall be revealed in us* (Rom 8:18). Resurrection fixes everything! The hope of resurrection sure helps things here.

You need the certain hope of eternal life, whether you face your own death, or the death of a loved one, *that ye sorrow not, even as others which have no hope* (1 Ths 4:13). Even with hope, we still sorrow at death, but we sorrow not like those who have no hope.

The certain hope of eternal life brought Paul to proclaim an unworldly view about dying: *For I am now ready to be offered, and the time of my departure is at hand. I have fought a good fight, I have finished my course, I have kept the faith: Henceforth there is laid up for me a crown of righteousness, which the Lord, the righteous judge, shall give me at that day: and not to me only, but unto all them also that love his appearing* (2 Tim 4:6-8). As Paul faced death, his certain hope of eternal life saved him.[1]

Paul had spoken many times of the connection between hope and resurrection. He was convinced of the certainty of that hope of a resurrection, which the God who cannot lie had promised. Paul had seen his resurrected Lord, who died for him, and Paul could hardly wait to see Him again. He had often groaned within himself waiting for the resurrection. He was ready to fight his final battle, even ready to be offered as a martyr for Christ. Paul's certain hope that eternal life awaited him saved him from his natural fears. This hope will save all God's children who are looking for Jesus as they face death.

The certain hope of eternal life will get you through life. It will get you through death. It will get you through anything and everything. The Lord is coming back. What a hope!

---

[1] Paul's hope of eternal life had nothing to do with how Paul would be saved to eternal life. Yet, Paul's certain hope that he would be saved to eternal life had everything to do with his being saved from despair, as he faced his death.

24
Why Are Primitive Baptist Worship Services So Simple?

Primitive Baptists believe that Jesus' church still belongs to Jesus. He built His church: *I will build my church* (Mt 16:18). He bought His church: *The church of God, which he hath purchased with his own blood* (Acts 20:28). He gave Himself for His church: *Christ also loved the church, and gave himself for it* (Eph 5:25). He is the head of His church: *He is the head of the body, the church* (Col 1:18). He is the husband of His church: *For this cause shall a man leave his father and mother, and shall be joined unto his wife, and they two shall be one flesh. This is a great mystery: but I speak concerning Christ and the church* (Eph 5:31-32). A Primitive Baptist church wants to defend her husband's honor, to lift up the one who is her head, to return love to the one who gave Himself for her, to praise the one who bought her, and to stand for the one who built her.

Jesus said: *I am...the truth* (Jno 14:6). He said: *Thy word is truth* (Jno 17:17). Jesus' church is to be *the pillar and ground of the truth* (1 Tim 3:15). Primitive Baptists not only feel the duty to defend the doctrinal truths of Jesus' church, but also to maintain the church practices that Jesus established. In one single verse, Paul not only taught that the church should defend Jesus' truths, but he also taught that she should know how to behave in the house of God. *That thou mayest know how thou oughtest to behave thyself in the house of God, which is the church of the living God, the pillar and ground of the truth* (1 Tim 3:15).

Since Jesus is the head, the husband, the redeemer, the builder and the possessor of His church, Primitive Baptists believe we should *'do church'* His way. We should know how we ought to behave in the house God. Jesus' church is not only to hold to His doctrines, but also hold to His practices. Thus we attempt to pattern, not only our doctrinal beliefs, but also our manner of worship after New Testament teachings. The New Testament describes a very simple and unadorned style of worship, even a worship service that could easily be practiced in a cave, but could easily become lost in a cathedral.

So what do we find in the New Testament about the proper behavior that is befitting to the worship service in Jesus' church? It might surprise many, but the New Testament worship service was comprised of only three simple things: singing, praying and preaching. The lists of things, which modern day worshippers have added to the simplicity of New Testament worship, far exceeds the short list of singing, praying and preaching.

First of all, we find that New Testament worshippers sang hymns and songs. *Speaking to yourselves in psalms and hymns and spiritual songs, singing and making melody in your heart to the Lord* (Eph 5:19). We see from this verse that singing hymns in the worship service is for the purpose of *speaking to yourselves*. As we further think about this simple statement, we question if musical instruments can fulfill this Bible-stated purpose. It is reasonable to think that vocalized *psalms and hymns and spiritual songs* can speak to those who sing and hear the words. Yet it is quite impossible for musical instruments to speak to the ones who are worshipping. Moreover, it is hard to imagine a piano being able to pull off *making melody in your heart.* Yet God blesses His children to be fully equipped, not only to make music with their lips, but also to make melody with the feelings of their hearts.

Let us look at another verse. *Let the word of Christ dwell in you richly in all wisdom; teaching and admonishing one another in psalms and hymns and spiritual songs, singing with grace in your hearts to the Lord* (Col 3:16). Just as it is impossible to accomplish *speaking to yourselves* with musical instruments, it is also absurd to think that a musical instrument can carry out the task of *teaching and admonishing one another in psalms and hymns and spiritual songs.* Just as a piano is not up to the task of *making melody in your heart*, it is also not likely to find a piano *singing with grace in your hearts*. On the other hand, human voices and Spirit-filled hearts are quite capable of all these things.

What is it to speak to yourselves in songs, or to teach and admonish one another through singing? The words of hymns speak messages. Some songs speak peace to troubled souls. Some songs proclaim the gospel message. Some songs tell us of scriptural teachings. So how can one worshipper speak to, teach, and admonish other worshippers? Primitive Baptists try to accomplish this in a rather unusual way. Our pastors and song leaders do not select the hymns. The leader simply pauses after the singing of each hymn, so as to allow individual worshippers the opportunity to request the next hymn. They may either call out the name of the hymn, or they may call out the number of the hymn in the hymnal. This promotes the Bible's idea of *speaking to yourselves* in hymns and spiritual songs. If a worshipper has some special feeling in his heart, he (or she) may request a song that would speak the feeling to other worshippers. Or if a worshipper is thinking of some Bible truth, he (or she) may call for a song that would teach and admonish others in regards to that particular truth. The singing of the words of well-written hymns is truly an important part of New Testament worship.

As we come back to the idea of adding musical instruments to New Testament worship, let us look at one more verse. *What is it then? I will pray with the spirit, and I will pray with the understanding also: I will sing with the spirit, and I will sing with the understanding also* (1 Cor 14:15). Surely no one would think that a guitar could *pray with the spirit* and *pray with the understanding*. Well if the guitar cannot do the first part of the verse, it seems strange that people might imagine that it can do the second part, even that a guitar might be able to *sing with the spirit* or *sing with the understanding*. Yet a worshipper is able to do both the praying and the singing, with both the spirit and the understanding.

Some protest that Old Testament worship included many kinds of musical instruments. That is a true statement. Yet it is an invalid argument. To claim the Old Testament manner of worship as the basis, authority, or pattern for the New Testament manner of worship is not a justifiable defense. Old Testament worship required the worshippers to assemble at the tabernacle or in the temple. Jesus made it clear to the woman at the well that the place of worship no longer matters. Old Testament worship required a priest in Aaron's lineage. We no longer need Aaron's sons in order to worship. Jesus is our High Priest. Old Testament worship required animal blood. It would be an insult to the blood of Christ for New Testament worshippers to bring the blood of a goat before God.

At Jesus' death the veil of the temple was torn from top to bottom. The Old Testament manner of worship was finished. New Testament worship does not need ritual and animal sacrifice. New Testament worship does not require pomp and ceremony. New Testament worship does not need priests in simulated Old Testament costumes. Altars with smoldering incense are no longer necessary. The seven lamps of the candlestick no longer need to burn. The Holy of Holies is no longer present. The Ark of the Covenant with its Mercy Seat is no longer the designated dwelling place of God.

If we honestly attempt to look at the full picture of Old Testament worship, we find that there is very little from the Old Testament worship service that belongs in the New Testament worship service. To try to justify the addition of musical instruments to the worship service, by arguing that they used them in the Old Testament, goes beyond common sense, and beyond scriptural reasoning. There is no mention of musical instruments when the saints assembled to worship in the New Testament. Let us not think that we can improve upon the church that Jesus built, even the church that He promised to sustain.

From a historical point of view, many great Bible men of the past attempted to stand against those who would add musical instruments to the worship service. Around 670 A.D. Pope Vitalian introduced the organ, but his newfangled addition to the worship service came with much objection from the monks.

Centuries later, John Calvin said, "Musical instruments in celebrating the praise of God would be no more suitable than the burning of incense, the lighting up of lamps, the restoration of the other shadows of the law. The Papists, therefore, have foolishly borrowed this, as well as many other things from the Jews." John Wesley retorted, "I have no objection to instruments of music in our chapels, provided they are neither heard nor seen." Martin Luther called the organ "an ensign of Baal". Charles H. Spurgeon preached for twenty years to thousands of people weekly in the Metropolitan Baptist Tabernacle, London, England, but they did not have musical instruments in the worship.

The learned Methodist commentator, Adam Clarke, wrote, "I am an old man, and an old minister; and I here declare that I never knew them (musical instruments) productive of any good in the worship of God; and have had reason to believe that they were productive of much evil. Music, as a science, I esteem and admire; but instruments of music in the house of God I abominate and abhor. This is the abuse of music; and here I register my protest against all such corruptions in the worship of the Author of Christianity."

In his book, *Fifty Years Among the Baptists*, the Missionary Baptist preacher, David Benedict, wrote, "In my earliest intercourse among this people, congregational singing generally prevailed among them... This instrument (i.e. the organ), which from time immemorial has been associated with cathedral pomp...at length found its way into Baptist sanctuaries... Staunch old Baptists in former times would as soon tolerated the Pope of Rome in their pulpits as an organ in their galleries, and yet the instrument has gradually found its way among them... How far this modern organ fever will extend among our people, and whether it will on the whole work be a RE-formation, or DE-formation in their singing service, time will more fully develop."

Some say that Primitive Baptists are inconsistent in their stand against additions to a worship service. They say, "You people have heat and air conditioning in your buildings. Where is the New Testament pattern for that? What's the difference in adding a piano and adding a furnace?" To this we say that some things are merely 'aids' to worship, while others are 'additions' to worship. Perhaps the distinction between the two can best be seen through illustrations. God told Moses to use gopher wood to build the Ark of the Covenant. A hammer would have been an 'aid' to doing what God said to do. Trimming the Ark in oak would have been an 'addition' to doing what God said to do. Jesus used unleavened bread in the Lord's supper. Using a plate to serve the bread is an 'aid' to the service. Serving beans with the bread is an 'addition' to the service. Burning natural gas is an 'aid' to worship. Burning incense is an 'addition' to worship. Songbooks are an 'aid' to worship. Seventy-six trombones are an 'addition' to worship. May God give us wisdom.

We further note that the New Testament makes no mention of choirs or 'specials'. The entertainment of others is not a stated purpose for singing. The New Testament repeatedly emphasizes the qualities in the heart while singing, but fails to mention the quality of the voice. Displaying the superiority of some singers (and thus implying the inferiority of others) may violate Bible principles, in that it could lead to pride in some, and discouragement of others. The singing part of worship is where all are invited to actively participate. Let us never hinder God's children from their rightful part of the worship service.

In addition to singing, the New Testament worship service included prayer. The New Testament church united in prayer immediately after Jesus' ascension. *These all continued with one accord in prayer...* (Acts 1:14). The New Testament church continued steadfastly in prayers. *And they continued stedfastly in the apostles' doctrine and fellowship, and in breaking of bread, and in prayers* (Acts 2:42). When the people of the New Testament church met together in prayer, the Holy Ghost honored them with His presence. *And when they had prayed, the place was shaken where they were assembled together; and they were all filled with the Holy Ghost, and they spake the word of God with boldness* (Acts 4:31). If one from the church was in need, the church met together and prayed. *But prayer was made without ceasing of the church unto God for him* (Acts 12:5). Paul ceased not to pray for the churches, and he encouraged the churches to pray for him. Prayer was an essential part of New Testament worship. They met together, and they prayed together when they met.

Beyond singing and praying, preaching (and/or teaching) was the centerpiece of a New Testament worship service. Paul told Timothy: *Preach the word* (2 Tim 4:2). Jesus said: *Go ye therefore, and teach all nations* (Mt 18:19). The apostles *ceased not to teach and preach Jesus Christ* (Acts 5:42). Paul *reasoned with them out of the scriptures. Opening and alleging, that Christ must needs have suffered, and risen again from the dead; and that this Jesus, whom I preach unto you, is Christ* (Acts 17:2-3). Paul *went into the synagogue, and spake boldly* (Acts 19:8). Paul *preached unto them...and continued his speech until midnight* (Acts 20:7). Paul persuaded *them concerning Jesus, both out of the law of Moses, and out of the prophets, from morning till evening* (Acts 28:23). Day and night, anywhere and everywhere, anytime and all the time, preaching was the focus of the New Testament church. The mission of the New Testament church hinged around preaching the gospel of the resurrected Savior. New Testament preachers proclaimed the salvation that Jesus had successfully accomplished.

God uses the foolishness of preaching to spread the story of Jesus. God sent an angel to Cornelius, not so the angel could tell the story. The angel told Cornelius to send for the preacher, who would tell him the story. The story of the salvation of sinners spreads from preachers to hearers, from one sinner to another, even from faith to faith. New Testament preachers felt an urgency to preach. New Testament churches heard all night preaching, everyday preaching, lots of preaching. Many of today's churches are truly out of step with the New Testament church. They have added so much to the worship service, that they leave little time for preaching God's inspired word to God's struggling children. They put what the New Testament church considered to be the centerpiece of the worship service, somewhere on the periphery. In Jesus' church, simple preaching beats pompous pomp.

A few months ago, a good friend asked for recordings of my sermons. After having listened to a couple of sermons, she began a conversation with words of encouragement about the messages. Then she hesitated, as if she was trying to find words that would not be offensive, and she asked me if all my sermons were over fifty minutes long. I tried to explain how Primitive Baptists put a lot of emphasis on preaching God's word to God's children. (Yet at the same time, I realized that Paul would have been ashamed of me for stopping at slightly less than an hour of preaching.) She told me that with all the extras, which are added to her church's worship services, there is only enough time for about a ten-minute message from the pastor.

I am thankful that this friend continues to listen to my long sermons, and actually seems to enjoy discussing them with me. Yet as a whole, I fear that we live in a time, when even the church-going people are starved for the word of God. *Behold, the days come, saith the Lord GOD, that I will send a famine in the land, not a famine of bread, nor a thirst for water, but of hearing the words of the LORD* (Amos 8:11).

As we consider that preaching is central to the New Testament worship service, let us interject the New Testament instructions that women are not allowed to teach, or preach, in the worship service. We look at a chapter where Paul is specifically teaching the proper behavior during a worship service, even when *the whole church be come together into one place* (1 Cor 14:23). In this chapter, and in the context of how to properly behave in a worship service, Paul stated: *Let your women keep silence in the churches: for it is not permitted unto them to speak* (1 Cor 14:34).

At first glance, Paul seems to be commanding women to maintain total silence in church. If this be the case, women could not sing, nor greet others upon arrival, nor whisper to a crying baby, nor speak a word in any way. Surely Paul does not teach total silence. The purpose and context of this Corinthian chapter is to teach the proper way to conduct a worship service, more specifically the proper way to prophesy (preach and teach) during the worship service. In the context of preaching and teaching during the church worship service, women are to be silent.

This idea of women not teaching in the church very much agrees with Paul's words to Timothy: *Let the woman learn in silence with all subjection. But I suffer not a woman to teach, nor to usurp authority over the man, but to be in silence* (1 Tim 2:11-12). Here women are specifically barred from teaching men, and also from taking a role of authority over men. Come let us reason together. The New Testament recognizes that preachers have at least some level of authority over the churches that they serve. *These things speak, and exhort, and rebuke **with all authority**. Let no man despise thee* (Titus 2:15). Thus if women are not allowed to have authority over men, and if the role of pastor includes rebuking with all authority, then the scriptures restrict women from fulfilling the New Testament requirements associated with being a pastor.

Furthermore, the New Testament recognizes only men, and not women, as bishops, or elders (the Bible's words for preachers). *A bishop then must be blameless, **the husband** of one wife...apt to teach* (1 Tim 3:2). *Ordain elders in every city, as I had appointed thee, if any be blameless, **the husband** of one wife...* (Titus 1:5-6). Surely preachers are to come from among the husbands, and not from the wives.

Though the New Testament precludes women as preachers, it recognizes the importance of women in the church. Outside of the worship service, the older women are to teach the younger women. *The aged women likewise, that they be in behaviour as becometh holiness, not false accusers, not given to much wine, teachers of good things; That they may teach the young women...* (Titus 2:3-4). Young women are to guide the house, which means to teach the children in the home. *I will therefore that the younger women marry, bear children, guide the house...* (1 Tim 5:14). Women may prophesy (proclaim spiritual truths) outside the church worship service. *The same man had four daughters, virgins, which did prophesy* (Acts 21:9). The angel sent women to tell of Jesus' resurrection. *Go quickly, and tell his disciples that he is risen from the dead...* (Mt 28:7). Jesus followed up with the same command to the women. *Then said Jesus unto them, Be not afraid: go tell my brethren...* (Mt 28:10). Women may even instruct a preacher concerning the truth of the gospel, but just not in the worship service. *And he (Apollos) began to speak boldly in the synagogue: whom when Aquila **and Priscilla** had heard, **they** took him unto them, and expounded unto him the way of God more perfectly* (Acts 18:26).

Our last point is that the New Testament does not recognize segregation in the worship service. There is no scriptural basis for having separate places for different individuals who come to worship. The New Testament recognizes the church as one body. *Now are they many members, yet but one body* (1 Cor 12:20). The New Testament acknowledges that at least some children have spiritual understanding. *As soon as the voice of thy salutation sounded in mine ears, the babe leaped in my womb for joy* (Lk 1:44). Children praised Jesus in His day. *The children crying in the temple, and saying, Hosanna to the Son of David...* (Mt 21:15). Jesus proclaimed that the Father reveals His truths, even to babes. *Jesus answered and said, I thank thee, O Father, Lord of heaven and earth, because thou hast hid these things from the wise and prudent, and hast revealed them unto babes* (Mt 11:25). Jesus further said that the mouths of babies are able to praise God. *Jesus saith unto them, Yea; have ye never read, Out of the mouth of babes and sucklings thou hast perfected praise?* (Mt 21:16).[1]

The New Testament does not recognize excluding children from the worship service. Jesus said: *Suffer little children, and forbid them not, to come unto me: for of such is the kingdom of heaven* (Mt 19:14). I know that having children in the worship service can be a struggle for moms and dads. Yet, should Christian parents deny their children the opportunities of hearing God's word spoken by a God-gifted preacher? Let the same pastor teach the same things to the one body. Jesus said to the preacher: *Feed my lambs...* (Jno 21:15). Jesus said to the preacher: *Feed my sheep* (Jno 21:16). Surely, Jesus' intention was for the same God-called preacher to preach to the entire flock.

Primitive Baptists believe that Jesus' church belongs to Jesus, and that Jesus' church should '*do church*' Jesus' way. Let the simplicity of the gospel be proclaimed in a simple worship service, so that the full focus of the gospel, and the full focus of the service, is only on Jesus.

---

[1] Surely I have heard babies singing along with other worshippers. They usually sing an extra note or two after the song ends, bringing smiles to all.

25
What Happens to Us When We Die?

Paul said: *absent from the body...present with the Lord* (2 Cor 5:8). At the death of our loved one, we very much understand that death is not imaginary. It is oh so real! The life that we loved is obviously no longer in its body. Yet that mystical thing that we call life has not ceased to exist. It has just changed locations. Our loved one is now in the presence of the Lord.

Solomon said: *Then shall the dust return to the earth as it was: and the spirit shall return unto God who gave it* (Ecc 12:7). The body came from dust, and it goes to dust. Yet as this happens, the spirit is not in the body. It has already gone back to God. Jesus told the dying thief: *To day shalt thou be with me in paradise* (Lk 23:43).

Jesus said, *Today*. What a transition! From hanging on a cross, to instantaneous being with Jesus in paradise! The thief's body has long since returned to dust, but the thief himself has been with Jesus in paradise for the last two thousand years. Jesus told the unbelieving Sadducees that God *is not a God of the dead but of the living* (Lk 20:38). Jesus' statement was in reference to Abraham, Isaac and Jacob. His point was that these men were not dead, but alive with God. This is true of the thief, and of Paul, and of thousands upon thousands of God's children from Adam to now. The scriptures teach that at the passing we call death, the spirit, even the very life, of the child of God is immediately whisked from this world to the next. Wow! If that be the case, then as the songwriter said, *'Death Ain't No Big Deal'*.

Let us consider what happens to our spirits when we die. Some are confused and mistakenly believe in what they call 'soul sleep'. They picture unconscious souls, which 'rest in peace' from the moment of death, waiting for a future resurrection. In one way, it is not such a bad idea to imagine the weary traveler, sleeping away the centuries until Christ returns. Yet, to say that sleeping away the centuries is just as good as being awake in paradise would be perhaps the greatest understatement of all those centuries.

The Bible does not teach the idea of 'soul sleep'. Paul said: *For I am in a strait betwixt two, having a desire to depart, and to be with Christ; which is far better: Nevertheless to abide in the flesh is more needful for you* (Phi 1:23-24). So what does this have to do with 'soul sleep'? Paul was *in a strait betwixt two*, that is, he was perplexed as to which of two possible outcomes would be the better. On the one hand, he was ready to die and go be with Christ. On the other hand, he wanted to live longer and continue to serve Christ. Paul somewhat acknowledged that the option of being with Christ was the better of the two, but he must not have been fully convinced, since he was still perplexed about it.

From his stated quandary, it is apparent that Paul did not believe in 'soul sleep'. If he had believed that several hundred years of 'soul sleep' was what awaited him after death, he would have had no dilemma. His predicament was not whether he wanted either fifteen more years of service, or fifteen extra years of sleep. Paul was torn between either fifteen years of serving Christ down here, or fifteen years of being with Christ in paradise up there. He knew that fifteen years with Christ would have been far better, but he sensed that his work here was not done. If 'soul sleep' is all there is, Paul would want to be alive still today, serving Jesus.

Jesus believed in consciousness after death. In Luke 16, Jesus told of the deaths of the rich man and Lazarus. Then He spoke of each man, so as to leave no doubt that each was fully aware of his situation. Jesus said of Lazarus, *He is comforted.* Jesus described the rich man as *being in torments.* The rich man said of himself, *I am tormented in this flame.* He begged for water. There is no doubt that these two men knew all about their surroundings.

Now here is the key point concerning 'soul sleep'. The rich man desired that Lazarus would go warn his five brothers, *lest they also come into this place of torment.* As this scene unfolded, the brothers were still alive on the earth. The setting is not eternity future, after the age of 'soul sleep' has passed. This all took place while the world was still here. There is no such thing as 'soul sleep'. When we leave this world, we immediately awake to experience the next.

Let us look at another record of a conversation that occurred in heaven, while men were still living on the earth. *The souls of them that were slain...cried...How long, O Lord...dost thou not judge and avenge our blood on them that dwell on the earth? ...it was said unto them, that they should rest yet for a little season, until their fellowservants also and their brethren, that should be killed as they were, should be fulfilled* (Rev 6:9-11). These souls in heaven were not asleep, but were talking with the Lord, even talking about how long things were going to continue on the earth. So this conversation took place sometime between these men's deaths and the end of time. Our state of existence between death and resurrection is not a state of unconscious sleep, but a state of conscious awareness.

Next, consider these verses that speak of the body and the soul after death: *The righteous perisheth, and no man layeth it to heart: and merciful men are taken away, none considering that the righteous is taken away from the evil to come. He shall enter into peace: they shall rest in their beds, each one walking in his uprightness* (Is 57:1-2). These words describe God taking one of His children on to heaven, in order to spare him from experiencing further evil in this world. At the time of his parting, this man is said to *enter into peace.* Then a more detailed statement explains what happens to the body and the soul at this time of death. While their bodies *rest in their beds* (perhaps laid out awaiting their burials), each of them is *walking in his uprightness.* While the body is laid to rest, the soul is walking in paradise. Jesus said to the thief: *Today thou shalt be with me in paradise.* And so he is. And so it is.

Thus we can see from God's word that we go straight to heaven when we die, and that we are conscious when we get there, but what will we remember of this world? Men's opinions vary on this one. Some reason, "We won't be able to remember anything from this world. Heaven would not be heaven, if we could remember the sin and misery of this world." Others rationalize, "What will be the point of singing praises to the Jesus who saved us from our sins, if we cannot remember that we were sinners?" Each believes he can defend his position with earthly logic, but worldly reasoning is probably of little use, when we ponder about heaven. When this world's logic goes to its logical end, reasonable men conclude that there is no such thing as heaven.

The Sadducees came to Jesus (who had come from heaven), in order to prove to Him that there could be no such thing as heaven. They presented to Jesus a story of a woman, whose first husband had died. According to their account, this woman then married her first husband's brother. This second husband also died, so she married another brother. The sequence continued through seven different brothers, and after the death of the seventh husband, the woman finally died. They had set their stage. They thought they had Jesus backed into a corner. So their spokesman popped the impossible-to-answer question: *Therefore in the resurrection whose wife shall she be of the seven? for they all had her* (Mt 22:28). Jesus answered: *Ye do err, not knowing the scriptures, nor the power of God. For in the resurrection they neither marry, nor are given in marriage, but are as the angels of God in heaven* (Mt 22:29-30).

Jesus stopped the Sadducees' mouths, but I admit that His answer troubles me. I am married to my high school sweetheart, and have been for forty plus years. She was my first date, and my only love. How can heaven be heaven, if she is not my wife? So I do not claim to be able to answer all the questions about heaven, in that I have my own questions. Yet I am very sure of one thing about heaven. When we get there, we will be perfectly happy. *I shall be satisfied, when I awake, with thy likeness* (Ps 17:15).

Jesus' statements about marriage prove that at least some relationships will be different in heaven. The former relationships of marriage will not exist in heaven (or at least will not exist in the same way that they existed in the earth). Yet, will all former relationships cease to be? Will all memories of earthly relationships be wiped out forever? What about the age old question, 'Will we know each other in heaven?' Paul's patent answer is: *Then shall I know even as also I am known* (1 Cor 13:12).

Yet there is much more in God's word about this than Paul's one statement. David's proclamation at the death of his son leaves little doubt that he thought we would know each other in heaven. He said of his deceased son, *I shall go to him, but he shall not return to me* (2 Sam 12:23). David faced his situation knowing two things. First of all, he knew the dreadful reality: *he shall not return to me.* Yet he also knew the glorious truth: *I shall go to him.* David had great anticipation of seeing his son again in heaven. Surely he was not disappointed when he got to heaven. Surely David did not find that he could not figure out which one was his son. I believe that David saw his son again, and I believe that he knew his son when he saw him.

Moses and Elijah had been dead for centuries. Yet when they appeared from heaven, Peter, James and John recognized them. *And, behold, there appeared unto them Moses and Elias talking with him. Then answered Peter, and said unto Jesus, Lord, it is good for us to be here: if thou wilt, let us make here three tabernacles; one for thee, and one for Moses, and one for Elias* (Mt 17:3-4). With eyes that could only see through a glass darkly, Peter, James and John recognized strangers who had come from heaven. If men on earth knew strangers from heaven, then it is only reasonable that men in heaven will know friends and family in heaven. If those, who only knew in part, knew enough to know somebody, then surely those, who shall know as they are known, will know enough to know everybody.

Moreover, from hell, the rich man recognized men in heaven. *And in hell he lift up his eyes, being in torments, and seeth Abraham afar off, and Lazarus in his bosom* (Lk 16:23). If the rich man in hell could look up to heaven and call Lazarus by name, then a man in heaven would surely be able to look around and recognize those who are in heaven. I look forward to seeing old friends that I have not seen for a while. I anticipate seeing new friends (even friends that I am yet to meet, but which I believe that I will already know), like a man named Paul. I look forward to talking to my Dad, and to holding my little Ellierose. Most of all I look forward to seeing my Jesus. I believe that I will know Him at first sight. Wow! To be able to put a face with that Name!! I do believe that we will know each other in heaven.

We now come to the question: Is there dying grace for the moment of death? Though we look forward to eternal bliss, we dread the path that leads to it. We do not so much mind the being dead part, but the dying part seems dreadful. Our fear of dying is natural, but I do not believe it is scriptural. *Yea, though I walk through the valley of the shadow of death, I will fear no evil: for thou art with me* (Ps 23:4). What a promise! When my time comes to go through death's valley, I will not be alone. My Shepherd will be there with me. As I think about dying, I imagine that I will be scared. Yet here I am told that *I will fear no evil.*

Along the same line, Jesus said: *I go to prepare a place for you. And if I go and prepare a place for you, I will come again, and receive you unto myself; that where I am, there ye may be also* (Jno 14:2-3). In anticipation of having us with Him, Jesus promised to prepare a place. Yet we need to look closely at the logistics of how we get there. When the time comes for us to go be with Jesus, He does not just call us home. He comes and gets us. *I will come again, and receive you unto myself.* I will not make that journey alone: *for thou art with me.* At my moment of death: *I will fear no evil.* I believe in dying grace.

As we think about dying grace, let me tell you my story of Norma McIntyre. Late one afternoon, Norma's son called me while I was at work. They had just brought Norma back to the nursing home from the hospital. The doctors could do no more. They had sent her back to die. Her son told me that she wanted me to come see her. I left work, and headed that way.

The hundred-mile drive was long, and I confess that I dreaded the visit. You see, Norma had been sick and in pain for a long time. I had visited her often, and prayed with her many times. Yet her anguish continued, and she had become very discouraged. After previous visits with her, I had often left her bedside feeling very helpless. Sometimes I had cried. It seemed that I had never been able to encourage her. Now she was dying, and asking for me.

Upon my arrival, Norma's son and daughter-in-law left the room, saying that they would give the two of us some time to be together. Norma had a death rattle in her breathing. She asked the nurse for a pain shot, and the nurse explained that the doctor had not yet sent the orders. (I tell you this, so that you will know that Norma was not under the influence of narcotics.) Norma asked me to pray. I prayed. Norma continued to writhe in agony.

Not knowing what to do, I began to softly sing *Amazing Grace*. I know what the Bible says about singing songs to those with heavy hearts: *As he that taketh away a garment in cold weather, and as vinegar upon nitre, so is he that singeth songs to an heavy heart* (Pro 25:20). Yet I did not know what else to do, so I just sang, and prayed within myself while singing. As I made my way through the verses, her writhing seemed to ease. She became still. I even thought that she might be asleep.

Yet as I finished the last verse, she opened her eyes, and said she wanted to go home. I knew that she spoke of her heavenly home. I told her that that was in God's hands. I told her that I did not know His times, but that Jesus knows those times, and that Jesus knows all about us. It was as if the Spirit gave me a song to sing. I began to sing:

> *Come what may of joy or sorrow, be my portion pain or rest.*
> *Jesus guides me and directs me, and His way is always best.*
> *Jesus knows – Jesus knows – All the way my feet must go.*
> *Jesus knows – Jesus knows – Him I trust who loves me so.*

When I got to the words, *Jesus knows,* a weak, trembling, alto voice echoed my words: *Jesus knows (Jesus knows). Jesus knows (Jesus knows).* Norma McIntyre was singing with me.

We sang *Blessed Assurance* together. When we finished that song, she opened her eyes and told me that she had felt the Spirit so strongly while we were singing, that she had thought she was gone. I told her that she had not yet heard singing, like she was going to soon hear. We then sang *It Is Well with My Soul*. After that, it seemed right just to sit and think of the Lord. She seemed to be so at peace. I know that I was.

Our reveries were interrupted, when her son, daughter-in-law, and two friends eased into the room. Norma was lying there with her eyes closed. One of them whispered, "How's she doing?" I said,

"I think she feels a little better. She's been singing." They looked at me, as if I was a fool. At that point, Norma came to my rescue, as she began to sing: *I am safe in His love, for a wonderful Savior is He. I am safe in His love. In His mercy, He saved even me.* When she finished, she said, "That's my favorite. They sang that when I was baptized."

The six of us sang *Rock of Ages* together. **While I draw this fleeting breath – When I close my eyes in death** – *When I rise to worlds unknown, and behold Thee on Thy throne – Rock of ages cleft for me – Let me hide myself in thee.* That was the last time I saw my friend, Norma McIntyre. She died two days later, hopefully still with a sense of peace. Soon thereafter, I preached her funeral. I look forward to singing with her again.

After this story, some would call me a naïve old preacher. They might say that it does not happen that way every time. I will be the first to agree. I know that everybody does not die in peace. I realize that some die horrible deaths in pain and agony. I understand that death is a curse, and that we are not to glorify it, as if it is some kind of wonderful blessing to get to die. Yet I still believe that the God of grace, whose grace has kept us thus far, will show us dying grace when we need it.

None of us knows how it actually feels to die. We may have watched what seemed to be an agonizing death. Yet, what appears from the outside is not always the same as what is happening on the inside. If we had watched Stephen die, we would certainly not have declared, "Now there was a man who died in peace." From all observation, it would have appeared that Stephen died a terrible death. Yet look what Stephen was seeing, while the boulders were crushing away his life. *But he, being full of the Holy Ghost, looked up stedfastly into heaven, and saw the glory of God, and Jesus standing on the right hand of God* (Acts 7:55). That is a picture of dying grace.

While his bones were being broken, his spirit was looking into the throne room of God. He saw Jesus standing, as if to greet a friend who was about to arrive. Being filled with the Spirit, Stephen prayed for forgiveness for those who were literally bashing out his brains. *And he kneeled down, and cried with a loud voice, Lord, lay not this sin to their charge. And when he had said this, he fell asleep* (Acts 7:60). Stephen fell asleep (that is he died), while talking to Jesus. *Yea though I walk through the valley of the shadow of death, I will fear no evil, for thou art with me.* What a way to die!

Christian history affords many such accounts. From *Foxe's Book of Martyrs*, we find where Thomas Haukes (or Hauker in some versions) had been condemned to burn at the stake. A little before his death, several of his friends desired that he should show them some token, while in the midst of the flames, as to whether a man might be able to endure such pains of burning. This he promised to do. It was agreed that if the rage of the pain might be suffered, then he should lift up his hands above his head towards heaven before he gave up the ghost.

Not long after, Mr. Haukes was led away to the place appointed for his slaughter. Being come to the stake, he mildly and patiently prepared himself for the fire. He poured out his soul unto God, and the fire was kindled. When he had continued long in it, and his speech was taken away by violence of the flame, his skin drawn together, and his fingers consumed with the fire, so that it was thought that he was gone, suddenly, and contrary to all expectation, this good man, being mindful of his promise, reached up his hands, burning in flames over his head to the living God, and with great rejoicings as it seemed, clapped them three times together. A great shout followed this wonderful circumstance, and then this blessed martyr of Christ, sinking down in the fire, gave up his spirit. Now that is dying grace.

I hold in high regard a preacher from our era, David Martyn Lloyd-Jones. I have read a great number of his books. I have studied in detail his many volume series on the Book of Romans. I do not agree with all that he said, but his writings have taught me much. I recently read his biography, written by his friend, Iain Murray. Murray gave an account of visiting Lloyd-Jones, as he lay on his death bed. His friend was in much pain. As Murray looked at him, he was grieved in his own heart, and said, "It hurts me to see you so weak, so tired, and so sad." It had been a while since Lloyd-Jones had spoken a word, but from somewhere he mustered the strength to say two words, "Not sad." That is dying grace! He wanted to reassure his friend that he was not sad. He was perhaps even then seeing the Jesus whom he had so long preached. It was not a sad time. He feared no evil. There is something wonderful beyond death. There is eternal life. There is a hope for tomorrow.

A blind man from our church, Harvey Purdy, had been in the hospital for a while, and had finally passed away. When I walked into the funeral home to express my sympathies, his widow said to me, "Brother Jeff, Brother Jeff, I have to tell you something." Considering the circumstances, her tone of excitement seemed most unusual. I said, "What is it, Ruby?" She said, "We were at the hospital. The doctor was in the room. Harvey was lying back in the bed, and all of a sudden he sat up and said, 'Look, Ruby, look'." (That old blind man had probably not said that too many times in his life. He had no eyes, but he had said, "Look, Ruby, look.") Ruby said to me, "I didn't know what to say, Brother Jeff. I looked at the doctor, and he nodded his head, like I should just agree with Harvey. So I just said, 'Yes Harvey'. About that time, Harvey said again, 'Oh! Look, Ruby! Look!'. Then he said, 'Isn't that beautiful!' After that, he just laid back in the bed." That is dying grace.

Ponder the excitement that the old man felt. He literally had no eyes, and had never seen anything. Yet now he was seeing. *Was blind, but now I see!* Yet it was not just that he could see. It was more what he was seeing. Listen to his words, "Isn't that beautiful!" I do not know what he saw. Maybe it was Whom he saw? Maybe he was seeing the Jesus, Whom Stephen saw. Whatever, or Whomever, Harvey used the word 'beautiful'.

There is really something out there, and it is much more wonderful than what is around us right now. At this point, the best we can do with eyes of faith is to see our hope through a glass darkly. Yet some day, we will say with Harvey (either as we are dying, or immediately thereafter), "Look! Oh, look! Isn't that beautiful!" What a day that will be!

26
Is Resurrection Real?

If resurrection is not reality — nothing else really matters. If there is no resurrection, all is futility. If resurrection is not reality, then the reality is, that anything and everything are no more than nothing. Without resurrection, even good ends up good-for-nothingness.

The triumph of all Bible doctrines hinges on the reality of resurrection. What is election, or redemption, or regeneration, without resurrection? Did God give His vast host of children to Christ in the Covenant of Grace before the foundation of the world, so the grave might be the end for those much-loved children? Did Jesus shed His precious blood of redemption for His people, so they might remain forever entombed in death? Does the Holy Spirit breathe regeneration into each of the heirs of eternal glory, so death's crypt might forever steal the life He had given? No! No! A thousand times, No!

Yet if resurrection is not real, all the glorious truths of the Bible become senseless. If there is no resurrection, Jesus is still dead. If Jesus is still dead, He did not ascend back to heaven. If Jesus did not go back to heaven, He is not coming back from heaven. If Jesus is not resurrected, nobody else ever will be.

Paul understood the nothingness of everything without resurrection. In response to those who doubted the reality of a literal resurrection, Paul countered that if there is no such thing as resurrection, then all faith is empty, all dead are perished, all hope is nothing, and all men are most miserable. *If in this life only we have hope in Christ, then we are of all men most miserable* (1 Cor 15:19). Resurrection is the centerpiece of the Bible. Resurrection is the exclamation point of all Bible doctrines. Resurrection separates Christianity from all others. The angel said: *He is not here: for He is risen* (Mt 28:6). Paul said: *But now is Christ risen from the dead* (1 Cor 15:20). Jesus declared: *I am the resurrection, and the life* (Jno 11:25). OUR MAN LIVES!!!

If resurrection is reality—nothing else really matters. If there is really such a thing as resurrection, all this world's terrible things will eventually amount to nothing. To know the reality of resurrection is to live a changed life. After Jesus' resurrection, the apostles were new men. No more striving over who was the greatest. Who cared about that anymore? No more denying that they knew Him. The cowards had courage. What was the worst thing that could happen? They might get killed for preaching Christ. So what! They had seen resurrection. They knew the reality of resurrection. They had seen His hands. They had supped with Him. They knew He was real. They had watched Him go through the cloud. They knew He was coming back. If resurrection was reality, nothing else mattered.

It is not just the apostles lives that are changed by the reality of resurrection. We also know that Christ is risen from the dead. We know that Jesus had the power to lay His life down, and that He had the power to raise it up again. We know that at the last day Jesus will again show His great power, when He shouts from the cloud and resurrects us from our graves. What a hope! What a wonderful, never-ending day that will be! If we know that resurrection is reality, the things of this world cease to matter. Resurrection is everything! Resurrection is the only thing! Resurrection is worth getting excited about!

The closer we are to death, the better the idea of resurrection sounds. Once upon a time, I was preaching to the lonely, imprisoned, dying souls at a local nursing home. From Matthew's account, I began to read about the women coming to Jesus' tomb. They found the stone rolled away, and the angel seated upon it. As I preached through the passage, I read the angel's words: *He is not here; for he is risen.* Applause suddenly filled the room. Cheers resounded. Those old folks were on 'shouting ground'. I am not accustomed to such interruptions. I was shocked, even kind of knocked me off my feet, but I must say that their excitement about an empty tomb was contagious. So I just got happy with them.

As I think back on the occurrence, I suppose that there were two things that I had failed to realize. First of all, I had not sensed the extent of the presence of the Holy Spirit in that place that day. Secondly, and to my shame, I perhaps had never sensed the true wonder in the words, *He is not here; for he is risen*. Yet those, who were near to that *walk through the valley of the shadow death*, cheered with anticipation at the very thought of resurrection. After many years of preaching at nursing homes, I have learned that "*Resurrection*" is their favorite subject. The closer we get — the better it sounds.

There was another day when I realized that the closer we are to death, the better the idea of resurrection sounds. I sat quietly observing a much-respected pastor. I was to assist in the funeral that he was to preach. The hour quickly approached, and he kept flipping back and forth through his Bible. He finally shut the book, confessing that he could come up with nothing different to preach at this funeral. With a tone of frustration, he said that he was just going to talk about the resurrection. I assured him that he had made a good choice. I told him that there is no better message than resurrection, when we face the hopelessness of death.

At the appointed time, he arose to his feet, and preached what had been preached so many times before. God abundantly blessed him with the message that we should just patiently wait for the resurrection, even patiently wait for the coming of the Lord. People from the back of the assembly began to 'amen' the message. As the preacher continued to speak of patiently waiting for the resurrection, I watched the saddened eyes of the family on the front row begin to focus on his every word. They began to 'amen' the message about a coming resurrection.

The '*Amens*', which came from those who faced death at the funeral home, reminded me of the applause, which had come from those who faced death at the nursing home. When we must face death, no message brings more hope and comfort, than that of resurrection. The closer we are to death—the better resurrection sounds.

We are more prone to think of death, when at a funeral home or a nursing home. Yet in reality, death can appear at a moment's notice, in any place, at any time. The phone rings. "This is the police. There has been an accident." Or, "This is Mom. It's your Dad." Or, "This is your pastor. I have bad news." Or, "This is the doctor's office. Your test results are not good." Suddenly, with no warning, we are facing death once again.

On a Tuesday morning at 9:40, the first text from my son read: "Saw a man die in front of our house late last night. Wrecked his car into the median. I tried to help and called 911, but they didn't get there fast enough. It's really bothering me...Can barely work."

I responded: "I'm sorry. Life is full of experiences. Some good and some bad, but many are for purposes we don't understand. You may need this for preparation for the future, or for awakening for the present. Or the man may have needed your presence for the moment. May God give you peace."

My son replied: "I just can't stop playing the reel in my head and questioning the speed of my response. It's crazy that he was alive one second, then dead the next. Guess I wouldn't have been a good soldier."

I answered: "Every good soldier has had to, and continues to, deal with what you are dealing with." My son did not immediately reply. So I further explained: "As I looked back on the previous message that I sent to you, I fear that you might have thought I was unconcerned. My heart aches for you, as it aches for many good soldiers who have watched men die. My point was that you are not alone in what you are feeling. Many have had these trials, but with the trials, God will give you strength that you may be able to bear it. The feelings you are having are common to men, and Jesus is touched with the feelings of our infirmities."

My son responded: "I didn't think you seemed unconcerned at all. I always appreciate greatly your counsel. I'm very fortunate that I've had limited contact with such things. However, that fact creates a disconnect with the fragileness that exists in our dealings with our brothers and sisters. The suffering that sin has created connects us all so deeply. Life is so fragile, and you never know when your service, words, or actions with others could be the last you or they experience. It was very much a perspective building experience. I want to learn who he was and write to his family. Thanks and love ya."

As I think of my son's words about what soldiers have seen, I am reminded of another recent experience. A preacher friend told me that he needed a favor. He asked if I would be willing to listen, while he talked about Vietnam. I told him that I never ask anybody about what happened in a war, but if he needed to talk, that I was more than willing to listen. For an hour, or more, I listened. It has been nearly fifty years, and my friend still cannot sleep at night. As has been said, "War is hell." Death is truly a monster.

These are two otherwise stable men, who witnessed death in two different ways. Both men are strong Christians, yet both struggle with what they saw with their eyes. The deaths they witnessed were not near as personal as the death of a loved one, yet just watching death happen is so difficult. Death seems so final, so cruel, so real. And at the same time, in some strange way, so unreal. When we sit with a stranger... When we look into his eyes... When he stares into our eyes... When he gasps his last breath... We ask the question: "Why?"

In some ways it seems like only yesterday when I watched a man die. This one was my Dad. While in the parking lot of the hospital, my dear wife and I received the phone call. "Where are you? Get here quick." We raced up to his room. My Mom, my wife's parents, and a nurse were standing around his bed.

We were too late. The nurse nodded that Dad was gone. In my sadness, I leaned over the bed, and said, "Love you, Dad." Much to the surprise of all, Dad muttered, "You too." Though it had seemed so certain that Dad was already gone, God's mercy allowed me to hear one last, "You too." It has been over five years, since I heard those last words. I still dream of him. We talk in the dreams. When I awaken, they are good dreams. One day soon I will awaken, and it will not be a dream. I will see him again. Maybe I will say, "Love you, Dad." Maybe he will say, "You too."

Surrounding the grave of that dear old man, we sang, *I'll Fly Away*. Someday my Dad is coming out of the ground. Oh, the blessing in knowing that we shall someday conquer death! We realize that we have no power to conquer the beast, but we find our hope in knowing that the beast has already been conquered. Jesus said that He would rise again after three days, and He did. Jesus conquered death in His own behalf, and through His death and resurrection, He has conquered death for us. We face death as mortals, knowing that our lives will soon fly away. Yet we also face death knowing, that as immortals, our very bodies shall someday fly away. Resurrection is reality. God is good!

God's word proclaims that God's plan of salvation will eventually, and certainly, end in resurrection. God's word praises the God, who purposed our salvation before time began, and whose purposes always come to pass. God's word honors the Christ who paid for our salvation, and who will finally have with Him all that He paid for. God's word exalts the Holy Spirit who gives us our salvation, by moving as He pleases to give eternal life to each of God's children. God's gospel preaches: *Salvation is of the Lord*. It shouts that Jesus hath saved us. It trumpets the successful Savior, and His certain salvation. It celebrates the waiting resurrection of all God's elect to eternal glory. There will be none missing. Everyone Jesus died for will be with God. From start to finish, God, and God alone, without man's help, even by grace, and grace alone, saves every one of His children from their sins. Resurrection is coming. God is good!

Paul wanted us to know these things. He knew that knowing these things would help us, when we face the deaths of loved ones. *But I would not have you to be ignorant, brethren, concerning them which are asleep, that ye sorrow not, even as others which have no hope* (1 Ths 4:13). At the death of a loved one, we still feel sorrow, but not like those who do not know about resurrection. If we believe that Jesus can and will resurrect the dead, then we are different to the world, *who through fear of death are all their lifetime subject to bondage* (Heb

2:15). The Bible is clear that Jesus will one day deliver His children from death to life. The knowledge that Jesus will do that, even now delivers us from the bondage of fear, to a life of peace. Paul preached the gospel of peace. There is much comfort in knowing the certainty of life after death. There is deliverance in understanding the truth and reality about eternity. By having certain hope concerning the reality of resurrection, we are saved from much despair as we face the loss of loved ones, or as we anticipate our own deaths.

It is a glorious thought to anticipate that our spirits, even our very lives, will go to be with Jesus when we die. To know that life does not end in death, but that we immediately go to paradise would seem to be a sufficient eternal outcome. Yet even the wonder of our spirits going to paradise pales in comparison to the thought of resurrection. The best is yet to come. Jesus is going to resurrect our bodies from the graves. What a day that will be!

Forty days after Jesus' self-resurrection, His closest followers watched Him ascend back into the heavens from whence He had come. *And when he had spoken these things, while they beheld, he was taken up; and a cloud received him out of their sight* (Acts 1:9). As if the ascension of Jesus was not enough astonishment for one day, while Jesus' disciples were staring in amazement at His going up, they perhaps had not noticed that two angels had come down. *And while they looked stedfastly toward heaven as he went up, behold, two men stood by them in white apparel* (Acts 1:10). To add even more marvel to the moment, the angels broke into their wonder with perhaps the most wonderful words of hope that have ever been spoken. *Which also said, Ye men of Galilee, why stand ye gazing up into heaven? this same Jesus, which is taken up from you into heaven, shall so come in like manner as ye have seen him go into heaven* (Acts 1:11).

We have a wonderful and certain hope. This same Jesus is coming back! Surely it was with a great sense of awe that Jesus' friends watched Him rise from the earth and disappear through a cloud. Surely it brought a great sense of joy to hear the words that He was coming back. If not for the angels' words, Jesus' departure might have been a scene of sorrow. Yet instead of being filled with sorrow, His friends were filled with joy, even filled with hope. Jesus is coming back. Jesus will return in the clouds one day with a purpose. He is coming to raise the dead!

Resurrection is the centerpiece of all that Christians believe. Christianity hinges upon the reality of resurrection. A resurrected Christ is the only hope of our salvation. Yet from early times, some have scoffed at the idea of a resurrection of the body. There were some in the church at Corinth who said there was no such thing. Paul asked that church: *How say some among you that there is no resurrection of the dead?* Paul began his answer to this challenge by acknowledging that *if there be no resurrection of the dead, then is Christ not risen.*

What if Christ is not risen? What if Christ is still dead? Paul proceeded to elaborate the 'what ifs', which would be true, if Christ is still dead. Paul said: *If Christ be not risen, then is our preaching vain, and your faith is also vain.* If Jesus is still dead, all that Christians preach, or believe, amounts to nothing. If Jesus is still in that tomb, then Christian preachers are liars. *Yea, and we are found false witnesses of God; because we have testified of God that he raised up Christ: whom he raised not up, if so be that the dead rise not.* If there is no such thing as resurrection, and if Christ is not alive, then our belief is in nothing. *For if the dead rise not, then is not Christ raised: And if Christ be not raised, your faith is vain.* If Christ is dead in a grave, then we are yet in our sins, and all men are perished. *And if Christ be not raised...ye are yet in your sins. Then they also which are fallen asleep in Christ are perished.* If the Christian hope is in a dead Christ, then the Christian's case is the most pitiful of all cases. *If in this life only we have hope in Christ, we are of all men most miserable* (1 Cor 15:12-19).

Yet Paul went on to declare that the Christian hope is not in a dead Christ. Paul said: *But now is Christ risen from the dead...* (1 Cor 15:20). Christ is indeed resurrected from the grave. Moreover, the Christian hope goes beyond a one-time resurrection of Christ. *But now is Christ risen from the dead, and become the firstfruits of them that slept* (1 Cor 15:20). Christ was the first fruit. He was the first to be resurrected. Someday Christ will shout and all His children's bodies will come forth to forever be with Him in glory.

The scoffer will ask how such a thing can be done. *But some man will say, How are the dead raised up? and with what body do they come?* (1 Cor 15:35). The Bible's extended answer to the question of how such a thing as this can happen begins with the two words: *Thou fool...* (1 Cor 15:36). It goes on to describe how the same God, who brings stalks of corn from dead seed, can bring a resurrected body from a dead one. The same God, who has made all manners of natural bodies, such as beast, bird and fish, can make spiritual bodies. The same God, who has made the celestial and terrestrial bodies of the universe, can make spiritual bodies. The point here is that only a fool would think resurrection is too hard for the Lord.

Paul said that the same body that is buried in the grave is coming out of the grave. Our natural bodies are buried in corruption, in dishonor, and in weakness. Yet those same bodies will be resurrected in incorruption, in glory and in power. *It is sown in corruption; it is raised in incorruption: It is sown in dishonour; it is raised in glory: it is sown in weakness; it is raised in power* (1 Cor 15:42-43). The '*it*' that gets planted is the '*it*' that comes out. God is not going to create new bodies. He is going to resurrect our bodies. You will be raised, as you. I will be me. The ones, we loved, will be the ones, we loved.

Our Jesus is the life-giving power behind the glory of resurrection. *For the Lord himself shall descend from heaven with a shout, with the voice of the archangel, and with the trump of God: and the dead in Christ shall rise first: Then we which are alive and remain shall be caught up together with them in the clouds, to meet the Lord in the air: and so shall we ever be with the Lord* (1 Ths 4:16-17). Resurrection will be instantaneous. *In a moment, in the twinkling of an eye, at the last trump: for the trumpet shall sound, and the dead shall be raised incorruptible, and we shall be changed* (1 Cor 15:52).

These mortal bodies will rise again. These mortals shall put on immortality. *For this corruptible must put on incorruption, and this mortal must put on immortality* (1 Cor 15:53). Jesus paid for body, soul and spirit at the cross. At death, our spirits go home immediately, but the day will come when Jesus will come back. He will shout. Our bodies will rise and be reunited with our spirits.

Death is swallowed up in victory (1 Cor 15:54). What a victory!! What a glorious Savior!!

Listen to Jesus' words: *For I came down from heaven, not to do mine own will, but the will of him that sent me. And this is the Father's will which hath sent me, that of all which he hath given me I should lose nothing, but should raise it up again at the last day* (Jno 6:38-39). What a plan of salvation! Before time began the will of God gave a vast host of people to Jesus. At God's appointed time Jesus gave His life for the people in that vast host. At the time of His pleasing, Jesus speaks the spiritual life of the new birth into each person of that vast host. At our deaths, Jesus receives our spirits unto Himself. Yet Jesus' final accomplishment in salvation is yet to come! At the last day, Jesus will shout from the clouds, and all that were given to Jesus, will come to Jesus. Nothing will be lost. Each and every one will be *gloriously* raised up the last day. All that the Father willed to Jesus, Jesus will resurrect.

To the praise of our Savior, none will be missing. To the honor of His integrity, none will be lost. To the glory of His name, resurrection is coming. What election determined before time began, resurrection will obtain when time is no more! From start to finish salvation is of the Lord. What a plan! What a Savior!

Resurrection is the only thing that really matters.

Resurrection is everything that really matters.

Resurrection is worth getting excited about!

Made in the USA
Middletown, DE
01 September 2018